To Ted

Enjoy your journey!

Jay Weber

I.D.E.A. to Exit:
An Entrepreneurial Journey

How Ordinary People Go From Basement to Big Time

Jeffrey Weber

Mill City Press
www.millcitypress.net

I.D.E.A.
TO EXIT:
An
Entrepreneurial
Journey

"How
Ordinary
People
Go From
Basement
to
Big Time!"

Jeffrey Weber

MILL CITY PRESS
MINNEAPOLIS, MN

Mill City Press, Inc.
212 3rd Avenue North, Suite 290
Minneapolis, MN 55401
612.455.2294
www.millcitypublishing.com

ISBN - 978-1-936107-60-5
ISBN - 1-936107-60-0
LCCN - 2010920871

Cover Design and Typeset by Peter Honsberger

Printed in the United States of America

CONTENTS

ACKNOWLEDGEMENTS

"If there's a book you really want to read but it hasn't been written yet, then you must write it."
—Toni Morrison, American writer, teacher, and editor
Pulitzer Prize for *Beloved*; Nobel Prize for Literature, 1993

To my wife, Lisa, who has supported me on every endeavor without question and without fail. None of what I have done would have happened without you and your support, hard work, encouragement, sacrifice, and love.

To my parents, Bill and Diana, who fostered a fantastic childhood for me and provided all of the opportunities which led me to where I am today.

To my in laws, Frank and Donna, who are just like parents to me and have entrusted me with their beautiful daughter.

To my children, Kaitlyn, Joseph, Nicholas, you each have tremendous power, talent, and potential that I can't wait to see revealed as adults. Understand your Risk Box and never let it hold you back from living an extraordinary life.

To you the reader, thank you for investing your time in my work. It is my desire to educate, influence, and motivate you to activate your entrepreneurial dreams to create new innovations that will benefit our society and the world. It's your turn now!

To Toni Morrison whose quote encouraged me to keep working hard to finish this book.

INTRODUCTION

My otherwise ordinary life led me on an extraordinary journey.

I report regularly to my job at an attractive multi-story office building situated in the very northern tip of the North Shore of Chicago. My car is left in a covered parking garage, which is particularly welcome in January when the cold Midwest winters make venturing outside considerably despicable. As I enter the cathedral-like foyer of granite and chrome, an oak-paneled elevator delivers me to my floor where I'll reside for the next eight hours.

State-of-the-art conference rooms and mini-kitchens exist on every floor, while a full cafeteria can be found on the penthouse level providing scenic views of the forested suburban landscape. Daily I fill up on company-provided coffee, cappuccino, or hot chocolate. Bi-weekly coworkers count on a delivery of doughnuts, cookies, scones and bagels. While ice cream bars are made available once a week in the summer months. During Halloween we get an afternoon treat of taffy apples, which I always take home to my wife who looks forward to this seasonal goody. My kids count on the introduction to spring when my company exclusively rents out the Six Flags amusement park to all employees and their immediate family.

This is not a high flying venture capital start-up as you may have suspected. Nor is this a description of the company I started as my corporate environment was far more humble than my current setting—far more humble. This is the home office of a Fortune 500 company where I reside in a newly created Business Development position. This is actually where my story ends, but where for many emerging entrepreneurs it begins.

In these rows of endless cubicles are people who dream of starting their own company. Many will dream it; few will do anything about it. It is this way all across America, and it was this way for me only in a different Fortune 500 company nearly 20 years earlier. I had been doing some dreaming of my own on the job lately, and I'm ready to head off in a new direction, but I'm getting ahead of myself. As I prepare to leave for the day, I look down at my desk to retrieve my one permanent daily message that I've carried with me from job to job for many years.

One Christmas several years ago, my wife gave me one of those cube-shaped daily calendars. You know the type. It has all 365 days on an individual 2.5-inch page that often features Dilbert, The Simpsons, or, in this case, a motivational quote with an inspiring graphic. I loved that calendar and took to heart many of its messages. Sure, some sound a bit cheerleader-like, but they resonate to me and I believe to all those who yearn for more in their career and personal life.

I adopted one particular daily entry which read, "If you do what you've always done, you'll get what you've always gotten." It's applicable to just about anything you do and reflective of the results. For me, it highlighted my mission to start and run a business on my own. I did not set out to be an entrepreneur per se; more so, my mind was fixed on having my own business—any business, and the independence it represented.

That quotation was symbolic for where I was at that point in my life. I was working a job, but it was that job—that well-trodden career path—that I found was holding me back. If I continued to do what I had always done, that is, work for someone else, I would continue to get what that effort had always provided. True, a predictable salary, benefits, and being on course for promotion and advancement is not at all bad, but my soul yearned for something more than these material rewards.

For me that job was not satisfying what I wanted in my life or how I wanted to live it. I was driven deep within to be an entrepreneur. The thought of working my entire life at a company was dreadfully scary and unsatisfying. Further, I found it to be risky. My fear was to commit a lifetime of work to a firm only to be laid off at an advanced age making it difficult to find comparable employment. I knew early on that I wanted to control my destiny and have the freedom to create my future. This feeling, this drive, started before I was in high school and grew stronger as each year passed. Don't get me wrong; I enjoyed the jobs I held, the companies I worked for, and the people I worked with, but routinely I thought of how I could go it alone. It was something that burned inside me. When I found that insightful phrase, I taped it on every desk I had throughout my career, even as president of the company I eventually founded. This became my driver and daily motivator, but at the time I had no clue as to what I wanted to do on my own—I was an entrepreneur in waiting.

My adopted phrase is attributable to the daily worker in any company. Do you want a raise, recognition, promotion? Then you can't do what you've always done on the job. I'm sure the phrase's author intended his work more for the masses than the stray entrepreneur, but its relevance and impact is applicable to all. In a way, it is a mindset that can bring an entrepreneurial spirit into any individual worker's repertoire. It serves to inspire innovation, desire, effort, ability, and passion, which is the core of the entrepreneur.

I know what most of you have inside and why this book is in your hands: you have that fire within. It's a compulsory desire to have your own business and create something new. I wrote this book because I would crave such literature when I was seeking my opportunity. I did not read success stories in envy or with a wish that I was that guy or gal. Reading other people's success stories is nice but serves of little assistance if they do not educate the reader. It's a bit like watching a segment of *Lifestyles of the Rich and Famous*. Seeing the material success of celebrities is nice, but what did they have to do to get to where they are today? I wanted to learn something from their experience. I wanted to do it for myself. I wanted the idea. I wanted to start something from nothing, and I wanted to build it to become a success.

This book is not so much to motivate, but to inform, guide, encourage, and coach. I will strive to push you out of your risk box and help provide the confidence you need to move forward with your dreams. I hope my experience will help you lower your frustrations while you await your opportunity to activate into entrepreneurship, will help you fully enjoy the elation during the startup of your business, provide focus while running your business, and lower anxieties when exiting what you've worked so hard to build.

If you already have started your dream, there is plenty of information inside these pages to keep you engaged and inspired to rethink your own business and to shake the routine out of you. I'll show how scaling, innovation, and leadership are the three most important entrepreneurial attributes during the running phase of your business. My main goal will be to prepare you for the ultimate last phase of your entrepreneurial career—your exit plan. This is truly the fruit of your labor and often the most overlooked aspect of an entrepreneur's planning and focus. It is my goal to share experiences that will coach you through the process and maximize the value of your business at sale.

This book is for the corporate worker who can do more and be more by adopting a sense of corporate ownership. That entrepreneurial spirit is within us all, and wouldn't it be great if you could express it now right where you are? Developing a method to foster innovation in any company is possible; it just needs a process—and I have one for you.

If you do what you've always done, you'll get what you've always gotten. To achieve your dreams, maximize your business's worth and to live an extra-ordinary life you can't do what you've always done.

PHASE I: IDEA

"The difference between great people and everyone else is that great people create their lives actively, while everyone else is created by their lives, passively waiting to see where life takes them next. The difference between the two is the difference between living fully and just existing."—Michael Gerber, author

Childhood really is a magical time. For most, it represents imagination, free thinking, no inhibition, no walls, and no boundaries. Compared to adult life, there are no demanding expectations. Eventually, life and the world start to confine, contain, and conform you. You begin to fit in to the order of society and how it works. Your conformity is protective and directs you to the next orderly step or phase of your life. You progress by learning more and more of this societal order. You adapt and learn how to navigate the world created around you and you try to "fit in," but inside is a desire to create your own world.

The society we live in broadcasts the dangers of creating your own world. It focuses on all the potential negative aspects that can occur and how risky such an endeavor can be. People repeatedly point out how you can lose some or all of what you have acquired if you leave this safe structure. It's a scenario reminiscent of the 1999 movie *The Matrix* in which humans are led to perceive an artificial world created by machines that pacifies and dictates the humans' actions. The artificial Matrix world is perfect and orderly. It becomes disruptive when one human attempts to step out of the routine and question not only the patternistic behavior but how the people may otherwise live their lives. I view the entrepreneur as that human rebel that breaks through the veil of The Matrix to see how the world truly functions and how he can choose to live in it.

Students who have completed entrepreneurship courses describe having learned a new way of thinking and an ability to pick up on the "not so obvious." Entrepreneurs have an inner drive to create their own destiny. This may seem to describe entrepreneurs as having an inflated sense of ego; that is not the intention. More so, it describes the deep inner self assessment and desire that an entrepreneur wants to seek in life. Most entrepreneurs in the long run will not be satisfied working in the formulated process of the world. It is too ordinary and too routine. The entrepreneur seeks the uncharted and the excitement and reward that discovery of the unknown brings. Further, entrepreneurs want to create their future and their destiny—not have it prescribed to them.

Therefore, in order to find their own way, they actively seek an opportunity that will allow them to follow their own direction. This mindset or internal clock of the entrepreneur is one sure way to assess your own fortitude for becoming one. If you have this internal gravitational pull that compels you to create your own destiny and manage your own life, and if you are constantly looking out on the horizon for the opportunity to bring you there, then you are most likely an entrepreneur at heart. Still others become accidental entrepreneurs by happenstance or opportunity and discover a world that is far more rewarding and enriching than what they had come to expect.

Author and professor, Elliot McGucken, PhD describes the entrepreneurial process to his art students through an analogy of ancient literature. He describes the first stage of the entrepreneur and that of the classic "hero" story as a journey in which the hero, or entrepreneur, "embarks on a quest that requires separation or departure from the familiar world." That separation or departure from the familiar world hits it right on the head. The entrepreneur moves into the unknown and the unproven. This is the world beyond the walls of what I will describe as our Risk Box and the second defining moment to becoming an entrepreneur. Departure from the familiar is what keeps many from not exploring their entrepreneurial world at all. However, before the entrepreneur can move into the unknown they must pass the first defining moment which is the I.D.E.A. that formulates entrepreneurial activation.

All of this serves to answer this: "How does one achieve the entrepreneurial dream?" This question is for entrepreneurs who have yet to activate a business of their own as well as existing entrepreneurs. Entrepreneurial success lies in how well a business scales, innovates, and successfully exits; aspects that some entrepreneurs are ill prepared to execute once they open their doors.

CHAPTER ONE
The Grove

I grew up in Glenview, Illinois, a very typical suburban village outside of Chicago. We moved in just prior to me starting first grade and it was a fabulous place for a child to grow up. Our development was new and was situated on the edge of a 123 acre forest preserve called The Grove. Our relatively small subdivision of about 70 houses on typical quarter-acre lots rimmed the eastern edge of The Grove. For 1972 standards, our home and neighborhood was something to be proud of in terms of style, size, landscaping, and amenities. Compared to the behemoths of suburban Chicago today, our home would be considered modest—but it was my castle.

What made my home particularly special was that The Grove was just one block from my front door. I would enter The Grove through a well-worn path near my best friend, Peter Johnson's house. I would cross over into the forest at a dead end street that abruptly ended at a gradual edge of grass, stones, and weeds. Further from the pavement small trees sprouted yielding to larger species that extended their branches over the forest entrance like the arch of a cathedral. The primary entrance path was wide and worn so well that bikes could easily navigate through the arch of branches above it.

I was drawn to The Grove by nature and curious exploration. To this day, I enjoy every aspect of nature from landscapes, to vegetation, to wildlife. My wife is often unsettled during our vacations to national parks where I confide to her that I could easily take up residence in the middle of a forest, mountain range, or wherever we happen to be visiting. I'm sure my love of nature and wildlife is innate, shared genetically with my self-proclaimed "tom boy" mother who grew up in Fox Lake, Illinois during a time of its very rural development. My mom spent her childhood days exploring the many ponds, rivers, and forests surrounding her home where she often found turtles, fish, and other exciting discoveries that she would temporarily capture then eventually release.

Regardless of where my passion was seeded, I was continually drawn to The Grove. Each exploration took me deeper into this world seemingly removed from the one I would return to prior to the scheduled dinner hour—if I was lucky. The Grove's one primary path briefly meandered from my neighborhood to an adjoining, more established neighborhood about 200 yards through the forest. The two neighborhoods were cut off from each other partly from the forest and the remaining reaches by a wall of backyards from peripheral homes in each subdivision that backed up to each other. That well-worn path was obviously the shortcut for many to pass quickly between the two neighborhoods. In fact, it was the only way to reach that community, shy of leaving the main entrance of my subdivision and following a single frontage road back to what seemed to be a foreign land in the eyes of a first grader.

The primary path was great fun to race through on bikes or to engage in hide and seek with our homes still in site through the trees. What was truly intriguing and drawing to me were the smaller, less visible arterial paths that branched off from the central dirt highway. These paths took one deeper into the core of the forest, and I would have to plan for these journeys as they would take hours to complete. It seemed every visit uncovered a new route and with it a new element of the forest system. There were large openings in the forest center of fields covered in tall golden grasses and wild prairie flowers. Swampy outcrops were especially appealing for the potential wildlife that may reside inside or under fallen logs. Certain areas would be so densely covered in tall trees that the ground would be almost bare with only pine needles, fallen leaves and branches due to the lofty canopy providing minimal sun penetration. The Grove even held some secrets that only few explorers ever came upon.

One was an old dumping ground of a religious retreat, which was located on the very opposite edge of The Grove from my home. The highlights of this small depository included what seemed to be a vintage automobile, probably a '60s era shell of a Chevrolet that apparently had no worth to entice someone to free it from its final resting place. A refrigerator and other half buried appliances sprouted from the ground between tall weeds and grasses. Then there was just a collection of stuff that did not seem to keep permanence in my memory, but the collection together was somewhat magical to a seven-year-old boy who happened to stumble upon its secret location.

The jewel of The Grove that I would only discover after dozens of solo journeys was further down a barely visible path that zigzagged around low-standing waters, fallen trees, and other formidable forest hurdles. The path faded at what would have been a magnificent backyard of a large two-story, wood-planked house that was a cross between a Victorian and a Prairie style home. Neglected and abandoned for what appeared to be forever, every aspect of the house shared the same rain-washed, colorless appearance from the doors, window sills, downspouts, and porch. As a kid you wanted that house to be haunted. I mean, who really ever gets to come across a true haunted house? Even better, this one was all by itself without another neighbor or structure in site and in the middle of a forest! How cool is that! But how could such a home just be abandoned? Where did the occupants go and why did the house not pass on to relatives or sell to new owners? Maybe everyone was murdered!

Rounding the house to the front one could tell that this was no ordinary home. The prominence of the front door, although simple in appearance, was ornate—something not expected of an abandoned home. The windows were all so thick with dust and dirt that it was impossible to see inside of the structure. Subsequent investigations would yield another dwelling not too far from what appeared to be the primary residence. I never entered either home even though I am sure it would have been very easy to do and within the law (in my mind), as clearly no one had claimed ownership of this property for quite some time. Yet, I still respected the property and its long past owners. Perhaps it was my upbringing not to break down a home's front door or break a window just to see what's inside. I'm sure that's what my parents would like to hear, or maybe I was just too darn scared to alert any ghostly inhabitants?

It would be years later that the home's story would be told to the entire Glenview community. Its former grandeur would be restored and its occupant's remarkable history would be revealed. It turns out that the home belonged to the Kennicott family. Dr. John Kennicott, the area's first physician and noted horticulturist, built in 1845 what is described as a "majestic gothic revival house" for his growing family. Today the exterior of the house has been fully restored with careful attention paid to each historical detail from the sharply peaked roof line to the rain barrels on the back porch. The interior of the house has been restored with 19th century furniture, including many pieces that actually belonged to the Kennicott family.

From the plaque that stands outside the house today, "Dr. Kennicott was a prominent Illinois physician, horticulturist, and educational and agricultural leader. Kennicott moved to The Grove from New Orleans with his family in 1836. He devoted much of his time to the study and promotion of horticulture and agriculture, developing The Grove into the first major nursery in northern Illinois. His son Robert Kennicott, developed an interest in nature at an early age, studying with his father."

The adjoining Tudor-style home I later discovered is today called The Redfield Estate, which was built in 1929 and was the home of various Kennicott descendents as well as acclaimed authors Louise Redfield Peattie and Donald Culross Peattie, who respectfully each authored *A Prairie Grove* and *American Acres.*

Robert Kennicott's story particularly interested me and seemed to symbolize early frontier entrepreneurialism. Robert was born in New Orleans but grew up in the home in The Grove. His fascination and exploration of The Grove behind his house was in direct correlation to my own only separated by over one hundred years. In 1853, Robert began collecting and cataloging snakes for the Smithsonian Institution in Washington DC. He would go on to help found the Chicago Academy of Sciences and the Northwestern University natural history museum all within a short four years.

In April 1859 he set off on an expedition to collect natural history specimens in the subarctic boreal forests of northwestern Canada and beyond the Arctic tundra. Kennicott became popular with Hudson's Bay Company fur traders in the area and encouraged them to collect and send natural history specimens and Indian artifacts to the Smithsonian in Washington DC where he would eventually reside in 1862. Robert and his younger brother actually lived for a period of time in the Smithsonian Castle during the American Civil War.

Like me, Robert Kennicott had an interest in snakes and was the original author of many new snake descriptions brought back by expeditions to the American West. In 1864, two years before his death from a heart attack at the age of 31, Robert was part of an expedition to Alaska funded by the Western Union Telegraph to find a possible route for a telegraph line between North America and Russia by way of the Bering Sea. He was buried at a Kennicott Family plot in The Grove, which is now a national historic landmark. You see, it was haunted!

Robert Kennicott was an ecological-entrepreneur adventurer, and I greatly envy his experiences. His entrepreneurial life, like my exploration of the forest, was reflective of Robert Frost's poem "The Road Not Taken." So many times in my life, both figuratively and literally, I have been faced with two paths to choose. Almost always, I took the one less traveled and that has made all the difference.

My discovery of the Kennicott house would not have been made if I stayed with the other kids, or was required to stay on the sidewalk that ran safely along the outer perimeter of The Grove. If I continued on the well-worn path that cut between my neighborhood and the other, I would not have discovered the magical dump and other treasures hidden within the woodland. By today's standards my parents might be thrown in jail for allowing their child to roam freely and unescorted into a forest where who knows what was lying in wait for them. I certainly would not allow my children to replicate my childhood in those respects, and unfortunately today we can't. The world is vastly different from when I explored.

Entrepreneurs take the road less traveled as Kennicott himself did over one hundred years ago. Who would imagine taking the life journey he did in terms of exploration of untamed lands? I relate and envy the works of Kennicott and perhaps I mimic them in a 21st century way as an entrepreneur of business.

The rules of society that I spoke of keep us safe and prevent us from taking the road that is less traveled. They tell us that it is safer and predictable by taking the well-traipsed path. They teach us to be weary and apprehensive of the less-traveled road because the outcomes are not guaranteed. There is considerable risk in taking this path, and they are right. However, this little analogy also shows us that dramatic and wonderful outcomes can happen by following the less-traveled path. People set out on journeys down unchartered paths for discovery, to find riches, to learn, to experience, and sometimes just for the freedom to do it.

Robert Kennicott went on a journey of exploration where he created the path resulting in the discovery of new species and land that would eventually be monumentally important for his country. I walked a path to discover a fascinating home that kept remarkable historical secrets right in my own backyard—perhaps a path created many years ago by a young boy around my age at the time who walked out his back door and headed out to explore the outer reaches of the forest he called The Grove.

Every journey starts with an idea to take the journey. Are you ready to discover your Grove?

CHAPTER TWO
Entrepreneur or Business Owner?

"Most new jobs won't come from our biggest employers. They will come from our smallest. We've got to do everything we can to make entrepreneurial dreams a reality." — Ross Perot

I was not an expert on the study of entrepreneurs, or entrepreneurialism for that matter, when I started to write this book. True, I was an entrepreneur—a "replicative" one—which I'll explain later. The mission and purpose of my book was well conceived and the core outline of the content I wanted to convey was equally well formulated. However, as I dug deeper into my content I realized something critical was missing. I discovered I needed to become a student of entrepreneurial studies myself. It was necessary for me to do this to validate my assumptions and methodologies and to earn credibility from you, my reader.

The ensuing research took a considerable amount of time and became increasingly more validating in the sense that my theories and assumptions on the entrepreneurial psyche, risk assessment, growth progressions, and ingredients for success were confirmed through multiple sources of empirical independent study. Through this research I realized it was necessary for me to define the word *entrepreneur*, the types of entrepreneurs, and explain how they differ from business owners in order for you to navigate your own entrepreneurial journey.

There is a significant difference between being a business owner and being an entrepreneur, just as there are significant differences between the various types of entrepreneurs. You may set off on your journey intending to be one thing, when in reality you are very much another. This understanding should help guide you toward appropriate resources and models that will help you avoid the cost and frustration of figuring things out through trial and error. The old adage, "if I only knew then what I know now" certainly applies to myself and knowledge gleaned from writing this book would have greatly impacted my own journey. Knowing what I know now would literally be worth millions to me during my journey, as I'll explain, and this knowledge may turn into millions for you!

Many a "would-be" entrepreneur has ventured out into his own personal Grove unprepared for the journey ahead. He either does so out of abundant self confidence, blindness to unforeseen pitfalls, or simply out of impatience in waiting for the right opportunity, thereby trying to force opportunity upon himself. These trial-and-error attempts are expensive both in terms of money spent on failed ventures as well as mental fatigue and erosion of self confidence.

If entrepreneurs are born from ideas then what do your ideas tell you about the type of entrepreneur you may be or want to be? The media portrays entrepreneurs as all being categorically the same and, for that matter, anyone who owns a business or conducts business on their own is considered an entrepreneur; however, that simply is not accurate. Entrepreneurs don't all come in a single shape and size or inclusively represent business ownership. The Wikipedia and Webster's definition of an entrepreneur are very similar with Wikipedia stating it "is a person who has possession of an enterprise, or venture, and assumes significant accountability for the inherent risks and the outcome." Commonly an entrepreneur is defined simply as a person who starts a new business venture. I would add my own abridgement to those definitions that "on a good day: it can be the most rewarding life experience, and on a bad day:

the worst decision of your life."

The wiki goes on to state that the word *entrepreneur* is often synonymous with founder and that "entrepreneur in English, as it is a French term, is applied to the type of personality who is willing to take upon herself or himself a new venture or enterprise and accepts full responsibility for the outcome." Debate has gone on for years as to whether entrepreneurs are made or born, and defining entrepreneurs as having a type of personality sways in favor of genetic predisposition. I agree that an entrepreneur demonstrates an organized set of characteristics that uniquely influences his or her cognitions, motivations, and behaviors in various situations, aligned to the definition of a personality type. However, as a personality type it implies to me that some would have this trait and others would not. My experience and study sees entrepreneurism more as an action born out of a situation and opportunity regardless of personality type. Granted, certain personalities like my own seem more predisposed to gravitate toward the entrepreneur, but I affirm all are capable.

A clear description distinguishes a *business proprietor* who starts up a business in order to pursue personal lifestyle goals from a *true entrepreneur* who has the vision and drive to create completely new products and services that may serve entirely new markets.

Early trait theory describes common entrepreneurial characteristics as traits derived at birth, where I would argue they are predominantly behaviors learned through experience and education. Entrepreneurs want to create something, not just manage a business. Through this creation they want to achieve great results and expand into unchartered areas. They are able to do this as they are creative, innovative, and continually generating ideas and variations of ideas in order to meet the needs of an opportunity that only they may see. Some describe entrepreneurs as overtly positive and having tremendous faith in themselves, their abilities, and their vision. They promote their vision actively and have tremendous powers of persuasion to engage others to satisfy the needs of their vision.

To me an entrepreneur is an action or a response. Many popular theories say entrepreneurs respond to opportunities that they feel only they uniquely see. The key here is opportunity. This response can take place in the actual creation of a business or a response to harness innovation within an existing business. On one hand the entrepreneur assesses all available information on the opportunity and on the other he assesses the environmental factors that may influence the opportunity's chances for success. Combining both sets of data allows the entrepreneur to make educated decisions on how and if to proceed. That process of educated decisions is called risk assessment.

Risk assessment to an entrepreneur is no different than risk assessment that a manager conducts within an existing business. William Gartner, a professor of entrepreneurial leadership, asserted that entrepreneurs' traits are rather similar to managers and the general population, which reinforces my assertions. The act of risk taking is more heavily associated with entrepreneurs because it is the individual personally taking on this risk, rather than a firm. Smart and successful entrepreneurs are not so much risk takers and gamblers, as the mythic image and definitions may popularize, as they are calculated strategists who are able to assimilate data and apply the results to a future vision that they alone can uniquely see.

Through my research and experience I have found that talented entrepreneurs are better described as being more risk averse. Entrepreneurs have to make decisions to launch their business and they do this based on "factors of production," which includes in basic form: land, labor, capital, and intelligence/knowledge/creativity. They assess the risk they undertake by calculating the success of a new innovation they want to bring to market. The innovative idea becomes the core essence of the entrepreneur and it represents the primary element that drives the Idea phase, which is the first phase of business creation. Entrepreneurs become the byproducts of ideas and innovation once they decide to take action. It's not the chicken or the egg. Entrepreneurs become entrepreneurs once they take action to make their idea or invention a reality, not before.

Why is it important for entrepreneurs to exist? Simply put, entrepreneurs are the catalyst of all economic creation. Now that's a pretty tall statement, but one historians, economists, and theorists have all agreed upon through their study of entrepreneurs in our economic ecosystem. Entrepreneurs claim this title over business owners because they develop new markets through effective demand; discover new sources of materials; mobilize the resources of land, labor, and capital; introduce new technologies, new industries, and new products; and create employment growth.

Peter Drucker, notable author and management consultant, stated, "Entrepreneurs redirect their resources toward progressive opportunities and they use change as a catalyst to deploy those resources." The business owner that fails to offer something new and stays the status quo remains just that, a business owner. When resources are not risked on new opportunities, they are kept to maintain the current state and you simply have a business being managed.

This notion of putting resources at risk reminds me of the Parable of the Talents in the Bible (Matthew 25:14-30), where three servants are entrusted with their master's funds each according to his ability. Two put their funds to work and increased their "talents" while the third buries his out of fear of losing them as he explains to his master. The first two servants are praised for their faithful service and the third is cast out for laziness and fear of taking risk. How do we as individuals act with the gifts and talents that each of us have been given? Do we use our abilities to return greater achievements or do we horde them to ourselves?

By no means is this to assert that business owners are any less important or worthy than entrepreneurs. More so, it serves to distinguish an entrepreneur and what makes him different from a business owner who is generically referred to as an entrepreneur. They are not equals, but nonetheless both vital to our economy. It is the business owner who typically serves a product or service fulfillment need within a community. His business model is not necessarily devised to scale or to innovate but to sustain.

You might say I'm splitting hairs but the differentiation is significant to answer the question of whether our nation can remain globally competitive and why it is important for entrepreneurs to exist. We see our educational performance lagging in world comparison, particularly in mathematics and science, and we ask if we can remain competitive. Do individuals shy away from math and science because it's hard and they are afraid to invest in the challenge of the content? At times I see a "fatness" in our country. Not so much the physical fat that is the concern of our growing obesity rates, but in complacency that often results in non-physical or mental engagement.

Often I feel our country is sitting back and getting fat on our quality of life and all of the amenities and luxuries afforded within our borders. Like a spoiled child, have we become complacent, lazy, and unchallenged? Why innovate and why create if we have all these great things already at our disposal? The hope found in the answer to those questions is that we are innovative and creative people at heart. We have an educational system that increasingly focuses on entrepreneurial endeavors and thinking. We have a government that invites innovation and research and a society which rewards and admires these efforts. Most importantly, we still have people who want to pursue entrepreneurial dreams, and we still attract the foreigner to our shores, who views our country as the most likely and favorable place to make that attempt and take that risk. It is the entrepreneur who will create new businesses, new industries, and new markets that secure global competitiveness.

As we see old businesses die, like the bankruptcy of GM and Chrysler, we need new businesses to take their place and they will come from the entrepreneur. A descriptive quote from Professor Sumner H. Slichter of the Harvard Business School states that "a community in which everyone attempted to make a living by getting on someone else's payroll would be a community of unemployed." These are macro considerations for the value of the entrepreneur, but I want to focus on you the individual. Entrepreneurism is seeded in all of us yearning to maximize our potential, talents, time and human contribution that should not be wasted.

The Bank Account

Imagine you have a bank account that credits your balance each day with $86,400. The trick is it carries over no balance from day to day. Every evening it deletes whatever part of the balance you failed to use during the day. A wise man would therefore draw out and use those funds each day. We all have this bank account and it is called Time.

Time grants you 86,400 seconds each day. You can use these seconds however you wish, but you cannot carry them forward. Any unused time is written off as a loss. If you fail to use the day's deposits, the loss is yours. There is

no going back. There is no drawing against the
"tomorrow." Your dreams will always be dreams
if you fail to invest the time in making them a
reality and you're given 86,400 seconds each
day to try.

—Source Unknown

Everyone has ideas. Some of those ideas are businesses that
serve commercial, social, or environmental missions. These ideas are
the fuel for job creation, economic growth, and extraordinary lives.
What prevents us from taking action to make them a reality? Knowing
our "time accounts" are limited and reset each day, why don't we
maximize how we use them toward these purposes—our dreams?

CHAPTER THREE
A History Lesson of Entrepreneurs

The study of entrepreneurs and entrepreneurship is very young, even though the word was coined as early as 1800 by Jean-Baptiste Say, a French economist. As far as we know, the first documented courses taught on entrepreneurism in the United States were at Harvard Business School (HBS) in 1947. Myles Mace, who earned his MBA at HBS in 1938 continued to work at the school as a research associate up until 1942, when he was called for military duty to serve in World War II. It is said that Mace, being an economist, took careful note of the number of fellow servicemen who were sharing hopeful stories of returning home after the war to start businesses for themselves. The explosion of post war GIs trading their traditional industrial jobs for entrepreneurship, in my opinion, was due in part to their war experience lowering their risk barriers. That life or death experience made abundantly clear the value of following personal dreams. Where's the relative risk in starting a business after you've just survived the experience of war? When Mace returned from service in 1946, having earned the Bronze Star, he went back to HBS and started the first known course on entrepreneurism in higher education.

Growth of entrepreneurial study did not exactly explode, as I imagine society in general viewed the practice as an individual effort or personality trait that was not influenced by broader study or understanding. It took entrepreneurial courses in higher education nearly 30 years to grow to just over 100 by the mid-1970s. The focus in government and academics was centered on supporting big business as the primary source of economic development and employment. However, by 2009 it was reported that more than 80 percent of both two- and four-year-degree-granting accredited colleges and universities in the US had courses on entrepreneurism. That growth really only started during the mid '90s.

One of the great and philanthropic entrepreneurs of our time, Ewing Marion Kauffman was a World War II veteran like Mace who started a company, Marion Laboratories, several years after he returned from service in 1950. Kauffman started the company with $5,000 and it grew to revenues of $930 million by 1989 when it merged with Merrell Dow Pharmaceuticals. Kauffman is credited with creating over 3,000 jobs during his tenure at Marion Laboratories. One of the great societal benefits of entrepreneurialism is in job creation and in that regard we all owe respect to the men and women who continue to innovate and create businesses.

The greatest contributor to the understanding of entrepreneurship and the earliest researcher on the topic is the Austrian economist Joseph Schumpeter. Coincidentally, Schumpeter moved to the US prior to World War II to escape Nazism in 1927 and taught at Harvard from 1932 to 1950 when he died. I am sure to some extent he worked with and exchanged theories with our friend Myles Mace. Schumpeter studied business cycles and economic development and the role of the entrepreneur and political influence. It is worthy to understand Schumpeter's theory of the "stationary state" to acknowledge the influential progression of innovation to entrepreneurism and the critical bind between the two.

In his theory of economic development, innovation plays a critical role and it will be central to my discussion of the entrepreneur's journey. The theory states the economy should follow a circular flow; that is, firms provide goods and services to households, who in turn pay money for those goods and services. The circular flow of income can increase or decrease, thus providing economic booms or recessions. What can stall the economy are stationary states which are caused by the lack of innovation or innovative activities. This highlights the importance of the role of the entrepreneur and for you as a would-be or existing entrepreneur to understand that your role in your business is to innovate! Schumpeter's macro economic theory holds true at the individual business level too. A business that does not innovate will reach a stationary state of non-growth or worse, negative growth. This may sustain a successful business owner with a decent salary and consistent annual sales, but not an entrepreneur.

To Schumpeter, the entrepreneur is the one who harnesses a new idea or invention into something meaningful and useful with an economic outcome. It is the entrepreneur that saves the day by establishing innovation, creating a vision for its use, and putting it into action. Schumpeter's Mark I theory goes on to argue that it is entrepreneurs who are responsible for the innovation and technological change of a nation. As I said, entrepreneurs are the byproducts of innovation. They are the ones who take invention and innovation and do something with it. Trying to capture the essence of what drives and motivates the entrepreneur's desire to do this, Schumpeter coined the descriptive phrase "entrepreneurial spirit" which is used so prevalently today.

Schumpeter drew upon the term "creative destruction," pulled from the work of economists Mikhail Bakunin, Friedrich Nietzsche, and Werner Sombart's *War and Capitalism*. Schumpeter's own work, *Capitalism, Socialism and Democracy* uses the term to describe the power of innovation and creativity that destroys complacency and stationary states. Entrepreneurs convert new ideas into new products, services, and business models which challenge established companies and industries. Their revolutionary approaches catch the established companies off guard and immediately put those firms at a competitive disadvantage. The marketplace rewards the entrepreneurial firm with business and the old school firms either adapt or die. Creative destruction acknowledges that some businesses will fail due to other firm's innovation, yet the benefit of a more dynamic and efficient industry coupled with expanding economic growth dwarf the causalities in the process.

Like innovation, risk is closely associated with entrepreneurship and I'll specifically cover risk further along in our journey together. Both economist Frank H. Knight and management guru Peter Drucker described entrepreneurship as being about taking risk. They view entrepreneurs as individuals who make a commitment to themselves that can involve risking their finances, career, home, relationships, time and quality of life on an uncertain and unproven venture. The public perception of entrepreneurial risk seems so unilateral in the sense that if you take this action you may lose everything or win big, which adds to the allure as well as the consternation of being an entrepreneur.

What most would-be entrepreneurs should find very disturbing is Knight's classifications of uncertainty in regards to entrepreneurism. While it is popular to associate risk with entrepreneurism, the correct term to use is uncertainty. Knight established three types of uncertainty: risk, ambiguity, and true uncertainty, with risk being the least risky—oddly enough. Risk is defined by Knight as being statistically measurable. Ambiguity is hard to measure, while true uncertainty is impossible to estimate or predict statistically.

As you would guess, Knight classifies the entrepreneur as conducting in true uncertainty. This is not universally true of all entrepreneurial types and endeavors; however, for those who engage in new technologies and inventions, the likes of which create new industries and serve new markets, true uncertainty correctly categorizes their undertaking. True uncertainty may even be present in existing markets where entrepreneurs are introducing new competitive variations of an established product because there is still no guarantee that the market will accept the new player.

My Story Begins

Mine is not the high school or twenty something entrepreneurial whiz kid story; my journey starts several years after college. I attended Northern Illinois University, which up until February 14, 2008 was a college that no one outside of Illinois should have recognized. Due to tragic headlines of a mass shooting which injured 18 and claimed the lives of six including the perpetrator, NIU became well known around the world for becoming the site of the fourth deadliest university slaying in US history. Graduating nearly ten years earlier with a general Business BS degree in May, 1988 I found first employment with Allstate Insurance in Northbrook, Illinois.

I landed a management trainee position in the home office Operations Department, and I was really excited about the job. There certainly was a bit of pride and prestige being able to say you got a job with a Fortune 100 company right out of school. Allstate was a great—no, fantastic place to work. The well-landscaped grounds of the home office provided paths to take walks and ball fields for interdepartmental softball tournaments after work. Inside, well appointed offices or cubicles were provided to all, along with cafeteria service and other corporate amenities. Though people worked hard, it was a pretty strict 8-to-5 crowd.

I was fortunate to work with a great group of people who were nurturing and supportive of my career. In return, I gave 100% and did a pretty good job by incorporating minor innovative thoughts and procedures where I could. As a management trainee, I was rotated to various areas always managing a group of administrative co-workers. This provided me with extensive hands-on management experience of people which would prove to be invaluable in my career development. About two years after I began working at Allstate, I started studying for my Masters degree in business, which I would complete going to school at night on a part-time basis while working. When I earned my MBA in 1993, I not only received a degree but my first child too, a daughter named Kaitlyn Marie Weber.

Life was going great and I was itching to move up faster. I enjoyed the work at Allstate, but I didn't feel what I was doing really impacted the direction and success of the company. Operations was a supportive department responsible for shipping and receiving, mail room, security, building engineers, grounds, and other support services. We were not responsible for revenue, marketing, or other aspects core to the insurance business. Home office jobs were cherished and people built life-long careers ascending their respective departmental ladders. That however did not appeal to me and I wanted to make a change.

Armed with my new MBA and a sense of entitlement to grander things, namely a bigger paycheck, I set out to be the next grad school superstar to bless someone's doorway. In the early '90s MBAs were hot. Everything you read showed their additional earning potential over a typical undergraduate degree and now I had the golden ticket. My search led me to a Plant Manager position for a small textile manufacturing company in Chicago paying $12,000 more than I had been earning at Allstate. After a brief series of interviews I was offered the job. The comfort and amenities of Allstate would be replaced with a stone patch, four-car parking area behind a single story brick building erected in the 1930s or '40s. Lack of air conditioning was compensated by rows of hand-cranked vented glass ceiling panel sky lights surrounded by security bars. The work force I was to manage was Hispanic with little to no English as far as they would let on to me. Yes, I knew all of this when I took the job, but I was ready to rock the world and impact the direction of this company and make a few more bucks.

I had established relationships at Allstate and many of those I worked with were truly sad and disappointed to see me go. I was not prepared for that. I was internally focused and to a degree selfish. I made a career move based on the wrong reasons. I ended up hating every day in my new position. Each morning I would sit in my car in the weed-infested parking lot before work, dreading having to go in. Having no understanding of the product or the customer, I was struggling to innovate and create the efficiencies that the owner had hired me to develop.

CHAPTER FOUR
A History Lesson of Entrepreneurs

Two macro types of entrepreneurs, replicative and innovative, emerge from the aforementioned definition to help establish the type of entrepreneur you are or wish to become.

The Replicative Entrepreneur

The replicative entrepreneur is probably the most common. They start businesses that are very similar or even directly identical to ones that already exist. The replicative is so common because many entrepreneurs gain inspiration from businesses and industries that they know and are familiar with. They learn the business and, more importantly, the industry by working for someone else and then decide to go it alone.

To increase the chance of survival and growth, the replicative entrepreneur finds and develops a way to differentiate himself in the marketplace. Simply copying an existing business model often is not enough to guarantee success, especially if targeting the same customer base. Differentiation can come through operational improvements and cost cutting, to new methods to sell or deliver the product, or by incorporating new materials or processes. In the case of my story, I replicated what my former employer did and took it to a completely new market. As my company developed and matured, I "micro-innovated" to serve our customers in new and unique ways.

JetBlue founder David Neeleman stated in an article for *Fortune* magazine, "I never would have started JetBlue unless I had the experience of starting another airline." Neeleman cites his replicative knowledge from his first airline experience with Morris Air, which he co-founded and later sold to Southwest. Neeleman continued by saying, "I guarantee that I never would have started JetBlue at J.F.K. airport if I had listened to the experts, who said that you can't put a low-fare, customer-centric airline in New York. But I knew we could do it, and I had a wealth of experience behind me that I trusted to make JetBlue a reality."

The replicative models flourish particularly during periods of economic growth by providing needed goods and services to the community or customer base that they serve. Although replicatives are not best known for increasing overall economic productivity, per-worker or even per-capita new wealth creation, they do serve an important function to the economy by creating efficiencies using proven business models and providing increased employment.

If you wanted to, you could classify most business owners as replicative entrepreneurs. The dry cleaner, restaurant owner, gas station, copy center, franchise, retail store, and so forth. They certainly serve a purpose to their community and they launch based on existing business models and practices. What earns the title of entrepreneur and a true replicative is when they innovate and scale their business. Where replicative business owners respond to demand, the replicative entrepreneur creates demand.

The Innovative Entrepreneur

Innovative entrepreneurs are the ones who grab the headlines for introducing revolutionary new products and services to market or by virtue of their innovation they create new markets entirely. They take inventions and make industries out of them. For instance, research and development yields unique inventions in the form of new technology and substances. These new inventions may have been created for a single purpose or multiple uses and businesses can be created to take advantage of the discovery. However, it is up to the entrepreneur or an entrepreneurial company to turn that new invention into a useful product. This is the action I spoke about earlier in defining entrepreneurs. Entrepreneurism is not so much a personality trait that exists as it is an action and response to an opportunity at hand.

Innovative entrepreneurs create wealth by boosting productivity, which in turn establishes a higher standard of living for the economic base touched by the innovator. Nobel Prize winner Robert Solow, an American economist known for his work on the theory of economic growth, had conducted extensive research on innovation and described it as the "cornerstone of economic growth." Innovative entrepreneurs are the elite that fuel progress and national growth.

Entrepreneurial Name Tags

Understanding the role each type of entrepreneur plays should shape your business plan and influence your acquisition of available resources. There are more granular entrepreneur types which fit under either the replicative or innovative models. For instance, there are social entrepreneurs—someone who identifies a social problem or issue and creates an organization, fund, enterprise, or some other entity to address that issue or problem. The goal is to alleviate, mitigate, or solve the social issue. Often the measurement of the goals and objectives of the social entrepreneur do not directly align with the traditional financial benchmarks that we envision. Success is measured less in dollars and cents and more in the impact to the cause, resulting in a social profit. Similarly a rapidly emerging entrepreneur definition is the green entrepreneur who is focused on environmentally friendly outcomes with an eye on profits.

The entrepreneur I admire most is the serial entrepreneur. This person has continual radar for opportunity and can apply innovative ways to exploit it. Serials have already started, successfully run, and exited a business venture and they go on to start new businesses. Sometimes ventures are started in succession or other times simultaneously. I have to believe that these individuals see no barriers to creating what they dream or envision. They see the world through a completely different lens where they find the resources they need with relative ease to start their next enterprise. Often these individuals create very different businesses, each unique to the next. That is because the mind of the entrepreneur is often not so fixated on any one thing in particular, but in how needs develop and improvements can be made. I am a huge fan of Sir Richard Branson who as a serial entrepreneur created many different types of significant businesses in vastly different industries from transportation, music, mobile telephony, travel, financial services, publishing, and retailing. The Virgin Group boasts 200 branded companies worldwide, employing approximately 50,000 people in 29 countries.

Many can identify with the serial entrepreneur's scattered interests in that you have probably had dozens of ideas to start a business and all of those ideas were very different from one another. The serial entrepreneur sees or visualizes the market opportunity for their particular product or service regardless of segmentation. Many entrepreneurs who successfully start a business continue to have new ideas while running their business and after they exit. They just can't shake that mode of viewing the world. The deliberate serial entrepreneur enters a business knowing he won't be satisfied with just one. He wants to grow the business to a sustainable level so that he can then move on to his next idea. The mindset is completely different from that of the solo entrepreneur and he is far more difficult to predict in terms of where he'll wind up next.

The Internet entrepreneur is one who creates businesses solely focused on the Internet as his storefront. These innovative businesses often shape the direction of commerce on the Internet and challenge the traditional brick and mortar establishment. Larry Page and Sergey Brin of Google aptly fit this description as would Jeff Bezos of Amazon.com. These are more often the sexy, high-profile companies that grab our attention. They also probably represent one of the greatest areas for entrepreneurial growth in upcoming years. The digital revolution is in its infancy and it is exciting to imagine the new resources, services, conveniences, and business models that will emerge from these Internet entrepreneurs.

A term presented to me that I credit to Ron Brumbarger, a replicative social entrepreneur from Carmel, Indiana, is Evangelpreneur. By his definition this is a faith-based approach to entrepreneurialism and entrepreneurial success. Ron's assertion is that an individual must have a faith and belief that his entrepreneurial efforts will bear fruit and that starts with a firm belief in his God. I found the notion of faith to be an interesting perspective which I carry forward in subsequent chapters. Faith in yourself, your idea, and your God is a pretty strong trifecta that manifests itself in the desire or passion of the entrepreneur.

Ron continued his evangelpreneur explanation to include a focus he has on delivering entrepreneurism to other countries as an educational deliverable wrapped in a faith-based foundation. Ron's vision is to develop faith-based entrepreneurs in the Ukraine. He wants to go to the Ukraine to teach the principles of entrepreneurship so the citizens can create businesses and develop a sustainable economy. The twist is that he wants to instill in these entrepreneurs that they can't do it alone; they need faith, specifically a faith in their God.

Bill Hybels of Willow Creek Community Church in South Barrington, Illinois could be considered an evangelpreneur for his creation of one of the nation's largest and most successful mega church. I suppose every spiritual leader would like to consider themselves a spiritual entrepreneur by their own evangelistic charter, however, few are able to scale and grow their organization like Hybels. Through innovative use of music, drama and multimedia, and targeting a niche market of the un-churched, Hybels created a church whose facility holds the largest theater in the United States and welcomes weekly attendance in excess of 20,000 people. The Willow Creek Association became a spinoff of the success of the mother church in 1992 and connects like-minded churches around the world with training and resources. They now boast a network of over 11,000 churches. In 1995 the Global Leadership Summit was formed out of Willow Creek, which serves as an annual training event to sharpen member leadership skills. Summits have reached over 70 international sites touching 80,000 attendees!

The Power of the Entrepreneur

As you can see there is great variation in the definition and explanation of what an entrepreneur is. Someone who buys an existing business or opens a sole proprietorship is not necessarily an entrepreneur, he is a business owner. He doesn't fit the description of an entrepreneur and he doesn't fulfill the promise of an entrepreneur. The crux of the definition is that a true entrepreneur is someone who takes an idea, innovation, or invention and develops a business which fully exploits its potential. In doing so, new supportive businesses are created, new industries may be started, job creation expands, the economic base grows, and wealth generation occurs. Entrepreneurs are not merely interesting news stories; they are an integral foundation to any economy and hold the promise of sustaining the nation's standard of living. Harvard Business School professor Arthur Cole put it best stating, "The entrepreneur provides an economic service" marrying factors of production with economic enterprises. To Cole nothing in economic life happens without the entrepreneur who is, "the central figure in economic society and whose actions create all economic change."

Fired with Children

I had been working three months at my new job as Plant Manager of a small manufacturer of infant bedding products when the owner who hired me stopped in to talk with me. She took me aside to the conference room, which happened to be the emergency exit to the courtyard between our building and the body shop behind us. She quickly delivered the news that I was to be fired. I should have been relieved, but I was shocked and scared. I had never been fired before, and I was working hard to increase production line efficiency. With a new baby girl and house to take care of, a million things were going through my head. My ego that got me into this mess popped like a balloon in a cartoon. Here I had just received my MBA and had a successful run with a large Fortune 100 company and I was getting fired from this dinky little bootstrap company?

I was to learn a great lesson from this experience: results trump hard work. I could put all the time in and expend great effort, but if at the end of the day I'm not making a difference or driving greater results, I'm not needed. The expectations here were far higher and more time sensitive than they were for me at Allstate. It was the right decision to fire me as it would have been a long time, if ever, before I was successful in that business. This was my first career failure. It stung and became influential in steering the outcome of my professional career moving forward. Foremost it enforced the need for humility and not getting too big for my britches.

Suck it up!

I immediately went into job search mode and reluctantly heeded everyone's advice to file for unemployment benefits immediately. About a month into the search, I desperately went back to Allstate Insurance to see if they would hire me again. Thankfully, they didn't. A good rule of thumb to follow is not to offer employment to an employee who has quit, regardless of what type of a performer he was. If they left once, they will leave again. This same rule should be heeded strongly by new entrepreneurs. Once an employee quits or is fired, let them go and wish them well—don't take them back. Small companies are very susceptible to this as the investment in training is high. You may feel that as long as the person understands your world he is an asset, but employees that are not 100 percent committed can become very costly to an upstart business. The expectations are higher in a smaller company because each individual's contribution is so significant and visible.

It took a grueling five months to find my next job. In that time, I answered ads, went to job fairs, knocked on company doors unannounced, and had maybe three or four interviews. I simply could not get anyone to look at me. It was an awful market. Fortunately, great friends of ours, John and Pat Laystrom, followed my plight, and Pat shared an open position with the firm she worked for. Pat had gotten in pretty close to the ground floor with Educational Resources and was truly on the fast track. Educational Resources was a reseller of computer software to the education market right when the PC was going mainstream. A reseller is another term for a retailer or dealer. All of Educational Resources' sales were conducted via mail order and over the phone. The company had been growing dramatically since inception in the late '80s and they were hiring for all sorts of positions.

I applied for a marketing product manager position. The product manager was responsible for a variety of software publishers that Educational Resources represented. This position was the central interface between the publisher and Educational Resources, helping to facilitate product information internally to the sales and operation teams and externally to the customers in the form of catalogs and other direct mail pieces. The product manager's responsibilities included: establishing a product's price and profit margin, determining what type of promotional efforts to conduct to market a product, developing inside sales training, and performing a variety of other duties which really sounded interesting to me. I was truly excited about this job and the company, and I wanted in.

After meeting the hiring manager and president I thankfully got the job. My MBA was a plus in the eyes of the hiring manager, but personal networking probably had more influence. When I started work I busted my butt to learn the business. There was no training; things were moving way too fast and no one had time for it. Sink or swim was the motto and no one had time to see you drown either. I began reading every industry trade journal from cover to cover as soon as it hit my desk. Knowledge was paramount in this industry and especially in my position. Information was changing rapidly as technology was improving and creating new products at an exponential rate, and the product manager was responsible for finding new products to represent.

In this capacity, I was responsible for managing my as-signed product lines from cradle to grave. Meaning: we brought on a manufacturer, positioned them into marketing vehicles, put the products in our enterprise resource planning (ERP) system, estab-lished competitive price points, communicated internally relevant product information, and eventually released the line if it no longer served to be a profitable performer.

Rockin' & Rollin'

At the time, Educational Resources was primarily a catalog-based company that provided technology products to the primary and secondary education market. We sold software and hardware peripherals to K-12 schools across the country. I joined right at the heyday of the technology boom. Personal computers were finding their way into schools and they were being heralded as the next new super tool to deliver the basics in education—reading, writing, math, and science. Software publishers were popping up all over California and the rest of the US creating what would later be phrased as "edutainment" games for the PC and Mac.

These arcade-like edutainment titles quickly evolved into well crafted educational learning tools. Most often designed by educators themselves, these products focused on teaching the four R's in new engaging methods using this exciting new technology called the personal computer. The rate at which new software publishers were coming on the scene was nothing short of amazing. An entrepreneurial story in and of itself were these mom-and-pop publishers on a gold rush of sorts in this new age of technology. Schools could not get enough of technology. With brand new budgets created to procure hardware, software, and training for a population of teachers who had never touched a computer before, businesses were springing up everywhere to serve the need. The environment was exhilarating. I loved this job, and I was doing well at it too.

Part of my job, along with two other product managers, was to review new products to determine what we wanted to sell. It took a bit of assessment to essentially guess what would be the next hot title and earn a decent ROI on the catalog real estate we would devote to promoting the product. More often than not, the title was a dog if the publisher was an unknown. With people jumping in the game quickly and calling themselves a programmer after six easy lessons, there was no shortage of new software releases. At one point, I could have been looking at five new publishers a week and the vast majority of them had no clue how to get their product to market. Their product may have been good, but they failed to understand the channel of distribution and how to market it. Most publishers naïvely assumed that the reseller would generate demand simply by putting their product in a catalog. Rarely would a title grow legs without the publisher himself generating a multi-pronged marketing launch.

The other part of my job was selling cooperative advertising space to these publishers. Known simply as co-op, this was advertising money that a publisher would pay to the dealers to help promote their product. Co-op drove the dealer channel. The savvy publisher with the right venture capital backing would have an ample—seemingly limitless—supply of money to pour into advertising. These publishers, regardless of the product's quality, would often see success, although it would be short lived if the title lacked substance. However, if the product was high quality with sound educational content and theory it could explode.

I would scratch my head as publishers of unsuccessful titles would come back catalog after catalog with co-op check in hand ready to pay for the next full-page advertisement. Educational Resources was the number one catalog-based K-12 dealer at the time. If a title did not sell with us, it simply did not sell. I wondered why these people kept pouring good money after bad. I was partially compensated and goaled on how much co-op I could bring in as it paid for the printing and postage on the catalog. I could afford to drop a few cash-paying dogs into the catalog to help supplement the cost of production. The catalog was very expensive as it exceeded 200 pages and was mailed to virtually every school in the country and thousands of individuals.

Some publishers just didn't get it—their product wasn't any good. They were too close to that fact. After all, it was their dream; the dream of creating something, building it into a company, and making it a reality. The only problem was that no one wanted to buy what they had created and they did not know when to reinvent or to let go. They also failed to look into all the necessary aspects needed to be a software publisher. They knew how to code, but were clueless about the dealer channel, marketing, and customer needs. Others had another agenda. Their dream was not tied up so much in the entrepreneurial baby they had created, but in their exit plan.

The '90s were boom times for technology. Bill Gates and Steve Jobs really just got started in the '80s and computer technology had finally evolved to providing practical applications to be used by the masses. We had moved away from mainframe green screens to individual PCs with screensavers. Because all this was so new and exciting, standards had not been established and no one knew where things were going. Mergers and acquisitions were the talk of the town. This was how to get rich: selling your business not your product. It almost didn't matter what you made, someone was ready to buy it and venture capital firms were all over it.

That's why the co-op dollars flowed so well. These venture capital-backed software publishers just wanted to make a splash, gain some positioning in the market, and get buyout offers or go public. The relationship worked fine for me. I gave a publisher some ad real estate which shows they are in the channel and ripe for big sales, and the publisher gets to position their company for sale and a big payout.

Without having any type of technology background—and having just been fired from my last job—I immersed myself in my new surroundings. I sought information to learn as much as possible and as fast as possible about my job, the manufacturers, and the industry. I did so out of a sense of urgency and fear that my lack of knowledge would spell my doom. What I did not piece together at the time was that my peers were in the same boat as me in terms of knowledge and experience. No one went to school to do what we were doing or had previous work experience because our industry was brand new. We were all learning at the same time and the rules were regularly changing. The people who would make it and do well would be the ones who put in the extra effort and had the desire to be successful. I intended to be one of those people. I quickly outpaced my more seasoned product managers and, for that matter, company executives. Not only did I master the publishers and products that we represented and sold, but I became an expert in the channel.

Because the job and industry were new to me and I wanted nothing more than to succeed, I poured everything into my job. My creative and innovative thoughts were channeled into what I could do new and differently, something I could not do at my last employer. The result was fantastic. I created new ad layouts, new bundles, and new methods to market and to promote publishers. I was in an entrepreneurial environment, and I was flourishing.

Through my own self study and complete absorption of the business and industry, I was able to foresee where the industry was going. Even though the technology industry itself was moving at warp speed, I was able to make predictions and bets on new products better than anyone in the company. I had developed not only a passion for the business, but a natural, almost instinctual understanding of the industry. I knew I would be going places here.

CHAPTER FIVE
Entrepreneurs and Family

E veryone rightfully says they put their family first in terms of their personal priorities. However, when starting a business, an entrepreneur needs to place the needs of the business first, at least in terms of his time commitment. It's just a reality that launching a business is going to take a significant time commitment, and it will pull the entrepreneur away from family and friends, which is all the more reason to pursue something that you love foremost over money. It must be understood that this time commitment needs to be for a temporary period and not for the duration of the business. The entrepreneur must remember the significance of personal time as well as time devoted to his business.

It can and will be hard on family when the entrepreneur is absent and it is equally hard on the entrepreneur. When the entrepreneur activates to start a business he can be fully immersed into the process and become neglectful of anything else. A selfish and self-centered mindset can develop that says "this is so important everyone just needs to understand." This can cause discord at home which can complicate an already stressful period of development.

The entrepreneur who has yet to activate is trapped in an entrepreneur's body and is struggling to get out. Those living with that person have to endure the struggle along with the entrepreneur, and it could honestly drive them absolutely nuts. The would-be entrepreneur is always coming up with ideas and complaining about their desire to start something but is unable to come across the right idea. Living with a new entrepreneur isn't any better, and it can be a bit like living with a mad man. The new entrepreneur will experience mood swings, bursts of enlightenment, sudden lows, crazy talk of farfetched ideas, and late night scribbling of ideas on random pieces of parchment. You should almost pre-screen a spouse to determine if these entrepreneurial desires are present to understand what you might be in for. I was blessed to have a very supportive and understanding spouse, in-laws, parents, and children who actually did not know life for me any other way.

The family is continually tested as the entrepreneur dedicates himself to the start of his business and throughout the life of the enterprise. The family often adapts to the entrepreneur and the business becomes a part of the family. More often than not, family members are drafted into some form of support and quickly come to realize that the business is the sustaining economic structure for the family and a sense of responsibility toward it develops.

With such a high rate of divorce in our country, it is imperative to adequately account for the impact your entrepreneurial decision will have on those you love the most and understand that this is not all about you. The attitude that these things are understood and do not have to be spoken is not good enough. You need to incorporate your personal life into your business plan. I have three primary steps to establish family planning (no, not birth control) into your business development.

1. Get family buy-in.

Discuss your business plans and expected time commitments with your family. Let them know why you are doing this, and what it means for you and your family. Explain what sacrifices may need to be made and why you think they are worthwhile. Establish what your anticipated time commitment will be to the business and when you estimate you can establish a more favorable work/life balance. Talk about hypothetical scenarios for what would be acceptable: to miss, to be late for, what you will give up doing, being at, committed to, hours to work and so on. Ask your family if they agree or have alternative suggestions. Finally, obtain their buy-in and support to your plans.

2. Set personal life goals and a time table.

Establish a goal and related time table for when you will restore family balance and describe what that balance looks like. Perhaps it is a gradual increase in non-work activities or maybe certain activities must come back on line faster than others. Your vision of restored balance may be entirely different than what your family envisions. Eliminate surprises and disappointment by discussing your goals and estimated time frames before you get too far down the launch pad.

Keep in mind that your personal life goals are not just to bring peace to your loved ones. They are also for you. You should have a life outside of work and a new business can become all too encompassing, swallowing the former you. Hobbies, interests, and activities outside of your venture should not be abandoned. They lend themselves to the wellness of the individual, which, in return, benefits the health of the enterprise by having a founder who is mentally and physically prepared to face the challenges of the endeavor.

3. Incorporate your personal life goals into the written business plan.

Your personal life is intertwined with your business life and, therefore, your goals should be as well. Developing a "personal business plan" to parallel your formal business plan is a good way to keep the two in focus. A personal business plan is for you and encompasses the personal goals and targets that you outlined above. This may include coaching a child's sport team, involvement in the community, volunteering, running a marathon, vacation time, personal growth and development, taking an art class, family succession plans, or other personal milestones. The goals and timeframe you establish to rebalance your work and personal life need to be written down in your personal business plan and interlaced with your regular business plan in order for you to maintain their focus.

Entrepreneurs are fiercely independent, which is a characteristic that allows them to go off on their own and take the risks associated with starting a business. They can easily take on that burden and pressure solo, and inadvertently establish barriers that prevent family inside their world, where they could be helping the entrepreneur to alleviate such strain. Active family engagement in the endeavor takes a tremendous amount of pressure off of the entrepreneur, spreads understanding, commitment, and creates a sense of unique family pride.

Learning the Business

I was putting long hours in at Educational Resources because the pace of new marketing initiatives was so rapid. As a team of six in Merchandising, we were putting out two full-line 200+ page catalogs, four quarterly catalogs, and several side marketing projects each year. It was our responsibility for each project to solicit the co-op advertising, find new products, determine competitive pricing, select images, obtain copy, and other marketing details. I was meeting deadlines with relative ease, due in part to the hours I kept and the commitment I made to be successful. That's not to sound boastful. I was still scared of getting canned and I was putting in twice the effort of any of my peers because of that fear.

While most product managers hated selling co-op, I enjoyed it. I had mastered knowledge of the two things necessary to be successful: the product we sold and the customer who bought it. In my case, the product was our advertising and the value of our company in the marketplace, and the customer was our publishers and manufacturers. I became the top co-op producer and that had an impact on the company's bottom line. I could see that the job I was doing was relevant and made a difference to corporate results and that motivated me. Leaving Allstate and being fired from my last job all stemmed from not being able to make a significant contribution to the company where I worked. While at one job I was viewed as a success and the other a failure, at both I was unfulfilled for not being able to utilize my talents completely or effectively. Now my talents were optimized and that propelled me to another career problem.

Ideas on how to improve, grow, and innovate poured out. However, now the company was not running at the same pace I was and there was not a clear corporate vision other than to keep growing. Learning about the products we sold, the channel they were distributed through, and the customers who bought them was constant. I was always looking to find ways to improve on our internal processes. The business was extremely fast paced and technology was advancing at a mind-spinning rate. As soon as I learned a product, it would be obsolete by better, faster, flashier technology. For the most part, the rest of the company had their job and they did it. They did not necessarily look to see how they could improve on their processes or methods, merely just how they could get by on them. I started to question everything we did, striving for improvement.

Innovation is something I feel I've nurtured at every job I've have, and it is a basic genome of an entrepreneur. I would constantly bring up ideas or new methods to do things at Educational Resources; whether marketing tactics in product placement in the catalog, bundle offers, developing product kits, procedural advance-ments, or improved process flows. Because Educational Resources was a young, entrepreneurial company I practically had complete autonomy to act on any of my ideas. I worked hard and dedicated a great deal of time to that job. I did so because it was so personally rewarding and satisfying.

I was highly competitive at Educational Resources. I wanted to advance, and I wanted to beat out everyone in the company—everyone. I could see my own evolution from when I entered the business with very little knowledge or experience in the industry to surpassing the most seasoned sales and marketing coworkers in a short amount of time. Fear and survival were my catalysts. Fear, in the sense that I did not want to get fired, developed into confidence from the knowledge gained of how to do things better than the competition. The confidence I built from becoming the knowledge leader made me more competitive and hungry to advance.

I had reason to be concerned about my survival as casualties were numerous and merciless at Educational Resources. New and existing employees had to keep up with the growth of the company. There were no excuses for lack of training or non-performance. If you didn't perform, you didn't last. I would give my new employees an analogy of a leaf floating down a stream, where the stream represents the industry, and they were the leaf. Survival was gained by floating atop that rushing water being pushed along at the same rate as the stream. They either need to go around objects in their way or get pushed over them. Failure to do so meant that you sunk and the rest of the company would go rushing by unable to stop and help them. Rather dramatic, but true.

One bottleneck in the organization was our sister department Purchasing. Closely related to my department, Merchandising, in terms of vendor and SKU management, my team relied on

Purchasing to keep pace with us on creating SKUs for new products, managing inventory, and ordering product to meet demand and customer expectations. Purchasing was locked into how things had been done and became internally focused on developing procedures that met their needs, not necessarily the requirements of both their internal and external customers. Purchasing was becoming a real problem for my team and the Sales Department in that they were slow, unresponsive to our needs, and failing to properly manage inventory. This began to cause considerable conflict between me and the head of Purchasing. It was becoming clear that the resolution to be forced upon management would be that only one of us would prevail.

I suggested combining departments to create a bonding synergy and sharing of labor to become more efficient and responsive. The argument from my counterpart in Purchasing was for my department to follow their rules and fall in line. My plan prevailed. Our departments merged with me as the leader. An unfortunate and somewhat unexpected casualty of our conflict was that my Purchasing counterpart lost her job. I certainly did not intend or want that to happen, and I never did get the entire story as to why she was let go after being on board for several years. If I had to guess, her conflictive personality and fiefdom mentality had much to do with it, as she became a rock in the stream. You see, rocks don't budge but sink to the bottom and get set in place, whereas leafs float on top and rush right over rocks.

Knowing our company's history, I had a concern during the conflict that I could lose my job. As hard as I worked to earn my position and as much as I feared the prospect of unemployment, I was not going to yield in my drive. I found that the confidence I held in my performance and the conviction I had to correct the deficiencies affecting the company was far stronger than conceding safely into the status quo. My motivation was to advance, not so much to earn more money, but to advance to a level where I could implement my ideas without having to campaign. I wanted to have the power to come up with bigger ideas and freely execute them, and now I had more ability to do just that. I would find, however, there were other rocks in the stream, and as my ideas grew grander the rocks became larger, and they would be the ones who were writing my paychecks.

Shortly before I came on board, Educational Resources was sold to one of the top K-12 publishers, Davidson & Associates. I was not aware of it at the time, but things were changing. The founder of Educational Resources had made a lot of money with the sale, and his focus was shifting toward creating his new future. Although still at the helm, his role was changing and he was now answering to executives in California. Long-term employees started to change too in conjunction with their leader's shifting focus. Some developed entrepreneurial plans, and more "outsiders" were being brought in as "experts" to manage specific departments.

The founder of Educational Resources, Forest Barbiari, was a very innovative entrepreneur. He was working at CBS software, one of the very early developers of educational software. He learned the business at CBS and then got the idea that this market needed a dealer channel to distribute the software to schools. What you have to realize is that companies like Educational Resources did not exist prior to the computer revolution. They were one of the many by-product businesses of the ingenuity of the personal computer.

Forest developed a relationship with another interesting entrepreneur, Jan Davidson. She was a school teacher in California who had been lucky enough to be in the classroom at the dawn of this new technological breakthrough. Computers were being bought by schools, but without software they were rather useless. Jan Davidson was blessed to be in a school district that could afford these great new tools, but she was frustrated by the lack of true educational publishing content coming out of the market. So what did mother necessity do? She created her own software.

From school teacher to software developer overnight, Jan Davidson created one of the premiere educational titles and an eventual series called Math Blaster. It was a combination arcade game mixed with number facts that took "drill and kill" to an exciting new level for the kids in her classroom. Along with her husband Bob, the Davidsons started Davidson Publishing out of their home.

Davidson had a successful IPO at the birth of the pre-dot com era and new titles quickly sprang up; a Science Blaster series, a Reading Blaster series, and more. It was during this time that Forest met up with the Davidsons and a marriage was quickly made between the two companies. I believe the story goes that Bob Davidson analogized software publishers and software dealers to the great movie houses in tinsel town. MGM would not only create the movies, but own the movie houses that they played in to guarantee an audience and distribution channel for their content. Forest and the Davidsons believed that model would be just as relevant in the new software industry.

Their vision paid off. Educational Resources became the number one educational software reseller in the US and Canada, while Davidson Publishing grew to become one of the largest and most well-respected software developers in the country.

CHAPTER SIX
The E-Formula: Activating the Entrepreneur

Defining Moment Number One

T he preceding pages cover what an entrepreneur is, but I have not answered how one becomes an entrepreneur and you may be asking yourself that question too. How do I become an entrepreneur, and can I?

Researchers have looked at the common characteristics of an entrepreneur and conducted psychological profiles to help identify potential entrepreneurs. They try to discover that illusive entrepreneurial DNA. Their studies determine common skill sets and qualities that make up successful entrepreneurs. They ask candidates to respond to a list of questions and conclude that if they answered yes to 18 out of the 25 statements they must have the qualities to be an entrepreneur. Such questionnaires tend to be more entertaining than useful. Sure, certain characteristics, traits, and skill sets are predictive of a successful entrepreneur, but in my opinion such qualities are learned and refined along the way, not necessarily genetically implanted. I don't know if I was born an entrepreneur, but I am sure my life experiences heavily influenced my outcome.

An entrepreneur cannot be inspired "into being" an entrepreneur. You can't bring a person into a seminar, get them so fired up on the virtues and thrill of being an entrepreneur that they then go out and become an entrepreneur. An individual may get motivated and inspired by such speakers or influencers, but it is not enough for him to spontaneously take action and create a business that would be successful. If he does, it is most likely acted out of foolishness than any new-found ability. The individual has to come across situational factors that correspond to a business opportunity that often come about at an unpredictable point in time.

Therefore, my sentiment is that entrepreneurs are made and that everyone has the potential of becoming an entrepreneur. There are those actively looking and longing to become an entrepreneur and those who seemingly accidentally stumble upon it. Those longing for the entrepreneurial experience, seek out ideas, listen for opportunities, and actively strive to find the right opportunity. To increase the odds of entrepreneurial fission, I suggest increasing your activity level in seeking opportunity. Listen to what existing business owners do, read the paper, stay current, look for future trends, and build relationships. The more information you are exposed to, the more likely you are to find that one special opportunity.

Nobel Peace Prize winner Muhammad Yunus, an economist who is known as the "banker to the poor" by making small loans in impoverished countries stated, "I did something that challenged the banking world. Conventional banks look for the rich; we look for the absolutely poor. All people are entrepreneurs, but many don't have the opportunity to find that out." An entrepreneur in his own right as founder of the Grameen Bank, Yunus developed the concept of microcredit as a method to help fund entrepreneurs who would not qualify for any other type of loan. He believed in creating economic development from the lowest tier of society and saw that the entrepreneurial dream was defined to no man; it was a gift to all.

So you, dear reader, want to know if you are an entrepreneur? It would be so easy to draw your blood and see the entrepreneurial DNA floating about and qualitatively state, "Yes, she is an entrepreneur!" But what good would this do? There still would be so much lacking outside the control of simple DNA to activate the entrepreneur within you.

Unlocking the Entrepreneur

"I would not have seen it if I had not believed it."

The yet-to-be entrepreneur spends his time agonized by dreaming and not doing. You may be that entrepreneur who is constantly thinking of new ideas and businesses to start, but never taking that fateful step of actually doing it. I categorize the idea phase of the entrepreneur as a time of frustration. The years leading up to me starting my company were spent conjuring up idea after idea of new business ventures that never materialized. I described it as a curse; longing to start a business, but unable to because the right idea had not triggered action. A better reflection on that time spent is summed up by author Wilfred Peterson who said, "Big thinking precedes great achievement." That statement can provide solace in knowing that one has to go through a period of significant brainstorming before something clicks. Focus less on the frustration and more on the fact that each idea is a lesson learned to strengthen the next.

I have said on many occasions that the hardest part of being an entrepreneur is starting, or as Walt Disney said, "the way to get started is to quit talking and start doing." The hardest part is making the move to actually do it. To move beyond writing notes on napkins and half-started business plans, and to make that move to do it full time and rely on it to generate income for yourself. Eventually the entrepreneur makes the decision that not following his dream is worse than all of the potential outcomes of trying. He obtains courage to act through a belief in his dream. The ironic maxim, "I would not have seen it, if I had not believed it," for me says that I would not have seen my company come to life and exist if I had not believed in my dream. Once the decision is made and supported by faith, all other aspects of the business come with comparative ease or, as I like to say, by gravity. Once the idea is put into action is when things seem to fall into place fluidly. This chain reaction can take place provided you have met the requirements of the entrepreneurial formula, or "E-Formula" for short.

This is a very important part of our journey together. We are going to talk about the first defining moment to become an entrepreneur and what causes him to "activate." I use the term activate deliberately. Deep inside all of us lays the entrepreneurial spirit. It may manifest itself in different ways at different points in our lives. A stay-at-home mom may ignite her entrepreneurial spirit in the ways that she attends to her household obligations and child rearing. A student may apply his entrepreneurial spirit to his school work, an executive at a corporation to her job. In other words, it may not always be directed toward starting a new business venture, although that is what we are primarily concerned with here. My point is the entrepreneurial spirit exists in all of us, it is always there whether we are cognitively aware of it or not and whether we are trying to resurrect it or not.

Those of us who have an entrepreneurial passion try to force it out of us. We want to engage in an entrepreneurial venture so badly that we try to make it happen by creating business plans, seeking out ventures, or even going so far as to buy a business. These are the impatient entrepreneurs who are trying to make their activation happen. There is nothing wrong with these activities, and certainly many entrepreneurs do establish their base by purchasing a business that they then transform and grow based on their vision.

However, the entrepreneur has to be careful to recognize his own impatience from the real or perceived opportunity at hand. One has to recognize when the entrepreneurial formula is complete in order to feel secure that when they activate they will be successful. The impatient entrepreneur runs the risk of failure by jumping into endeavors that he may not be fully prepared or educated for. Simply abiding by the thought that if you can dream it you can do it is not good enough—you need the full E-Formula.

The E-Formula, like the entrepreneur, starts with the I.D.E.A. The basis of every entrepreneurial endeavor starts with an idea that the entrepreneur transforms into a vision upon which the business is built. The idea is the building block and a successful one contains four components which ensure the likelihood of success. The true measurement of an entrepreneur's efforts is success. It does not have to be a level of success measured in dollars, but a success in that the idea becomes a viable and sustainable venture. That's what we're shooting for.

The E-Formula

We all understand what an idea is and we have them all the time. The idea is the central nuclei to a start-up. This is where it all begins, and so much goes into the makeup of an idea. I created the I.D.E.A. as the starting equation in the E-formula and it takes the following form:

Innovate
Desire
Effort
Ability

Innovate: *Innovation is the **substance** of the I.D.E.A.*

"INNOVATION is the specific tool of entrepreneurs, the means by which they exploit change as an opportunity for a different business

or a different service. It is capable of being presented as a discipline, capable of being learned, capable of being practiced. Entrepreneurs need to search purposefully for the sources of innovation, the changes and their symptoms that indicate opportunities for successful innovation. And they need to know and to apply the principles of successful innovation."—Peter F. Drucker

Innovation is what starts the entrepreneur's journey and, aptly, it is the first integer in the I.D.E.A. component of the E–Formula. Innovation is the dominant characteristic of the idea-generation phase and it will serve as the foundation of everything moving forward. After an idea is formed, it is used to innovate. The innovation is the core deliverable of the entrepreneur's venture. Innovation is the seed of what an entrepreneur is and what he ultimately creates. The primary difference between the manager, the business owner, and the entrepreneur is that the entrepreneur seeks and uses innovation to propel his business into unchartered areas of the market or creates a new market for himself entirely in the process.

"Just as energy is the basis of life itself, and ideas the source of innovation, so is innovation the vital spark of all human change, improvement and progress."
—Ted Levitt, Harvard Business School Marketing Professor

Innovation is the substance that makes up the entrepreneur's idea. It will become the intellectual property and basis for market differentiation. The innovation will separate the entrepreneur from being another "me-too" business to a revolutionary business that forces change upon the existing establishment.

Desire: *Desire is the **emotion** needed to accomplish the I.D.E.A.*
"Nothing stops the man who desires to achieve. Every obstacle is simply a course to develop his achievement muscle. It's a strengthening of his powers of accomplishment."
—Eric Butterworth, author

Where innovation is the substance of the idea, desire is the emotion that compels and sustains the entrepreneur to accomplish his vision. The desire to see an idea through closely resembles the passion that erupts to support an entrepreneur's idea. Starting a company is no easy task; a great deal of work is needed upfront before the doors even open. Many an idea has died on the doorstep of grand opening day. Without a long-standing desire to accomplish what you are setting out to do, your idea will fail. Desire becomes a motivation in which your thought fuels action. The desire embodies the belief and faith in the idea that this is the right project to pursue—this is the one!

"It sometimes seems that intense desire creates not only its own opportunities, but its own talents."—Eric Hoffer

As mentioned, the true measurement of an entrepreneur is success in that the idea itself becomes a viable and sustainable venture. Wilfred Peterson stated, "Success is focusing the full power of all you are on what you have a burning desire to achieve." Desire becomes such a critical component of the idea's development because it drives the entrepreneur to accomplish what he set out to do. He has achieved a vision of the final outcome and he can see the finished product—he must make it happen. Desire stirs all of the internal dreams to become an entrepreneur with the viability of a sound business plan giving hope that success is achievable.

"There is a boundary to men's passions when they act from feelings; but none when they are under the influence of imagination."
—Edmund Burke

At this point, quitting is not an option for the entrepreneur. Notice I did not say failure because failure still may be an outcome of the entrepreneur's efforts and the entrepreneur realizes this potential. Even though the entrepreneur is driven by desire to transform his idea into a tangible reality he is not blind. He realizes that it will take all the components of the I.D.E.A. to be successful but even with his best efforts he still may fail, yet he chooses to move forward. He carries on because he is fully aware that it would be far worse to have quit his dream than to have tried and failed.

Effort: *Effort is the **physical** needed to accomplish the I.D.E.A.*

"Genius is 1% inspiration and 99% perspiration. Accordingly a genius is often merely a talented person who has done all of his or her homework."—Thomas Edison

I will provide a greater focus on effort in the following chapter on startup as that phase represents the greatest need for desire and effort to succeed. The physical construction of the business, whether it is mental exertion or actual labor, requires an investment in effort that goes far beyond normal levels. The efforts of an entrepreneur combined with desire, vastly exceed those of the average man. Entrepreneurs start with nothing and very rapidly need to create a business and every facet of that business. They must do this in the shortest timeframe possible, and even after the business is created they still must continue on a rapid trajectory to grow and sustain. During this time the entrepreneur cannot rest, cannot sit back, and cannot take a break. Sweat equity and the long hours and sacrifices that accompany it are the hallmarks of the entrepreneur.

"The bitter and the sweet come from the outside, the hard from within, from one's own efforts."—Albert Einstein

Ability: *Ability is the **skill** needed to accomplish the I.D.E.A.*

"A man of ability and the desire to accomplish something can do anything."
—Donald Kircher, former president of Singer Manufacturing Co.

Everyone has certain abilities and talents that are either learned or innate. Successful entrepreneurs can identify the abilities that they lack and find corresponding talent to involve in the endeavor. Entrepreneurs manage the collection of abilities that they and others bring to the table. They utilize their own self discipline, self confidence, financial aptitude of profit and loss, leadership, time management, and exceptional organizational skills to manage the collection of abilities. It's been said we rate ability in men by what they finish, not by what they attempt.

Ability is the dominate characteristic of the running phase of the business. Once the effort and desire is poured into startup and the business is viable and sustainable, the focus centers on ability to properly manage the business. Certainly ability is needed through every phase, but the longest running and most enduring phase is running, and this is when your skills will be called upon the most.

"Success is the maximum utilization of the ability that you have."
—Zig Ziglar

Formed but Incomplete

Now the I.D.E.A. is formed and its components are ignited and ready to deploy. The utilitarian vision of the innovation at hand will commit the entrepreneur's desire to extend extraordinary effort and complete utilization of all available abilities to see a functional result achieved.

"Take up one idea. Make that one idea your life - think of it, dream of it, live on that idea. Let the brain, muscles, nerves, every part of your body, be full of that idea, and just leave every other idea alone. This is the way to success."
—Swami Vivekananda, brought Hinduism to the
status of a world religion

When an idea takes hold, it is exciting. After personally assessing dozens—maybe hundreds—of ideas, you've hit one that you believe enough in to stand behind to commit resources. This is a very exciting time; however, the I.D.E.A. alone is often not enough for the entrepreneur to be successful and may not be enough to activate the entrepreneur. A great idea alone may not make you rush out and get a second mortgage on your home to fund your start-up. There are still two more parts to the E-Formula that are needed to make it complete. The appropriate situation and the necessary opportunity must intersect to provide a fertile ground for the I.D.E.A. to grow. The complete formula looks like this.

I.D.E.A. + Situation + Opportunity = Entrepreneurial Activation

Situation

"Meanings are not determined by situations, but we determine ourselves by the meanings we give to situations."—Alfred Adler, psychologist

Situation represents a particular condition or set of circumstances that are happening in your personal and professional life, as well as environmental factors. Aspects in your personal life would include your marital status, children, health, economics, family, ability to relocate, education, hobbies, religion, and so on. Professional factors represent your current employment status and all of the circumstances surrounding it including benefits, vacation, salary, location, prestige, title, tenure, relationships, future outlook, and level of satisfaction. Environmental factors would include things such as war, recession, inflation, taxes, global events, legal factors, resource availability, weather, and so on.

When the personal, professional, and environmental situational factors are in a neutral state, they will neither negatively or positively impact the entrepreneur's efforts in moving forward with a new venture. When situational factors are in a disruptive state, they can negatively impact the entrepreneur's efforts at starting a new business and can increase the downside costs should the venture falter. Positive situational factors will increase the upsides and enhance the entrepreneurial efforts.

Let's take, for instance, a negative personal state in which you have a child that has a long-term illness. Your professional situation is positive and provides you with health insurance, and environmental factors are neutral. You may come across a tremendous I.D.E.A. that you know will be successful, but you fear moving forward and losing your much-needed health insurance coverage. Certainly the level of risk is greater for this individual than a single person on their own right out of college ready to tackle the world.

Ideally, all of these factors should be in a neutral or positive state to launch your entrepreneurial dream. An entrepreneur can probably move forward if one of the situational factors is in a disruptive state. It would be very difficult, however, to move forward if a disruptive state were present in all three situational variables, not to mention multiple negative variables within a situational state magnifying the potential impact.

Opportunity

"Most successful men have not achieved their distinction by having some new talent or opportunity presented to them. They have developed the opportunity that was at hand."—Bruce Marton

Arthur Cole, the economic historian who organized the Center for Research on Entrepreneurial History (closed in 1958), established that there are four types of entrepreneurs; the innovator, the calculating inventor, the over-optimistic promoter, and the organization builder. He presented that these types are not traits of personality used to describe the entrepreneur; rather, they reflect the types of opportunities the entrepreneur faces.

Entrepreneurship has been defined by William Bygrave, professor of entrepreneurship at Babson College, as the "process that involves starting a business venture to pursue a perceived opportunity." Minorities and immigrants are well noted and documented for establishing small businesses and pursuing entrepreneurial endeavors. This group in particular is heavily influenced by situational circumstances. Often due to language, educational, and cultural barriers this group's quickest road to prosperity is to establish a business of their own in a field that they are familiar with. The opportunity for this group is the relative ease to start a business in the US compared to anywhere else in the world. Their situation, of being the outsider, may be considered a negative to most, but in this case it actually forces a positive.

"The entrepreneur in us sees opportunities everywhere we look, but many people see only problems everywhere they look. The entrepreneur in us is more concerned with discriminating between opportunities than he or she is with failing to see the opportunities."
—Michael Gerber

The treasure of opportunities is that not everyone can see them. They are sitting there waiting to be picked off the vine, by only those who are acutely aware of their location. The collapse of the US auto industry shuttered hundreds of dealerships and sent General Motors, Chrysler, and various suppliers into bankruptcy. For most budding entrepreneurs this would seem to be the industry to run the furthest from. However, for those with the right idea and situation, this dramatic event may have been the most opportune signal to jump in the pool. The timing will be brief and the entrepreneur will have to act fast.

"Entrepreneurs are simply those who understand that there is little difference between obstacle and opportunity and are able to turn both to their advantage."
—Niccolo Machiavelli (1469-1527 Renaissance man)

This quote by Machiavelli makes the entrepreneur sound like a sort of business superhero. I suppose many are just that and can truly see little difference between obstacles and opportunity. What's true is that most successful entrepreneurs have removed or reduced obstacles through careful planning and understanding of their idea. The idea is closely aligned to the opportunity and both are perishable. An opportunity is present when favorable circumstances align at a suitable time. If action is not taken the opportunity fades or is acted upon by someone else.

What distinguishes idea and opportunity can be demonstrated by the innovation of the intermittent windshield wiper blade invented by Dr. Robert Kearns. Kearns idea was sparked through his own customer experience of the original wiper blade motor that operated at a single speed regardless of the variability of rain conditions. The opportunity was that all of the Big Three had been working on developing an intermittent wiper motor themselves with no success. There was urgency in the rival automotive engineering teams to invent this technology and Kearns had it. Idea meets opportunity.

Summary of the E-Formula

I've always analogized starting a business to the act of jumping in a pool of less-than-warm water. I drew this correlation from my youngest childhood days when I took swimming lessons at the YMCA. I must have been in kindergarten, and I still have a clear picture of standing at the end of the low diving board stretched over an Olympic-size pool. I don't know if I was afraid to swim or if the water was cold—probably both. That feeling of tension, apprehension, fear, anxiety, and on a rare occasion, excitement, would build up as I stared out into the vast pool at a height from the diving board that seemed to exceed my current height three fold. (Did I mention I don't like heights either?)

The pent up feelings in pre-jump would not leave the child until they hit the water and resurfaced paddling toward the exit ladder on the side of the pool. Those anxious feelings would be immediately replaced with relief, exhilaration, joy, and happiness. That same circulation of feelings builds up in a similar fashion in the soon-to-be entrepreneur. They too may sometimes need a push into the pool of entrepreneurialism in order to kick off their experience. Once they actually take the leap and hit the water, there too is an immediate feeling of exhilaration, joy, and happiness. It can't be explained, only experienced. It's one of the greatest feelings I've had, next to the birth of my three children.

The purpose of the E-Formula is for you to be able to self assess using the model (IDEA+S+O=Activation) to determine if you are ready to activate as an entrepreneur and if you're ready to jump in the pool. The formula does not include money, time, talent, or resources. Those are the things found in business plans. The formula is used to prevent forced or impatient entrepreneurial attempts of leaping into opportunities too soon without proper readiness. After all, you can drown.

The formula is also there to help alleviate the would-be entrepreneur's level of frustration in waiting for the right opportunity and situation to develop. By recognizing how your I.D.E.A. elements, situation, and opportunity align, you can save yourself, time, effort, expense, and energy by assessing whether your idea is viable and worthy of full commitment. Walk yourself through each component of the formula and determine if, at this point in time, this is the right opportunity and situation.

An entrepreneur takes an idea into action. That action defines the separation between everyone else who has a great idea but never acts on it. The activated entrepreneur is created when all elements of the formula are in sync, and then the entrepreneur's vision conveys how those elements will be applied. An entrepreneur cannot be categorically defined because both the circumstances or situation and the opportunity which occur to activate the entrepreneur are variable and always changing. In my own case, if my career had not proceeded the way it did, I may not have happened into the IT industry and started my company, thus not becoming an entrepreneur. Or perhaps my life would have gone in a different direction, and I would have been an entrepreneur in the health care industry? Or maybe I would have gotten too old and would have given up on my entrepreneurial dreams?

For ten years, Arthur Cole researched and tried to define the entrepreneur and he was unsuccessful. He came to the realization that everyone on his team had "some notion of it" but applying personal beliefs, perceptions, and independent study to its definition all lacked consistency. There are separate bodies of research, ranging from economists, psychologists, and sociologists that apply their theories and definitions to entrepreneurs within their silo vantage points. The E-Formula postulates that an entrepreneur can be a blend of each school of thought and those disciplines are contained within and influence both the situational and opportunity aspects of the formula.

Greatest Achievement

In an early form of industry consolidation, affiliate programs led by top publishers like Davidson would take on the marketing and distribution for small upstart publishers. Davidson would pick up the Knowledge Adventure series and Blizzard's World of War Craft, which at the time seemed a bizarre partnership. The Blizzard title would go on to produce over a billion dollars in revenue by 2007. This affiliate consolidation would be a forerunner of acquisitions to come in the software industry. Davidson & Associates itself would eventually sell to Cendant Corporation along with Sierra On-Line in 1996 at an astounding $2.2 billion. Rival publishers would consolidate with The Learning Company fetching a whopping $3.5 billion being sold to Mattel toys in 1999. I find it interesting that these explosively growing entrepreneurial companies were almost exclusively purchased by large corporations who subsequently did little with the investments they made. In the case of Mattel, the deal caused the company's stock price to fall and forced the exit of its CEO. Regardless of the eventual dot com bust that slaughtered the ROI on these deals, the acquirers had no long-term vision or industry knowledge for what they were buying.

Meanwhile, my ideas were exploding at Educational Resources and I was itching to kick one of them off to do something really big and significant. Through my relationship with a distributor who had a primary focus serving college bookstores, I started looking at the other education market—higher education. My primary lines as a product manager were the productivity publishers which included: Adobe, Filemaker, Novel, Symantec, Corel, and the flagship Microsoft. No one else wanted these lines because they felt they were difficult and confusing to manage.

Once schools became acclimated to computers and edutainment, they began to think about productivity tools. They started to learn about new titles such as Word, Works, Pagemaker, Filemaker, Photoshop, and how they could be used in the administrative offices of the schools. Along with these releases, viruses were being developed which established the need for a new breed of high-margin security products from Symantec, McAfee, and Computer Associates.

About one year into the job, I made probably the greatest contribution to Educational Resources' success and future for the next 20+ years while managing these productivity lines. Microsoft products were really not being embraced at Educational Resources. Even though they were quickly becoming one of the higher volume publishers, like most productivity applications, our staff was intimidated by these products because they were so different from the familiar educational titles that built the company.

Microsoft sold software through single-version copies as well as through two-volume license programs. The first program was called Open and all authorized Microsoft dealers could sell it. The second was a more flexible and deeper discounted program called Select which only nineteen dealers in the US were authorized. These dealers were called Large Account Resellers (LAR) and their pricing was vastly better than ours. Microsoft closed the LAR program to new dealers as they wanted to control the number of big fish in the pond: too many and they would start to feed upon one another and erode margins and the intended service level of the program. Volume licensing was considered complicated and Microsoft wanted to have a dedicated channel of dealers who were capable of fulfilling the program's requirements and only the very largest of dealers seemed capable to meet those qualifications.

Although Educational Resources was big in the education niche, we were nothing compared to the LARs who included Hewlett Packard, CDW, Compaq (pre-HP acquisition), Dell, and other resellers exceeding hundreds of millions in revenue and a few exceeding the billion mark. Manufacturers like HP and Dell were granted LAR status due to their large volume personal computer orders where software like Microsoft Office would be included in the original image. I wanted to make Educational Resources a LAR, and in my opinion we would need to be a LAR if we intended to remain the predominate dealer in education. The challenge was that Microsoft was not open for creating new LAR authorizations. I was about to embark on a year-long process of lobbying and selling. It would take confidence to leverage existing Microsoft relationships to introduce me to influencers and decision makers close to the LAR program. All of my knowledge of Educational Resources and our K-12 customer market would be drawn upon to establish a business case that ultimately addressed the needs of our market. Along with this knowledge, I would need a lot of luck.

The business case I was building was far less about Educational Resources than it was about Microsoft and the end user. By listening to the customer, I discovered the pain points in purchasing Microsoft licensing through the current LAR channel. A case was made showing how these pain points potentially negatively impacted Microsoft sales and drove customers to alternative products and licensing models. This over simplifies the casework accumulated, but boils the approach down to its basic roots. End users had issue with the LARs servicing them, and it was adversely impacting Microsoft's potential revenue in this vertical segment.

Educational Resources would fill the gap through an innovative and customer-centered approach to selling Select licensing. Since Educational Resources was an education-only dealer, there was no need to ask for full LAR access. Granting authorization for education only would be fine and would be an easier argument internally at Microsoft.

With the help of the Microsoft dealer account manager assigned to Educational Resources, I built a strong position for authorization based on the knowledge I learned about Microsoft and our mutual customer, K-12 schools. My case was centered around Microsoft's need to authorize Educational Resources rather than Educational Resources' need to be authorized—basic sales strategy, yet skillfully executed.

To meet the stringent requirements of Microsoft, several commitments in terms of personnel and training were necessary and I had another selling job to do internally with my executive staff. Eventually, everything came together and Educational Resources became the first education-only LAR and now had a significant competitive advantage over every education dealer in the nation. Microsoft turned out to be a chum bucket for gaining the licensing business of just about every other productivity publisher. Since volume licensing was a consultative sale, not a transactional one, customers came to rely on Educational Resources as an expert. If the dealer supplying their Microsoft products did a good job then they would entrust all of their big ticket productivity needs to that same dealer. And what customer wasn't buying Microsoft?

Microsoft sales would account for the bulk of Educational Resources' revenue in subsequent years, long after my tenure would have ended. Educational software demand would dry up in future years and their establishment in productivity titles would prove to be the saving grace to sustain the company and allow them time to branch into new product categories and services.

CHAPTER SEVEN
Insoluble Problems

"We are continually faced with a series of great opportunities brilliantly disguised as insoluble problems"—John W Gardner

On the PBS Web site devoted to his biography, John W. Gardner is described as "the quintessential American hero,". . . "a man who has transformed this nation through ideas and action that improved the lives of millions." In essence, Gardner was a social entrepreneur. He was the spark of innovation that created Common Cause, the first non-profit public interest group in the United States as well as Independent Sector, a leadership forum for charities, foundations, and corporate giving programs. In addition, the Experience Corps, Physician Renewal, Medicare, White House Fellows Program, Positive Coaching Alliance, and the Corporation for Public Broadcasting (PBS) all were created under Gardner's leadership or involvement.

Entrepreneurs and inventors continually generate ideas that solve difficult problems. The greatest of these are the insoluble problems: those perplexing issues that seemingly have no solution or explanation. They can't be "solved." Thankfully, there are people in the world like Gardner who challenge these problems. Challenge being the key word. Their passion and desire drives them to solve a problem others had conceded. The insoluble problem I faced at Educational Resources was to obtain the Microsoft Select authorization even though the program was closed to consideration of new dealers.

Imagine the insoluble challenges of the past: to fly, to breathe under water, to walk in space. As humans, we are often faced with what seems to be the impossible, but there will always be someone, most likely an entrepreneur or an inventor, who challenges the issue. This is the first stage of the creation process—identifying the problem. In the second step, the "solver" can go in one of two directions.

In one direction, he will view the problem and develop a theory to solve it. He may believe deeply in the need to solve the problem, and he may also develop a firm belief in his theory to solve the problem. However, what he most likely doesn't realize is that the E-Formula for success is not complete. The components that trigger action are missing. As a result, the entrepreneur begins to dispel his own theory. He starts to poke holes in the reasoning and probability.

He may lack confidence; fear may take over; the risk may seem too great. These factors have an impact because one or more portions of the E-Formula of success may not be present or are not present in great enough degree for activation. The entrepreneur may find he does not have as strong an attraction or passion for the problem now that action is required. He may not have a clear vision, or the situation may not be right and he may abandon his dream. This may seem like a failure, but it actually reflects the weighted risk assessment that an entrepreneur conducts in making decisions. In this situation, the risk was too great based on the variables that make up the E-Formula for success. The formula was not complete and therefore unable to activate the entrepreneur.

The obvious other direction the entrepreneur can take would be to work toward solving the problem. He will develop a theory: a blueprint of how to solve the problem, and then he will take action by trying to prove his theory. He will ignore the majority who cast doubt on his efforts and trials. He will continually question and have doubts about his efforts, but he will persist. He will continue despite being compromised financially, mentally, and physically.

What drives the person in this second scenario? The question people ask is, "What makes that entrepreneur tick?" The better question is, "What activates the entrepreneur?" The question is less about what makes an entrepreneur than what activates or triggers the entrepreneur into action. Again, we are all capable of being entrepreneurs. The DNA is in all of us but that alone is not enough. The entrepreneur must identify and align with an opportunity that solves a problem. That's where passion comes in.

Don't Hesitate

Five years prior to writing this book I identified an insoluble problem, one that I developed a desire and passion. My first stage, identifying a problem, was complete. The problem was the lack, or non-existence, of personal health care records for individual patient access and portability in digital form. The associated problem was the resulting costs to the healthcare system and the individual's ultimate care by not having digital access to health information.

People don't think about their medical records until they are presented with medical issues themselves. Suddenly faced with having to provide family medical history, their own medical history and the tremendous redundancy in reciting this information to different providers since records are not electronically linked or easily shared is daunting and frustrating. The efficiency and accuracy that can be gained through electronic records is obvious today, but due to HIPAA and other artificial barriers, it seemed impossible at the turn of the latest century. People change jobs more frequently than in prior generations and that often leads to a change in insurance carriers and providing doctors. The process to transfer records is not difficult but does take time. My primary concern had long been that the individual was not in possession or control of their own health information. They were held hostage by the health system.

For the United States, our greatest advancements in the medical field certainly have not historically included the back office administrative management of patient medical records. So my thought for stage two was to develop a system to make medical records digital; organize the information in a universally transferable format, and house in a central repository that would provide access to the patient and all providers anywhere in the world. What happens if you are on vacation in Italy and brought to a hospital unconscious? The doctors and nurses don't know anything about you or your family's medical background. Wouldn't it be helpful if you had an ID card that would allow that hospital to access a primary database that described your past conditions, allergies and so on?

As I mentioned, the first stage of identifying the problem was completed. The problem was real and it was big. So big, most did say it was insoluble. The second stage of creating a system to solve the problem was conceptually sound. What most entrepreneurs do next is to test their problem's theory with family and friends for validation. Just about everyone I spoke to said this was insoluble. Great idea and very much needed, but there was no way this could ever happen. Many wanted this problem solved but they felt it was impossible due to the size and fragmentation of the healthcare industry. Further, the technology that was being used and deployed into the provider market came from hundreds of proprietary solutions that were not designed to communicate with each other.

The primary objections that "experts" cited as to why digital records would not come about included proprietary software publisher systems that did not communicate with rival systems, HIPAA compliancy and concerns over patient privacy, doctors' resistance to change, and related costs to upgrade. For these reasons the problem seemed insoluble.

I would occasionally revisit the problem over the years, always receiving the same negative response and again accepting that logic and putting the topic back in my idea cabinet. Well, one day something triggered. I either knew that the naysayers were dead wrong, or I had been faced with far too many examples of why this problem was one that needed to be solved. It was then that I started designing my blueprints for a cloud-based application of personal health care records. My system would be a Web-based application that anyone could access with an Internet connection. Further, there would be a download feature of the application for those doctor offices without constant Internet connection, and then data uploaded when appropriate.

The application would centrally house records in a hierarchical structure allowing the patient to share the most granular of data with specific entities of their choosing. A network of primary care providers, first responders, and more would be established to link data in and out of these protected records. Users would be able to link their records to family members in a method similar to today's social network platforms.

Search engine functionality would be used to search existing electronic records in doctors' legacy systems to map data into the cloud records. That same search engine could be used to search patient records and then search the Web for helpful research, information, products, support groups, and more. Information housed in database tables for patients could anonymously be shared with agencies for research, census, donor, or other purposes that the patient would elect to participate in. For instance, the patient's blood type along with geographic information could tell hospitals or central blood supplies where the greatest source of type O positive blood exists in their area. The possibilities to streamline, share, and view information has staggering possibilities and enormous potential for good.

An elaborate patient-driven methodology of permissions-based management would allow or disallow outside access or sharing of these records. Of course, the entire system would be protected by the latest in security software and firewalls comparable to systems in place protecting your centrally stored financial records with the four trusted consumer credit rating agencies that exist today.

Although my blueprints were more a collection of notebook sketches than computer aided design documents, the theory was being written into concept. As time progressed, the consensus was less about whether it could be done and more that it could not be done due to HIPAA privacy concerns. Coming from the IT industry, I knew that was the least of the concerns in terms of constructing my cloud-based system. If that were the final common objection, I knew I could overcome it and this system could, and would, be built.

Just as in sales, I waited until the customer objections could all be met. In this case, the final objection was security and patient privacy. This told me my theory on what was needed to solve the problem was being accepted, and I knew the final objection could be answered. Therefore, the only thing left to do was to launch the business. However, I had waited too long. I hadn't trusted my instincts. I had required too much information to eliminate risk.

I stumbled across beta versions of Google Health and Microsoft Health Vault: two products of similar scope and purpose to my designs. My designs were practically identical in function to what I saw in beta screen shots leaked on the Internet. It was amazing to see my concepts and visions right there before me. I am by no means saying that these were copies of my efforts. It was the simple fact that I wasn't the only one in the world with this brilliant idea or recognizing that this insoluble problem could indeed be solved.

There was an opportunity at one point in time, but my situation did not lend itself to urgently pursue my idea.

Seeing the advancements made by these two superpowers and knowing the resources behind them, I eventually succumbed to disproving my theories of being able to launch the business. I'm too late. I lack the resources. I lack the knowledge of the industry. Too much additional information would be needed. The competition is too big. These reasons were all substantial, but if I had been drawing blue prints five years ago, the story may have been different.

At the point where I should have decided to jump into the pool, fear was trumping the power of the Entrepreneurial Formula. I was waiting for more validation—I wanted people to say "yes, go for it." Even though the size and scale of the challenge of centralizing the nation's personal health care records was immensely appealing, I had to be a realist at the same time. I was not afraid to go up against Google and Microsoft. In fact, I think I had a better product. I just had so much to learn about the healthcare industry and how to develop the product and I had waited too long. At this stage it would have been difficult to attract investors knowing that Microsoft and Google were capable of using their marketing muscle to roll their concepts out in mass scale.

This was my first hand experience with an insoluble problem. From this, I was reminded of the need to trust my instincts, just as you need to trust yours. If you believe there is a need then it is likely many more people see that same need. Perhaps finding that next great idea is a lot like playing the stock market . . . when everyone is fleeing the market, it signals a great time to buy. When people are buying you're often too late. Edward de Bono, a leading authority in the field of creative thinking wisely stated, "If you wait for opportunities to occur, you will be one of the crowd." Find those opportunities that people are fleeing from that they feel are insoluble. If you wait till when most of the risk is removed you're going to be too late.

Glimpse of TRC

I started to take notice of the number of higher education customers appearing on our sales reports at Educational Resources. Under the radar, more and more higher education institutions were purchasing from us. Educational Resources had no focus on this market and further no structure internally to work on it either. We were K-12 focused and everyone was very comfortable with that direction. The Educational Resources sales representatives were trained to call solely on K-12 schools. A field sales team developed and matured into representing a more solutions-oriented sale focused on staff development and curriculum-based integrated learning systems. This further limited Educational Resources' ability and desire to branch into emerging markets like higher education.

It so happened that the line of products that I managed were equally attractive to the higher education market, especially Microsoft. In fact, productivity titles were more strongly positioned for higher education than they were for K-12. This knowledge piqued my interest, and I started to investigate what these schools purchased and how they obtained product. This led me to a distributor named The Douglas Stewart Company out of Madison, Wisconsin. The Douglas Stewart Company was started in 1956 and had a focus on distributing various products to college bookstores who, in essence, were resellers like Educational Resources. Publishers of productivity applications flocked to bookstores as a reseller channel because there really was no higher education reseller channel in existence. Out of necessity, many publishers established direct relationships with college bookstores and college academic departments because of the lack of focus in the channel. That in itself seemed to be an obstacle to entry, but I saw it as an opportunity.

The Big Idea

With this new-found intelligence on the higher education market, I figured this is the big thing I can bring to my manager that will propel my career. Here's a great idea to add incremental growth and revenue to the company operating off of our existing core competency. We have virtually no barriers or cost to enter the market. This was exciting because I felt like I had a leapfrog idea; one that would provide an entirely new market, advance my career, and possibly create a new dedicated division. I could lead this new division! I could run the show and grow this segment and be recognized and rewarded for those efforts.

My next step was to write up a business plan and present it to the divisional vice president to whom I reported. I prepared the business case showing what was required to enter this new market and the advantages of being first to enter. The big day to do my dog and pony show finally came and within 15 minutes it was over. I was told that they had considered the higher education space before and determined that it was not worth entering. Thanks Jeff for the idea, good job, but let's get back to what we do best . . . what we have always done.

Man!—did that take the wind out of my sails. How could they not see what a great idea this was? The entrepreneurial parent in me wanted to defend my baby—my idea. Perhaps it was a face only a parent could love? Through their lens my idea was something that had been reviewed and deemed unworthy. To me it was an untouched market representing incremental growth. How could they not see the potential and greatness in it; had they no vision? Well, they didn't and that was the end of it. Or was it?

Won't Let it Die

Determination is a great word. It's about continuing on when others drop off and quit. It is about believing in something or someone so much that you stick with it or with them until the end. Determination is what winners have and it is what separates them from others. It is the element that differentiates an entrepreneur from a dreamer.

I had been the dreamer for years, actually, most of my life. While at Allstate and through my months of unemployment I conjured up all sorts of business ideas. I must have had a hundred of them, but pursued none. They all seemed good enough, but nothing seemed to motivate me to take action. The truth is I would let my ideas die by finding reasons not to pursue them. This idea, however, was different. It was something I was really determined to follow through on. Instinctively, I knew I could commit everything to it. I was racking my brain for years trying to come up with a great business idea and here one was. This was it, and I would not let it die.

Entrepreneurs are a bit like inventors. They often fail repeatedly at their trials before they succeed. An entrepreneurial failure in the idea phase is often in the form of rejection from people who say the ideas are no good, silly, or dumb. The breaking point comes when determination trumps what people say can't be accomplished. The entrepreneur says, "It can be done, I know how to do it, and I'm going to do it." Entrepreneurs don't prove Einstein's definition of insanity in the process of doing the same thing over and over again expecting different results. They may fail time and time again, but they study their failures, learn from them and redesign their plans and try again. My series of failures came in the form of failed ideas, albeit ideas that I did not act on. Pretty safe failures but, nonetheless, I studied why I thought they would not work and used that knowledge in assessing my next idea.

The point in time when you commit yourself to an idea and make the decision to move forward is truly miraculous. It is like a shot of adrenaline. This is the point when you "jump into the pool" to prove to you alone that you have the guts to give it a try. It's not just talk anymore, you are going ahead with it and that is really damn exciting.

The decision to act fosters faith. It is this faith that leads the entrepreneur through the rough and dark times of developing the business. When I was told thanks but no thanks by my manager, I was crushed because I felt dependent on this manager and his opinion. Then I realized I had the ability to see the idea through. I had passion for the idea, and I knew it could be successful. It felt so right because for the first time, one of my ideas matched an opportunity. The higher education market was untapped and it was completely logical to assume that they would use computers and software to the same degree as K-12 schools. This created a sense of urgency for me to act. But something was still holding me back. I still was not thinking that I should actually do it myself. It was my situation and the E-Formula was not complete.

Positive Rejection

Just a couple months later my boss quit and a replacement was needed to fill his role as Vice President of Marketing. That job was for me. I earned it and was certainly the most qualified; after all, I just established Microsoft LAR status. After interviewing I waited weeks in anticipation for an answer. The decision would be made to hire an outside candidate with a portfolio of marketing experience unrelated to our industry.

Was I disappointed? You can't imagine. I put in a great deal of time and effort into this company, had tremendous results, created new programs, and established numerous cost saving efficiencies. I felt like I got slapped in the face. With my career path blocked, my professional situation had just abruptly changed and almost instantaneously the E-Formula had fully activated. I paused and thought I should just do it myself! I would start a business that sold software to the higher education market, and I would be one of the first to do it.

Any anger over the rejection of the VP position was gone. For years I was coming up with fabulous new business ideas, seemingly only to read about them months later in the newspaper or as a highlight story on the nightly news. They were the ideas that someone already thought of. That someone else had started and got off the ground while I was just thinking about them. I was beginning to believe in the famous statement by Charles H. Duell, Commissioner, US Patent Office, who in 1899 said that "everything that can be invented has been invented." But now, here I was, sitting on something that had not been invented—could this be true?

I had vision into a market that was new and had a need for a service that would certainly grow at a rapid rate for at least the next ten years. I knew the products, the manufacturers, the method of distribution, costing, marketing, and I had relationships that would help me. I could do this! Everything in the E-Formula from my personal, professional, and environmental situation to the opportunity itself was positive. I was always striving to understand how someone could start a business. I finally understood. It was relatively simple when it came down to it. When the E-Formula was true, I just had to jump into the pool.

CHAPTER EIGHT
How Entrepreneurs Think

The entrepreneur has been dissected over the years in an effort to uncover what makes him tick. Researchers look for the type of entrepreneur and what traits they possess, what skills they need, and how they think. I believe the entrepreneurs' thought processes differ significantly from the traditional worker, but this heightened way of thinking only emerges once activation occurs. Once the full burden of responsibility for an enterprise is cast upon an individual, it seems all of their senses and cognitive resources are directed toward that entity and its survival.

Entrepreneurs are able to critically think better than most. They scrutinize closely, the "what if" scenarios, weigh risks and rewards, and are able to confidently conduct risk assessment better than the traditional worker. Why? Because the entrepreneur is directly accountable to himself. The psychology of subordinate working relationships is removed. What will happen if I make this decision? What will my boss think of this decision? Will this decision hurt my career? In subordinate working relationships, the concern is first for the individual and secondly for the enterprise. For the entrepreneur, there is no difference between himself and the business. The feeling of freedom and complete autonomy starts to impact the thought processes of the entrepreneur over time creating a spirit of confidence. It develops a confidence in making decisions freely, quickly, efficiently, and solely in the best interest of the company.

The entrepreneurs' thought process is what probably best defines the allure of the phrase "being my own boss." It's the ability to freely make decisions without any concern of scrutiny and to be self-reporting, focusing all attention toward the business. Some term this way of thinking "ownership." My understanding is that ownership is an experienced talent, not a taught behavior. You can't put someone in a classroom and teach them this line of thinking. They have to experience it or be in a culture that fosters it. That's not to say you can't teach entrepreneurism, you'll just never graduate the complete package. The role of the classroom is to prepare for entrepreneurship, but not to create an entrepreneur. That only happens through the E-Formula. Learning how to truly think like an entrepreneur only comes about from hands-on experience when success or failure is on the line.

A big part of entrepreneurial thinking comes from the gut. Only the founder has the intimate knowledge and feeling for what is right and what is wrong for his business. Many of my best decisions came from my gut rather than through the result of strenuous deliberation. In a challenging position, my wife Lisa would always ask, "what does your gut say," and that would usually be my best answer. My gut answers were quickly formulated by processing all the available and experienced information. This is the heightened and differential way of thinking of the entrepreneur. The entrepreneur is truly connected to the business like a spider is connected to its web. The entrepreneur can pick up any vibration and instinctually form a response.

I play a game with myself in guessing people's nationalities. When I see their face, features, color, and hear their accent I try to guess their country of origin. I've started to get pretty good at it and find it a great way to engage with new and interesting people. It's funny how many people guess my locality to Chicago, due to my "Chicago accent." I tell them it's not me with an accent; it's everyone else that talks funny.

I try the same game with far less success trying to guess

professions of individuals I meet. The characteristics of a doctor, accountant, butcher, cashier, or nurse are less transparent than those of national origin; however, I still have fun with it.

Where I do tend to have incredible success is at picking out an entrepreneur. It is difficult to attribute physical or verbal characteristics when identifying an entrepreneur. What stands out is what I can best describe as an ambience or aura that an individual gives off that helps me identify them as an entrepreneur. It is very hard to explain, and perhaps I could only master this sixth sense after becoming an entrepreneur myself—a sort of secret handshake we learn. However, the vibe I sense from entrepreneurs is a combination of confidence, satisfaction, deliberateness, and happiness that, for lack of a better word, glows from them.

Sure, an entrepreneur's life is not rosy every day and they are certainly challenged on an ongoing basis with decisions that may make or break their kingdom and dream. However, even just living in the moment and knowing that they have the opportunity to make those decisions is satisfying and exhilarating. The tough decisions come with the job and there is no one more equipped to make those decisions than the entrepreneur himself—and he knows that. He knows how to solve his problems, where to go to get information or guidance. It is he who makes the decision, and he wouldn't want it any other way. It's what sets him free.

What Others Think of Entrepreneurs

How many times in conversation at a wedding, dinner function, church, or at the neighborhood barbeque has someone asked that well-worn conversation starter of "where do you work?" It always comes up, especially with relatives you have not seen in a long time, and they don't know what other personal question to use to jumpstart a discussion. But people are genuinely curious about other people's careers, and it's something I enjoy inquiring about too. Where others may use the line of questioning to fill time while in line for appetizers, I genuinely like to hear what other people do for a living and to briefly explore their profession for interesting tidbits or connections.

I love when I find a connection to my business or to a new idea. I like exploring in conversation to see if their expertise can help shed light or validate my thoughts. Seeking confirmation from sources is a characteristic of an entrepreneur seeking validation to his ideas.

When I find someone who is on topic to what I am pursuing or have an interest in, I first want to mine them for information and learn from their mastery. Second, I want to obtain from them their understanding and their opinion of my vision in their field. Am I just crazy, or does this idea have legs? Is the idea feasible, does it have merit, or is it way out there? Are there things I have not considered that will dispel my thesis?

So when I'm asked that question of "what do you do for a living," I open up my resume. I give a brief history of where I've been and how it led to where I'm at now. I share my primary objectives in the position I hold, and then give a glimpse into the future of what I would like to do or what I've been thinking about doing. My hope is somewhere on that continuum I'll hit some commonality with my guest for a deeper discussion. Ideally, you want to share experiences, skills, or uncover a network of people who somehow intersect your six degrees of separation. You probably know the theory.

Six Degrees of Separation

The theory goes that every person is a single degree of separation from all the people that they personally know. And they are then two steps away from all the people that those people know. And they are then three steps away from all the people that those people know. This continues on to the fourth, fifth, and ultimately sixth step which legend signifies you knowing every person on earth. This experiment is best drawn out on the social networking Web site LinkedIn. As you link your profile to those that you know you start to develop contacts. All of your contacts have contacts, which then become your second degree of separation to them. And all those contacts have contacts and so on.

—*Source Unknown*

At the time of writing this book I had 588 contacts on LinkedIn which created a network of 2nd and 3rd degrees of separation of 5,200,200 people. What's cool is that this is probably the first time in history that the theory of six degrees of separation has actually had a living model created to test its theory. Never before could I have not only created my six degrees of separation, but actually map out who makes up my network and have a method to reach them. Bam! All of a sudden I can "theoretically" reach out to over five million people based on a common relationship—albeit possibly two or three times removed. But heck, we've counted cousins this way forever, so it must be legit.

So back to that question, "what do you do for a living?" I've found that I've received two different types of reactions to this question and I've answered it in two different ways based on my career status. When asked, I and most people who work for a company would normally respond with "I work for XYZ Company" or "I'm a manager for XYZ Company." The one asking the question would then relate to the company, field of work, or related thread and conversation would continue down that path.

However, as an entrepreneur I would respond with "I own XYZ Company" or "I started XYZ Company." The one asking the question would then go in an entirely different direction with an entirely different level of engagement and responsiveness. It's hard to describe, but I can best say that there is an immediate level of curiosity and enthusiasm that develops. Questions start to fly about what the business does, how long it's been around, and how did I start it. Responding with "I own my own business" is a bit more appealing and rewarding than the former. I don't view it as an ego stroker, but I guess in reality it is. It is an ego stroker in the sense that you bust your butt to create a business and you work harder and take on risks greater than the average Joe, and a bit of recognition for that is welcome. So, yes, a little ego stroking is always gladly accepted.

Out of all this, the interesting point is not the level of self gratification that the entrepreneur receives during this engagement. What's interesting is what is going on in the head of the questioner. Why does that person have a heightened interest in the conversation and in you? Why the genuine curiosity and probing that results? Is it envy?

Many might like to think so. However, I believe it is far less about you than it is in about what you've done. Everyone is an entrepreneur at heart. When they encounter one of these elusive beasts in the wild they want to study it and learn from it, because ultimately deep down in their heart they long for an opportunity to do it themselves. I sense that there is a level of admiration and intrigue when one meets an entrepreneur. I know there is for me and I'm an entrepreneur. I have the same curiosity, admiration, and mystery when I meet an entrepreneur. It never gets old for me. I love hearing the stories, the vision, and the tone of excitement when I engage with an entrepreneur. Even though I did it myself I always want to hear about their story to see what I can take away from it.

CHAPTER NINE
Corporate Culture is Your Passion

"The work of art must seize upon you, wrap you up in itself and carry you away. It is the means by which the artist conveys his passion. It is the current which he puts forth, which sweeps you along in his passion"—Pierre-Auguste Renoir, French impressionist artist

An entrepreneur follows an inspiration or passion and is able to motivate others to follow them because of that passion. That motivation and passion is far different than what you find in, say, a typical manager. It is pure, genuine, and comes from the soul. This may sound hokey or weird, but it is true. The passion of the entrepreneur radiates in his presence. Those involved in the organization are touched and affected by the environment it creates. It causes them to take on a different understanding and ownership for the business that can only be kindled by an entrepreneur. When studying entrepreneurs' companies, the passion described for the business is actually conveyed through the culture.

When I started my company, I deliberately wanted to establish a culture. I now had a business, and I could create any culture I wanted. I saw this as a really cool opportunity to do something fun. There were so many examples of companies that let you bring in pets, had a basketball court, foosball tables, bean bag chairs, stocked kitchens, outdoor adventure outings and more. My focus in planning a culture soon became centered on creating this physical culture. It seemed exciting and unique to create what are really no more than adult day camp activities and sensory stimulants to make the workplace fun or energetic. I tried some of these initiatives but they really didn't seem to do much. What I soon observed and discovered was that the culture emerging at my company was coming from me and my behavior, not from my forced activities. I couldn't have planned for that or even altered it from happening. The culture was me.

The entrepreneur sets the tone for everything in the company. The culture that organically emerges is reflective of the values, habits, and personality of the entrepreneur. If I bought ping pong tables and other such amenities it would not reflect my desired culture and I probably would not even utilize them. I'm a bit boring in the workplace because I work—I would say to a fault. I incorporate work into my entire day and don't allow much time for fun and games, which I do believe are beneficial to relationship building and just letting your hair down.

I've noticed that the culture of a company changes when the entrepreneur leaves the business. There is a chemistry that resonates purely from the entrepreneur, which is evident from a statement found on the Virgin home page talking about founder Sir Richard Branson. It says, "The final word on our philosophy must go to Richard, the man who continues to inspire it: A business has to be involving, it has to be fun, and it has to exercise your creative instincts." Branson's team respects the man and his values and they understand the autonomy granted to them.

The culture that grew at my company was reflective of winning, striving for excellence, quality, innovation, and driving change. To achieve these things, you worked hard and that became our culture—hard work and great results.

Don't put too much thought and energy into creating a culture. I don't think it's worth your time as it will manifest itself on its own based upon whom you are. Those who try to develop a culture counter to their personality will build a schizophrenic environment likely to stress employees rather than motivate and inspire them. Finally, companies that try to create employee "ownership" without a culture that fosters "ownership" will be equally unsuccessful.

CHAPTER TEN
Entrepreneurial Exercises

A business is about to be born and this is when the hard work will begin. The mental preparation was frustrating for me in wanting to be an entrepreneur but failing to have an idea to act on. Once the idea was able to activate through the E-Formula I was on my way, and I had much to do to establish my business plan and all the related research involved in knowing how to actually incorporate. At this point I'm ready to go to work on my business idea, but I have to spend a tremendous amount of time understanding the legal and administrative aspects of setting up a company. Planning and preparation could have made this phase significantly easier if I had put myself through some Entrepreneurial Exercises prior to activating my big idea.

Entrepreneurial Exercises are my way of preparing to be an entrepreneur before you actually are an entrepreneur. These won't apply to the accidental entrepreneur that stumbles upon entrepreneurship, but they will help those who know in their heart that entrepreneurship is their desire and someday they will find their opportunity. Entrepreneurial Exercises are designed to prepare you to start a business before the opportunity presents itself. The purpose is to shorten the business launch time from idea to startup.

Entrepreneurial Exercises are a series of preparedness and fact-finding activities that require no financial expenditure and are centered on generic research applicable to any business or service. By completing these exercises now you can reduce time later when you are anxious and ready to start your venture. You may be tempted to go out and purchase office supplies, design a logo, obtain licenses or equipment. Please don't, as it may be years before you have the right idea to take action on. By knowing the industry you are targeting you can get more specific in these exercises, but for most a generic approach is best. To start your exercises you need to get organized and prepare a dedicated space and storage location for your Entrepreneurial Exercises.

Entrepreneurs in waiting gather a lot of material based on their ideas, and they need to be organized for future reference. You will forget why you tore out that newspaper article or copied that URL address months later. Organizing your storage of entrepreneurial ideas and material will be extremely useful for when you are ready to act. A physical file cabinet with hanging folders is best for me to library print material, while others may simply use a multi-folder portfolio or electronically scanned documents. Replicating those folder and file topics on your computer is the next step to capture your digital content. All of the ideas, examples, news clippings, industry data, experts, resources, and potential competitors can be organized using the following Entrepreneurial Exercises.

Preparation Exercises

Every entrepreneur must conduct a linty of administrative research when he activates. Many things have to be done to establish a business and it is often unchartered water for the entrepreneur. Researching this information in advance and filing it in an organized fashion will pay big dividends down the road.

- Research the type of ownership structures and the implications of each specifically on tax, liability, and ownership transfer.
- Learn what is involved to incorporate a business and how to do it.

- Articles of incorporation
- Federal tax ID
- Certificates

• Explore what certifications are relevant to a desired service or industry.
• Obtain and review business plan templates.
• Develop social networks now to expand your reach to resources and to communicate awareness of your company when ready (LinkedIn, Plaxo, Facebook, Twitter, etc.).
• Seek out experts, coaches, and mentors who own businesses or are in your desired field.
• Read actively and retain anything you feel is relevant for your journey.
• Seek out information on best practices and global business topics such as search engine optimization, social networking, technology, etc.
• Subscribe to relevant news services, groups, societies, clubs, etc.
• Understand your own knowledge gaps. Most entrepreneurs are not accountants so taking a basic "understanding financial statements" course at a community college may be a good investment. Even though no expense should be incurred in Entrepreneurial Exercises, furthering education never hurts.

Resource Exercises

There are several resources you will need regardless of the type of business you start. For instance, most likely you will need a Web page and you'll need a developer, hosting service, and source to buy a domain name. So much information is free on the Internet today that a bit of time invested should yield answers to your most basic resource questions. Documenting information online and researching experts you would like to use will take a lot of pressure off the entrepreneur when he is ready to activate.

- Accountant or accounting firm
- Web site developers, domain registration, and Web site hosting
- Graphic artist
- Information technology specialist (voice/data, networking, back up, mobility, email)
- Lawyer (generalist, patent, contractual, intellectual property, etc)
- Tax
- Software tools (accounting packages, CRM, Web conferencing, etc.)
- Insurance assistance (life, business insurance, workman's compensation, etc)
- Payroll service
- Employee benefits and human resource intelligence (401k, federal and state employment law, etc)

Financial and Funding Exercises

Most startup businesses are self funded or known as "bootstrap" financed. Others may obtain loans from banks, family, or friends. Start to investigate and understand the methods to finance a business and resulting obligations and requirements.

- Talk to a banker now to understand the business loan process
- Understand business bank/checking account fees, services, etc
- Start building personal savings and establish your current personal living expense budget
- Reduce or eliminate your own personal debt

- Investigate credit union and "micro loan" establishments; their fees and requirements
- Determine how to structure your personal assets from the business entity to protect yourself. Look into the benefits of creating Wills and Personal Trusts.
- Understand what is involved with personal bankruptcy
- Obtain examples of pro forma financial statements and learn their components

Few startup businesses will attract or require sophisticated funding; however, if you think yours will, then start to investigate the pros and cons now of funding via Angel, Venture Capital, or Private Equity.

Operational Exercises

The actual running and administration of a business is considered the operational aspects. These can be a tad more granular in research, but should prove beneficial even if alternatives are ultimately incorporated into the operational environment.

- Communications (phone systems, cell, virtual capabilities)
- Office space and rents (location, county tax differences, calculations)
- Determine how FedEx Kinko's, temp staffing, US Postal Service, and other service businesses can support you
- Ask business owners what services they use for cost savings and efficiency
- Research offshore development, services, and manufacturing knowledge if applicable
- Discover dealers of new and used office furniture, copy machines, or computing equipment
- Investigate merchant banking for e-commerce

You can learn more about Entrepreneurial Exercises by visiting www.jeffweberventures.com

PHASE II: START UP

One of the things I really enjoy in life and that I hold a personal passion for is the outdoors and nature. This deeply embedded sense is most likely a trait passed on to me from my mother. A self-proclaimed tomboy, my mom grew up in the country (as she likes to say) in a town far north of Chicago called Fox Lake. She can tell you plenty of stories about spending her summer days out on the lake fishing and, more importantly, stalking and capturing the grandest prize of all—turtles.

Turtles are one of my favorite reptiles too, and I had several as pets growing up. I'm still relied upon to bring home at least one live, large snapping turtle each summer to the delight of my kids. These snappers are the potential victims of the overpopulated suburban sprawl which has encroached on their instinctual land. Snappers burrow underground and hibernate during the wickedly cold winters in Illinois. In the spring they somehow emerge and return to the same place to mate and lay eggs. Roads tend to get in the way of these activities and the snapper will be driven to cross them to reach the destination engrained deeply in their behavior. I always pull over to help the turtle cross the road pointing them in the same direction that they were headed. Simply moving them off the road opposite of their original direction, they will turn around and head right back—certain to become road toast on the busy cement arteries that run along the numerous ponds and state forest preserves in my area. Sea turtles behave in much the same manner as the Illinois snapper.

Every two to three years Loggerheads mate and instinctively return to ancestral beaches to lay their eggs. It is like they have GPS beacons embedded in their brains. One particular sea turtle, the Kemp's Ridley, is known to nest on one single beach in the world found in Mexico. Regardless of who is on or using the beach at the time or if development has encroached, they will still rise up from the sea and move forward to deposit their eggs. Anywhere from 50 to 200 eggs are laid during the darkness of the night. They want their eggs privately buried before predators discover their location.

Those that are undiscovered by predators lie in the egg cavity for 45-70 days incubating. Once they break through their egg, the turtles may spend another three to seven days of effort digging their way to the surface of the beach. Most will emerge at night again instinctively, to avoid predators. Each turtle struggles to emerge and make its way across the beach, enter the ocean, and feverishly swim for an estimated 24-48 hours to increase their odds of survival. Ninety percent of turtles are lost to predators attacking the egg cavity or while exiting the nest and racing to the ocean. Once they grow and mature to their 4-6 foot lengths and 200-pound weights survival greatly increases.

Turtles remind me of business and the entrepreneurial spirit. Each egg is like a new business—each an entrepreneur's dream. Entrepreneurs who hatch new business ventures follow a similar journey of the sea turtle. Either due to funding, resources, confidence, or any other number of factors, a high percentage of businesses close between day one through year five. The reasons for closing vary greatly, but, nonetheless, the chances of a new business reaching the ocean tides are daunting. Like the sea turtle, entrepreneurs are driven by instinct with a sense of determination and passion to achieve what they set out to accomplish.

Let's see what it takes to move from idea to startup.

CHAPTER ELEVEN
Getting Started

When an entrepreneur finally has THE idea, he wants to jump in and get going. However, before any launch can occur, the critical step of planning must take place. For the entrepreneur, planning is one of the most difficult parts of starting a business because of impatience. Without proper planning an entrepreneur can be setting himself up for unforeseen obstacles including failure.

Planning a business is difficult. Having the organizational skills or tools to go through the process is critical. Considering all aspects of the business beyond the core of your idea is the offspring of what the value of planning produces. Take for instance the guy who comes up with the idea to launch a truly novel coffee shop. He creates a shop with great décor, ambiance, and a unique approach, but he has no idea how or where to buy coffee beans. Businesses that succeed are often ones where the founder worked in the industry in some capacity and then decided to break out on his own with an offshoot, direct replica or variation of the business where he cut his teeth. That's what I did; I was a replicative entrepreneur, as I'll come to explain. These businesses tend to succeed because the founder understood the entire behind-the-scenes aspects to his industry. He then developed a core competency in the business which differentiated it in the marketplace forming the basis of his idea. He knows the supplier channels, how much things should cost, where to get supplies, and how to maintain an acceptable margin of profit.

I started my business planning with a simple software package that helped lead me through the process of writing a formal business plan. I hated working on this. It bored me. It was agonizing because it had so many steps, and I just wanted to get going. However, it forced me to think about all aspects of the business before I invested a dime. It gave me the roadmap/game plan on how to make this thing happen. It helped convert my idea into business processes, where I could clearly see how lead generation efforts would turn into sales. At least I was smart enough to know that I had to go through this exercise to give myself a fighting chance of making it happen and actually pulling it off. I'd learned enough preparing for this moment to understand that I needed to write this formal business plan, even though I was itching to hang my OPEN sign on the door.

A business plan is required in order to obtain funding, whether it is as simple as a bank loan or as elaborate as venture capital or private equity. The type of funding you seek will dictate the format of your business plan, as template preferences exist in the varying funding circles. Most businesses are started with borrowed money. Often the bank of choice is family and friends. In that case the business plan is equally important. Think about it: if you are going to ask family and friends to loan you money on an enterprising effort, you owe it to them (and to yourself) to have a well thought-out business plan. The plan serves to communicate your understanding of the business to your investors or lenders. The plan will help establish the mental buy-in and commitment of these partners. The more these key partners believe in your vision and idea, the more committed they will be and the less you will have to answer to them. Further, should the venture not succeed, there is less chance of hard feelings or risk of broken relationships if everyone is equally committed and supporting of the concept.

After all, the next worst thing to having family and friends as partners or employees is having them as investors or lenders. You have to assume the worst when starting a business. Part of expecting the worst is failure. You'll need to consider the ramifications to family and friends whether they are engrained in the business by money, labor, or simply as a support line. When you go through the process of starting a business, all those around you go through it as well, whether they want to or not—most notably your spouse and your children. Time will be what you give up most, and in your planning you'll need to consider what will be required of you to make the business a success and what you will have to sacrifice in the process.

In my planning process, I committed myself to at least a solid year of minimum 14-hour days, consistently working 6-7 days a week, and foregoing vacations. I did not expect my hours to improve until year three because I was going to bootstrap it myself—no funding. First off, I weighed what this would cost my relationships. It meant I would spend less time with my wife and even less than the average dad with my brand new daughter. Further, it would cut into time with my parents, brother, friends, neighbors, and in-laws, who I enjoy an unbelievably great relationship with. Everything has to come second to the business—but only for a while. It cannot be indefinite. A leveling off period needs to be attained and then there will be a chance to balance work and family commitments. If this does not take place, both personal relationships and the success of the business are put in jeopardy. It is very difficult to run a business while having personal relationships crumble around you. These are not independent entities.

The business plan does not have to be a static document. I would first recommend just throwing all of your thoughts and research into the appropriate buckets designated in the plan (i.e. Marketing, Sales, Finance, etc). Don't worry about editing or fine-tuning the grammar. This will help you immediately identify the areas where more preparation is necessary. This is why the Entrepreneurial Exercises can be so helpful once you reach this point.

Entrepreneurs are a bit like men not pulling over to ask for directions when lost. They seem to put everything on themselves; while in any phase of a business, one should actively seek advice from everyone that will listen. It is ideal if you can establish mentors, people who will take an active role in your development and provide guidance and direction. Someone who has gone through it before that can offer relevant advice, knowledge, and experience is invaluable. Even if you don't find that father figure mentor, you should be able to find people you can bounce questions off. As you study your business plan, you will find areas that need refining or that require expert knowledge. You may have legal, banking, real estate or lease questions. Hopefully, you will have a circle of people that you can tap into for advice on these topics; if not, find them.

Use your six degrees of separation to find people who know people that you can reach out to. Sharing your need with everyone in your circle that you need help with XYZ and inevitably they will know someone they can refer. Thanks to the advent of social networking tools your six degrees of separation just got easier to navigate.

Get to know your local banker early on. You may be asking for money one day plus bankers know everyone in business. Odds are if you are seeking a specific talent your banker can introduce the right match. Most are eager to do so as they are in the relationship business. Since you're starting a business, you are now in the relationship business too. Just remember to pay it back and help the next budding entrepreneur when you get on your feet.

Winging it is a great way to get around Europe with a backpack, but not so great when starting a business. The temptation to just hang your open for business sign is tremendous. Resist, resist! I don't know the statistics on the percentage of businesses that succeeded by following the "wing it" business plan, but I'm pretty sure it's up there with the Chicago Cubs winning the World Series.

Don't get me wrong, I love the Cubs and have been a fan forever… and I've waited for a championship forever, which demonstrates my reference. I will say, however, that you can get started without having every duck in a row so to speak.

This may sound contradictory to popular thought, but when you are in the business-planning stage it is not necessary to do everything 100 percent. The reason being is that you're probably understaffed, underfunded, and short on time. You are wearing all the hats and if they all don't fit, that's okay. This is not an endorsement to produce a shoddy product or service—very much the opposite. Your product or service should be your best work. It is the reflection and image of the company and the reason why you are in business. However, all of the ancillary tasks and things that you need to build the company can wait or be completed merely to "get by." You almost have to adopt this mentality in order to keep moving forward.

I strive to be a perfectionist in my business. I want every facet of it to be rock solid; however, I'm also a realist. If I spent too much of my time on the minor details and nuances of the business, I would never get the product on the shelves. It becomes a fine line on how to adopt this approach, but for most it comes naturally, simply because time in the day runs out or important deadlines approach and something has to be dropped, sidelined, or put on hold. Your goal is to eventually circle back, clean things up, and improve on items that have been neglected or given a band-aid. That's prioritization and continual improvement at the startup level.

Recognizing upfront this need for balance within the business planning process is critical; especially for the perfectionist. The guy who won't raise the curtain until every piece of the set is perfectly positioned is at risk the most because he'll never raise the curtain to start the show.

CHAPTER TWELVE
Getting Past the Doomsayers

I am told my entrepreneurial story is both impressive and remarkable. I'm a bit shy telling my story to people as not to sound boastful or egotistical. (That's why I decided to write a book about it—right?) Seriously, I primarily seek the personal satisfaction of accomplishing my goals more so than any public admiration for doing so. A phrase I've adopted to describe myself and my accomplishment is, "be inwardly cocky and outwardly humble." Being cocky internally is merely to help assert your own confidence. The later portion of the phrase is most applicable as I have learned that the approach to be humble through my experiences will always outperform egocentric self promotion. Author Jim Collins described CEO leadership in *Good to Great: Why Some Companies Make the Leap...and Others Don't* as "a paradoxical blend of personal humility and professional will" where great leaders "channel their ego needs away from themselves and into the larger goal of building a great company." What a dead-on statement and so true of most entrepreneurs I know. There is no need or time for ego stroking as the complete focus is on the business and its survival.

Starting my company was no easy task just as it isn't for anyone creating something from nothing. The journey is daunting and many won't make it. I'm told, and I've come to learn, that my story is remarkable because of its rise and ultimate exit strategy. Less than one percent of businesses created will have an exit such as mine, which is not to postulate that mine was the most ideal conclusion. Rather I've sought such comparison to better understand the rate of entrepreneurs who start businesses and successfully orchestrate their exit. Sadly, this is an area where many entrepreneurs don't plan very well. The complete measure of success of a well-conceived plan in terms of entering and running a business is summarized by the execution of the exit. Too many entrepreneurs run a successful business for years only to fail in their exit.

Before a business exits it has to start, and one aspect of my research that kept recurring was the rate of new business failure, which can be very depressing if you take it at face value. I needed to dig deeper to understand why businesses fail, what failure means, what it foretells to someone looking to start a business, and what it says about my story.

It seems everyone wants to use these statistics to tell would-be entrepreneurs why they can't be successful and why they are likely to fail. These pessimists are usually the same people who have never tried to start something like a business on their own. Our world is full of negative prophets, just turn on the news. Perhaps it is our response to the fear we have within ourselves of taking risks and failing?

The "New Thought Principle" (with 18th-century roots) produced a phrase "energy flows where the focus goes," meaning things will happen and results will materialize where you focus your energy. Whether you believe in the metaphysical, spiritual, or cosmic beliefs behind the pseudoscience of this Law of Attraction, the phrase is powerful and has great impact for the entrepreneur. Entrepreneurs cannot focus on negative feedback as they attempt what has not been attempted. If they focus their energy and thoughts on the negative, they are more likely to find reasons to agree with the negative. The converse is true for positive thoughts. I tend to believe this is more human nature than it is a connection to quantum physics as theorist of the New Thought Principle's Universal Laws of Prosperity and Abundance propose. Regardless, if you start to believe the statistics that tend to be re-circulated on the rate of new business failures you would be crazy to start any type of business.

Statistics on Starting Business

Depending on what you read, the percentage of new business failures is high, very high. The popular published failure rate of new businesses varies but they all seem to center around 80 – 90 percent of ventures failing by year ten. That percentage is staggering, but even more so for restaurants that get pegged at a 90 – 95 percent failure rate within their first few operational years!

Why should non-entrepreneurs care about these statistics? Well, it is reported by the US Small Business Administration that our nation's small businesses employ about half of all private sector employees and pay almost 45 percent of the subsequent payroll. Small businesses created between 60 – 80 percent of the total "net new jobs" over the last ten years. Employment growth rates would actually be negative without the hiring from new start-ups and small businesses!

It is estimated that between 440,000 – 600,000 new businesses are started every month in the US; however, it should be understood that the bulk of this number includes single proprietors opening up local service-oriented businesses. It should also be known that this number helps replace the large number of small businesses that close and cease to exist every year. The net new is a little tricky to determine, but the desire to go out on your own is clearly present and has grown over the years.

What we want to see from entrepreneurs are companies that create employment. Per the Kauffman Foundation, "The number of net new jobs created by the corporations that appear on the Fortune 500 has been stagnant. Historically, big companies lay people off almost as fast as they hire them. In contrast, the companies that appeared on the 2008 list of the 500 fastest-growing private businesses added more than 116,000 new jobs."

When we say that 520,000 businesses are started every month on average, there are plenty of studies to say that nine out of ten of them will be out of business in five to ten years. Mohammad Al-Zubeidi, BS, MBA, MS prepared a detailed dissertation for his Degree of Doctor of Philosophy at the University of North Texas in May 2005 that reviewed several studies from noted economists and the National Federation of Independent Business that showed between 40 – 50 percent of small businesses fail within the first two years of operation. Yikes!

Bankruptcy is the ultimate badge of business failure. In 2005 there was an average of 169,903 bankruptcies per month in the US which saw substantial year-over-year percentage growth. In 2008 the average dropped to around 84,000. Don't get excited; the rate dropped in subsequent years after 2005 due to bankruptcy rule changes making it harder to declare bankruptcy. Since the rule was enacted, the growth rate in bankruptcies continues to be positive. The reasons for bankruptcy are many but you can bet a certain percentage can be attributed to business failures. Bankruptcy is the primeval fear that prevents many from starting a business and fuels those who are in business to succeed.

CHAPTER THIRTEEN
Why Businesses Fail

B efore you get frustrated and slam the book shut, let's peel back
the layers of this mythical failure onion or entrepreneurial urban
legend. The numbers do not necessarily reflect all the data and, more
importantly, circumstances surrounding what may be unjustly reported
as failures. Further, it is assumed by these statistics that when a business
closes, it has exhausted its cash and most likely has run its owner into
bankruptcy. That's not necessarily the case, as successful money-
making businesses close every year, and they are incorporated into
these statistics. By these definitions, my own story would be deemed a
failure, which I can tell you was very much the opposite.

Years of labor studies of small businesses by author David
Birch derived more encouraging statistics after dissecting the reasons
for business closures and those pessimistically deemed failures by the
US Bureau of the Census. Birch's research first found that the rate of
business closings was inversely related to both the employment size and
gross revenue size of the business. The firms with the fewest employees
and the lowest revenue tended to have the highest rate of closing. This
would seem to separate the hobbyist entrepreneur and the least-prepared
from skewing the percentage of closures higher. When incorporating all
of the reasons available for business closings, Birch derived business
survival rates that showed 85 percent of businesses surviving their first
year, 70 percent the second, 62 percent through the third. And once the
fifth year hits, odds of survival went up substantially.

Advanced study into the rate of restaurant failures is far more
encouraging when closely examined. From Ohio State University,

Professor H.G. Parsa conducted a study of Columbus, Ohio area restaurants from 1996-1999. He found that the failure rate closely mimicked that of traditional business, with 26 percent closing in their first year, 19 percent in their second, and 14 percent in their third year. Chances for continued operation again increased greatly after year five for restaurants. Certainly sustaining a business long term is statistically challenging, however it is not as daunting as popular reports would suggest.

The entrenched myth that says nine out of ten businesses will fail within a relatively short lifespan can be debunked by digging into the statistics to reveal four primary reasons why start-ups close. I discovered that far fewer businesses actually fail; rather, they change during the founder's entrepreneurial journey.

Closure Reason #1: Education

A great deal of study has gone into the correlation between years of accomplished education and the rate of start-up success. It turns out that education does make a difference in predicting whether an entrepreneur is likely to succeed or not in his business venture. Again I draw on Mohammad Al-Zubeidi's research which included all ethnicities, immigrants, ages, and gender in his studies, and he concluded that the common thread for increased likelihood of success lay in the number of years of education.

He found that the majority of people starting small businesses tended to have less than a college degree, at least in his exclusive sample drawn from Texas businesses, and they also tended to have the highest failure rate. He showed that advanced education helps entrepreneurs to be better prepared to make decisions and manage the business. Founders with minimal education that failed tended to have an "inability to recognize their own strengths and weaknesses and act accordingly." Al-Zubeidi's research found that "small business fails primarily because of incompetence, mismanagement and lack of experienced employees" which can be correlated to insufficient education.

So stay in school! Lack of formal or on-the-job education contributes to start-up failure.

Closure Reason #2: Preparation and Planning

Aside from education, lack of preparation and planning represent two other common reasons for failure. Preparation can again be traced back to insufficient education to prepare the founder for what he's about to jump into. This can include formal education as well as on-the-job experience especially when attempting a replicative venture. Planning deficiencies often include poor goal-setting abilities or failure to establish goals at all. Many failed businesses set a goal of just opening up for business without much of a vision for how the business should operate. They fail to set revenue, profit and operational goals, or milestones which act as beacons throughout the life of the company. Planning should include a visualization of the end game on all levels. What will things like marketing, accounting, and customer service look like on day one, in six months, one year, five years?

Poorly planned businesses (often due to a rush to get in and get started) account for plenty of failures or, at a minimum, result in costly attempts to get on track. We are an impatient nation full of impatient people who want immediate results. Those attempting to become entrepreneurs are no different and often dupe themselves into believing that simply starting something is sufficient to get it going to a sustainable level. This is not to contradict my earlier statement of pressing forward even though all ducks are not in a row. Mission-critical and core-competency items need to be as solid as possible. A business can survive if tertiary items are not completely up to code, so to speak. Roy Ash, co-founder of Litton

Industries said it best, "an entrepreneur tends to bite off a little more than he can chew hoping he'll quickly learn how to chew it."

Founders who prepare and plan poorly may not establish the proper legal structure for their business either. This can be truly disastrous in a business failure. For instance, establishing as a sole proprietorship, as most small businesses do because it is easy and inexpensive, shares the business's legal exposure to debt and liability with the individual founder. Incorporating a business establishes the business and the founder as separate legal entities. Each corporate structure has its own pros and cons and seeking professional guidance is advised.

Closure Reason #3: Money and Management

"A surplus of cash invariably leads to a shortage of sense."
—Simon London

Poor financial and operational management have become the death of businesses big and small. Money problems are so numerous I could write an entire book on the topic. The best example of poor— no, dreadful—governance occurred during the dot com era. In those days you were not a sophisticated entrepreneur unless you could boast the biggest burn rate of cash with the least amount of earnings. That's what founders talked about, their burn rate. Money was shoved down the throat of these typically inexperienced entrepreneurs who had no clue they were merely part of a numbers game with the venture capital firms controlling them. The game was to throw a bunch of money at ten prospective companies hoping one would hit the home run. That win would provide the venture capitalist a profit beyond all of the money spent on the ten combined. When the other nine didn't produce, their funding was cut and they died on the vine.

There is absolutely no fault in the venture capitalists in this simplified scenario. That's the calculated risk they take. Many of the founders who received venture capital money spent it on image instead of having a keen focus on the customer and their product. Elaborate office furniture, inflated head count, and well-stocked kitchens were common. The initial Web development firm for my company fit the dot com spending spree to a tee. They were out of business in a year—never showing a profit for the untold sum that was poured into them. They most certainly would still be around today if they had not burdened themselves with such elaborate expenses that rapidly eroded the founder's equity and chances of ever going into the black.

Taking on debt to establish a business is another way to get you off the ground or go to the next level, but you have to be extremely conservative in your future cash flow to determine the level of debt to take on. When a venture capitalist throws money at you they are taking ownership in the company. When you borrow money from the bank they are taking claim to your assets—business and often personal. Not properly factoring or being overly optimistic in your future sales prospects to cover your debt obligations is a very tricky formula and hedging yourself too favorably can cause disaster. Have patience to grow into your business; that truly is half the fun and reward. As a society we may want what we want now, but when it comes to starting a business, patience prevails.

Jerry R. Mitchell, president of The Midwest Entrepreneurs' Forum and Advisory Board member of DePaul University's Coleman Entrepreneurship Center regularly addresses the virtues of bootstrapping to start a business, particularly technology oriented start-ups, in his "Bootstrapping" newsletter. Challenging the prevailing thought that in order to launch a successful high-tech business you need to secure substantial funding and recruit the very best talent, Mitchell encourages bootstrapping. Mitchell says, "Bootstrapping ensures that you build your business on a legitimate, real-world value proposition. When you're bootstrapping, you're forced to deal with customers and to fulfill their needs from day one." External funding can distract the entrepreneur from the real point of focus: the customer.

Nothing drives entrepreneurial urgency more than time and the need to make money. Funding, especially generous funding reduces that urgency and diminishes the need to get out and sell and develop a selling process. So much is learned and incorporated into a product or service through the selling process. The bootstrapper has to start selling immediately and that becomes a top priority allowing him to get to market quickly. There is a great advantage gained by thrusting yourself into the market with your complete focus and attention behind your product to ensure it meets and exceeds customer expectations.

Lack of a fat bank account spurs creativity in all aspects of the business and as Mitchell says, "forces unconventional thinking." When problems need to be solved they are done creatively and dictate out-of-the-box approaches opposed to just writing a check to make the problem go away. I'm convinced bootstrapping sharpens all of the entrepreneur's senses far beyond his well-financed counterpart. Critical thinking skills are put on the front line to assess all aspects of the business constantly; whereas, funded ventures simply hire people to solve problems and fill roles. That can really serve to dilute the entrepreneur's intimacy with his product, company, and customer.

Bootstrapping develops the greatest ownership skill of all and that is money management and respecting the value of money. I went to a seminar where the keynote speaker discussed his boom-to-bust venture capital start-up story. What struck me was that he didn't sound like an entrepreneur; he sounded like a manager or a corporate MBA. He didn't relate any of the struggles and tribulations of startup because he never experienced them from his vantage point behind a protective layer of cash.

He did remorsefully acknowledge his disregard for cash management by citing how they would call on $300-an-hour network technicians that they knew were absurdly over priced, but were convenient. Financial metrics were focused on their estimated, and inflated, company valuation, which is rather meaningless to a start-up. Who cares what the company is worth unless you intend to sell it? That was simply how they regarded their business—as an investment—internally focused.

The vision or purpose of your business needs to be, as author Michael Gerber says, impersonal. A personal purpose, one that serves you and your desires, is destined to fail. The business has to address your customer's needs and desires foremost. If you go into business to make a bunch of money, have flexible hours, be your own boss then you are not really an entrepreneur.

Starting out with too little funding or going at it "on the cheap" is probably worse than being laden with debt or selling your ownership. Debt may cost you more with interest payments, but launching a business only to run out of cash with no reserves or sources to tap as bridge financing simply reflects poor planning. Insufficient capital, typically due to improper preparation in forecasting expenses and revenue, can quickly kill a company that could otherwise grow to become sustainable. Again, it usually comes down to impatience. I'm just going to do it! After all, the motto for success is "Go for it." You should only "go for it" once you've conducted proper preparation and planning on all fronts of the business, especially projected cash flow and related pro forma statements.

"Success is not the key to happiness. Happiness is the key to success. If you love what you are doing, you will be successful."
—Herman Cain

When it comes to startup motivation, greed can come into play. Focusing on starting a business for the monetary aspects is not part of the E-Formula. Money becomes a result of the E-Formula executed properly. Virtually all the entrepreneurs I've talked with personally, or studied, were led into their business as a result of an innovative idea that intersected with the right situation and the right opportunity. Harvey Mackay said, "Find something you love to do and you'll never have to work another day in your life." The "get rich quick" plans either never launch or they close in a very short timeframe. Your business needs a mission and purpose and if that mission and purpose is focused on you making money, you'll be hard pressed to find customers that are going to appeal to that value proposition.

Failing to share your success when the company is doing well can be a form of greed that hamstrings growth. Sometimes key employees need extra incentive to be retained and rewarded in order for the business to grow to its next level or eventual exit strategy. Founders can get stingy with retained earnings and equity. I heard Silicon Valley serial entrepreneur Jerry Kaplan say "don't hoard the equity" because doing so creates a fundamental mistake in growing your start-up. He quotes, "Equity is like shit. If you pile it up, it just smells bad. If you spread it around, lots of wonderful things grow."

Fundamentally, running a business requires exceptional skills involving management of all aspects of the enterprise, including financial. Researchers blame most start-up failures on "managerial incompetence" on behalf of the founder. Embedded into misman-agement comes poor decision making and an inability to lead. Failing to recognize your own inability to manage or to find appropriate talent will certainly jeopardize your chances for success.

A common mistake founders make as managers that can cripple their start-up is hiring people they know or like over hiring the talent they need. Regardless of the type of business you have, there will always be a line of friends and relatives waiting for employment. It's easy to hire a familiar face and somewhat problematic to turn them away. However, it is very difficult to let them go if they fail to perform the basic duties of the job.

Planning and preparation of such hires needs to be fully considered and openly discussed, including the prospect of termination. What will happen to the relationship should that decision be warranted and will you be able to do it? It is often easier to avoid having to ask the question by not putting yourself in the situation to begin with. My point is not to make a statement that hiring friends and family is to be avoided. Certainly trust, loyalty, and hard work can be gained from nepotism; my only point is that such recruits require more scrutiny than an ordinary hire which may seem counterintuitive.

Closure Reason #4: Owner Migration—The Myth Buster

The first three reasons for business failures are factors of the founder being poorly prepared, educated, or capable. Often these entrepreneurs are lacking the I.D.E.A. components—the desire, effort, and ability to pull it off. However, what I call owner migration actually accounts for much of the statistics in terms of a business closing or ceasing to exist. To get around the hype, it is important to differentiate business closing from business failure.

Many businesses that get lumped into the failure bucket have actually been sold. They cease to exist after the sale but they did not fail. In most cases they were a success! Sure some businesses get sold when they fall upon duress or other factors that necessitate the owner to bail, but many others sell at a profit and provide new-found wealth for the founder. Another factor is when the owner decided to change the type of incorporation, thus killing one business by name or tax identification and generating life into a new company again by name or tax identification only. Think about sole proprietors that move to incorporation. Statistics do a poor job of differentiating the reasons why a business no longer exists, they simply see that it is closed and the public then assumes a failure.

Founders may exit a business because they want to try something else. Entrepreneurs are a wily bunch and some just switch gears and decide to do something new. They may close or transfer ownership of a perfectly good business simply to explore new interests. They may have entered a business late in life and have now reached retirement. Personal circumstances such as divorce, health, death, or other life-altering events take place that attribute to the closure of a business too.

Some businesses may close just shy of bankruptcy. For instance, the owner may not be able to make the business scale and generate sustainable profits and simply gets tired of running it. The owner may see substantial loss potential on the horizon due to competitive shifts, political circumstances, tax changes, or outsourcing trends and decides to close to prevent future loses. While these are not attractive reasons to close a business, they fall far short of the dreaded bankruptcy, which most attribute to true business failure.

Still want to do it? I thought so.

"The greatest barrier to success is the fear of failure."
—Sven Goran Eriksson

The statistics may scare some off the entrepreneurial trail but once all of the E-Formula ingredients are aligned most are still ready to jump in the pool. The E-Formula is what compels the individual to start the business. The only real barrier preventing activation is fear. Fear no longer becomes a dominant topic during the running phase of the business because in most cases the fear is gone or greatly subdued. Confidence conquers fear once startup is initiated.

I've adapted a quote on love from author Merle Shain by substituting the word love with the phrase "going for it." It goes "Going for it can cost a lot, but not going for it always costs more, and those who fear going for it often find that want of going for it is an emptiness that robs the joy from life." This hits so deep for me because I came to realize that if I were never to start a business and experience what that had to offer I would have been robbed of an important part of what I wanted out of life. A quote from journalist Fulton Oursler has the same impact. "Many of us crucify ourselves between two thieves—regret for the past and fear of the future." It would have been worse for me to have lived with the regret of never trying than to have tried and failed dramatically. I could always recover from even the most damaging bankruptcy, but I'm not sure I could have ever lived fully having failed to try.

For most, fear turns out to be a shallow barrier, a façade of sorts. Behind the impending wall lay simple sticks propped up against what we are taught to perceive as a daunting fortress. We build up in our minds the cataclysmic outcomes of failed attempts and sadly attribute very little to the cost of not attempting. Well planned and managed risk-taking to launch a business carries far lower a price than what's been popularly advertised.

CHAPTER FOURTEEN
Opportunity or Obstacle

"Always do what you are afraid to do."—Ralph Waldo Emerson

I would describe my mom as an entrepreneur. Upon entering her child rearing years, she abandoned her corporate advertising life to pursue self employment as an artist. Because my father was employed she saw little risk in this decision and it provided flexible hours perfect for raising two young boys. As an independent artist for over 30 years, she built her business around her passion and talent.

My father was a risk mitigator. I would describe him as an old school conservative product of the '40s. He was extremely hard working and reliable. He supported his family and planned for his future. Ensuring stability, consistency, and predictability were his three horsemen. Oddly, he was in a 100-percent-commission-based sales business, which typically does not provide stability, consistency, or predictability. He earned a guaranteed $30 per week stipend (generously negotiated by his union) for collecting the insurance premiums from his clients. My dad was an insurance salesman for as long as I could remember. He retired from Prudential after 35 years of service and received a well-earned pension.

He was led into the industry by his father who also was a career agent with Prudential—the Rock, according to their advertising slogan. My dad was originally in human resources in the late '50s at Illinois Tool Works until he was laid off. Not knowing where to turn and newly engaged to be married, he followed his dad's advice to come work for Prudential. At the time, agents had to be married to get a job at

Prudential as a way of ensuring stability in their workforce. Selling insurance meant knocking on a lot of doors and the first ones to knock on would be friends and family. Once that list was exhausted in the first month, most ungrounded representatives left for easier work, whereas the married guys exerted more effort to become successful.

Insurance sales was a challenging field requiring advanced certifications and extremely good relationship-building skills. Most new agents never made it past their first or second year. They gave up because of the difficulty in developing a book of business. Back in those days, your insurance agent was a part of the community. Because customers were from all aspects of town life, a good agent would become well known. Subsequently, referrals would grow the agent's business as customers entrusted the agent's service to other family members and friends. It was this ability to forge solid, trusting relationships that made my grandfather a success in his career, and my father as well.

It was around his 15th year in business that my dad was presented with an opportunity. State Farm Insurance was growing, and they had a different model than Prudential in that independent agents owned and ran their own State Farm office. Much like a franchise, the agencies were similar to running your own business. The book of business generated by the State Farm agent was his and his to keep or his to sell to a new agent. State Farm wanted to add offices in the area and in particular they wanted certified life underwriters (CLU) to expand their product portfolio to life insurance from what had traditionally been home and auto coverage. A few agents in my dad's office made the switch as the commissions were greater and the prospect of ownership was appealing. The down side was the lack of benefits and retirement guarantees that my dad valued so much at Prudential, not to mention the risk of starting a new office.

State Farm approached my dad and wanted him because of his CLU certification and years of experience. He would have to start from scratch or convince his customers to switch to State Farm upon their renewals, but there was tremendous upside potential for his efforts. The only problem was that my dad was not cut out for ownership. His personality needed the structure and guarantees of an employer. He turned the opportunity down.

I'm sure a great point of consideration for not moving ahead with State Farm was stability and our family health insurance. My brother had developed diabetes when he was four years old. That existing condition would make it difficult and extremely costly to change to another carrier upon becoming an independent agent. My dad would have to leave the book of business he built over 15 years and basically start anew. There were significant risks involved but the overriding reason he turned it down was that he didn't want it. He chose his lifestyle and ownership did not excite him.

My dad was a tremendous success in his career and life. He was able to provide very well for his family. He put me and my brother through college loan free; he paid cash for his house; paid cash for his cars; bought me a car for college graduation; established a reliable pension; took wonderful family vacations, and built an incredible nest egg to retire comfortably on and provide a legacy for future Weber generations. He had a solid plan and that plan went far into the future, much like the products he sold. A neighbor of my parents did start a State Farm office and by all indications it was very successful. I hope my dad never regretted not making the change. I hope he never looked back.

People who don't move forward with a business idea often ask themselves—and probably those around them—would it have worked? Maybe not so much about the amount of money made, but would the venture have been viable and sustainable? Would it eventually provide stability, consistency, and predictability because none of those things are present when starting a business? Those questions reinforce Merle Shain's quote about individuals often finding that their want of going for it is an emptiness that robs the joy from life.

Creating TRC

After several discussions with my wife and gaining her commitment and acceptance to move forward, I started planning my new business. The first steps involved information gathering and putting ideas into my virtual parking lot. I needed to seek information that would validate my theory as well as disclose the nuances of this market. I knew higher education would be different from K-12 but I had no idea to what degree. Sure I had been ready for Educational Resources to jump into this market, but now it was my dime on the line. I reached out to publishers and distributors who could provide details on the higher education customer and what products they bought. I struggled to find publications focused on technology and higher education and found little aside from newsletters put out by a technology-focused higher education think tank named EduCause which would ultimately yield substantial insight.

After this period of research, it was time to formalize my business plan. Remember, in the early '90s the Internet was no help at all. I had to rely primarily on first person discussions and instinct. Finally, with the plan under my belt, I started to assemble the pieces to this start-up puzzle. My intention from the beginning was to be the biggest provider of software to the higher education market. I would take a replicative approach of what we did successfully at Educational Resources by producing a quality catalog manned by a skilled inside sales force. With that goal in mind, I wanted to start out of the gate establishing a customer perception that I was well beyond startup.

I would need an above-entry-level phone system, paying more up front on a scalable system rather than making multiple smaller purchases and upgrades as we grew. The phone system would be one of the closest links to our customers so it had to be of a high quality. To come on the scene creating the perception of being a bigger and more established company than we really were meant the catalog had to look top notch too. It was going to be big, four color, and on high quality glossy paper. Behind the scenes we needed computers, office supplies, and a chair or two. What I really needed was an extra pair of hands—actually several. I would need a graphic designer, someone to direct sales, marketing, and someone to work full time during the week while I was still working at Educational Resources since it wasn't in my plan to quit yet. Yep, that was me: fully committed yet still keeping one foot out.

The immediate need was going to be a graphic designer to create the first catalog. I turned to a college classmate from Northern Illinois University who was currently working as a print graphic designer. She graduated from the art program at NIU and was a classic overachiever. She was a workaholic always taking on multiple projects simultaneously and would be a perfect candidate. I would offer her sweat equity in lieu of cash to get the catalog done. She could work flexible hours around her current job just as I was doing. I would create the entire catalog layout, the product mix, pricing, obtain copy and images from publishers, and funnel that raw information to her. She didn't hesitate when I ran the project past her. In fact, she had already started an independent design firm on the side, and she took the perspective of growing my company into a premiere client of hers. She tended to think of me as her client more so than my partner. Her entrepreneurial dreams were focused on her business more so than mine. Regardless, I had a designer, and I couldn't have asked for a better one.

I needed a home base of operations where someone who knew the business could take calls during the day, and my house was not going to be suitable. Lisa was on board, but she was not going to answer customer calls regarding technology she knew nothing about. I immediately contacted Betsy Horlock who had been a product manager with me at Educational Resources. She left the company after her second child's birth to focus on her young family. I had heard she was looking for some part time work. Betsy knew the business, and she would be a great extra pair of hands. Since she was home during the day she could be the home base for the company, able to answer phone calls while I was working at Educational Resources. I approached Betsy with the same offer as our graphic designer and she quickly accepted. Now I had two partners, and I was about to work on two more.

I have over simplified and left out a very important portion of the story in establishing my first two partners, and that is the incredible influential power of the entrepreneur. When I approached both of them, I had nothing to show or offer other than a dream. What I shared was an idea for a business along with a rather extravagant exit plan for that business with no specific time frame. I felt strongly that our early entry into the college market would result in rapid growth and would attract the eventual attention of Fortune 500 suitors to purchase our company. I provided realistic scenarios as to how my vision would unfold, and I did so with a level of compelling and captivating exuberance that was completely spoken from the heart and not from an angle to "sell" them. Keep in mind I was painting a scenario that had less than a one percent chance of becoming a reality. That's the power of the entrepreneur: to share their story with others in a manner that naturally exudes enthusiasm and passion. It's influential and genuine not manipulative and for those who are looking to share the same passion it's compelling, powerful, and enlightening.

I wanted to bring on two more partners to fill what I deemed vital roles in sales and marketing. One would essentially become a product manager and the other a sales manager. During my time at Educational Resources, I had not really been exposed to sales even though my efforts were helping drive sales. I was a bit intimidated by this function because I had never worked in that capacity before. Sales quotas, commission plans, strategies, and the management of sales representatives were things I had no experience with. My plan to fill these positions was to confide in two employees at Educational Resources to come on board with me.

For the sales manager position, I turned to one of my former product managers, Dan Figurski who had subsequently moved to become the Inside Sales Manager and several years later would actually become the president of Education Resources. He is a character, an extremely personable guy with a great sense of humor, whom everyone enjoys being around. Dan's the type that seemingly gets along with anyone and can talk forever about nothing. Some may say the classic bullshit artist. In fact, we said that quite often jokingly within our team, but he was a good communicator and one that connected with customers. Dan was someone you could send out to meet customers face to face or send on a golf outing and know he'd come back with a sale.

For the marketing position, I chose another product manager, Nancy Ragont. Nancy is a very talented and confident professional with an incredible drive for success. Nancy wanted to advance. She wanted greater responsibility and she wanted greater challenges. She knew the marketing game. She knew products, had the contacts, and she could put it all together.

Taking a chance, I disclosed my idea to them. We discussed the roles I wanted them to fill and the offer of equity. I felt a certain level of confidence and security in approaching them as each had disclosed entrepreneurial dreams in the past. In addition, we had each developed a close and trusted relationship. Unfortunately, both turned me down even though they were very engaged and receptive to the proposal. Their main concern was the lack of income for an undetermined period of time and, I would presume, a doubt of my potential for success based on the bootstrap financing approach I had presented. That meant I was going to have to wear both of those demanding hats moving forward.

I suppose I was pushing my luck in thinking I could obtain four talented individuals, two of whom had very secure, well-paying jobs, to come work for nothing but a dream and a promise. Their denials got me to question whether I wasn't as daring an entrepreneur as I thought. Was I conservative to a fault? I could never afford paying salaries for these individuals right out of the gate with no immediate revenue stream, but having them all on board would certainly propel the business. I could have investigated a bank loan to secure funding or dug deeper into my personal savings to offer them a salary. By not doing so, was I not fully committed to my dream and would that jeopardize its success?

My dad had hammered into me that debt was bad, but that's not necessarily the case for a business. A garden won't grow without an investment. Planting the seeds takes very little investment at all. But to get them to grow requires an investment of time, labor, water, fertilizer, weeding, adequate sunlight, and protection from nibbling bunnies. By not taking on debt, more harm than good may be done because the growth of the business can be restricted—just like failing to put money into the supplies and labor for your garden. In my case it came down to my belief that personal sweat equity would be the wiser route to go opposed to debt at this stage. I have always been a hard and independent worker, and I figured I could do it all in the beginning if I had to and now I was going to have to.

CHAPTER FIFTEEN
Fear Factor

"Each time we face our fear, we gain strength, courage, and confidence in the doing."—Anonymous

If so many people have ideas and entrepreneurial dreams then why do so few take action to follow those dreams? The E-Formula shows how situational and opportunity factors align with an idea to activate an entrepreneur, but it is not a sure-fire formula for action. As I mentioned, the E-Formula was only the first defining moment required to activate the entrepreneur within. The second defining moment still needs to be mastered and its roots are made up of fear and doubt which manifest themselves as risk.

Many people standing on the threshold of their entrepreneurial dreams will say they are unable to commit out of fear and doubt. By definition the E-Formula should remove any doubt of the idea's potential or the entrepreneur's abilities, leaving us with just fear. And what is fear? It's really nothing at all, at least tangible. Fear is anticipation of something that is yet to happen or that may not happen at all. Being scared is an outcome of fear. Being scared is real because something tangible and definite has happened that causes you to be scared. It's scary when you lose your job. It's scary when you lose your house because it was collateral on a business loan. That's real because it happened. Fear is so damaging because it plants those seeds of failure, which may not happen, in the forefront of your mind.

Fear is very powerful. More often than not, it is more powerful than corresponding positive outcomes that seemingly have a greater probability of occurrence. What tilts the scale to achieving positive outcomes over negative is the strength of your I.D.E.A. How sound your innovation is and how well you apply desire, effort, and abilities toward its accomplishment. Fear is the barrier to doing, but it should have no place in your rational decision making. Because fear cannot be quantified, it has no place in the decision-making process at all. Business continuity managers recognize this emotional albatross and how it can impact well-informed and educated judgments and strive wherever possible to factor it out.

Fear is personal, and it typically attributes personal values that have no relevance to the business decision. The fear of loss is a real human fear and it is a powerful, innate characteristic that will skew and cloud probability decisions. The entrepreneur thinks of all the personal things in his life that he is about to put at risk and fear focuses on only the negative potential outcomes. I may lose money. I may disrupt my career. I may lose possessions or any number of other valuable items. Fear is preventive in that it builds up doubt so those personal items never have to be put at risk because if the action is never taken then the negative outcome will not take place.

In certain respects, fear can be a valuable emotion, helping to keep you safe from danger or disappointment. It is through life experiences that fear is learned and used to prevent injury and escape negative outcomes. An element of fear surrounds all of the decisions we make. Recognizing the potential results of fear's outcomes helps the individual avoid things like pain, expense, sadness, regret, and embarrassment. Fear's dual outcome is that it can prevent you from experiences. You benefit and learn from doing things that scare and stretch you. The fear that something bad may happen by taking action or choosing not to has prevented many from reaching their fullest potential and level of satisfaction. The challenge is recognizing when you are making decisions based on or heavily influenced by fear, and then knowing how to weigh that influence.

Time for Stress

In the excitement of launching this new venture much was happening. A somewhat controlled chaos developed in my life as I started construction on the new business during the early morning and night and reported to work at Educational Resources by day. Since I was wearing most of the hats I found myself doing an unbelievable amount of multitasking. There were clear priorities, like the catalog that had to get done first. I handled most tasks on my own or through Betsy and Lisa in order to avoid any extra expenses. Simultaneously, every part of the company was starting to come together.

Unfortunately, between the hectic pace of starting the company and being extremely frugal, I failed to get a legal agreement signed by my partners outlining our verbal agreement. Although, I did go to a lawyer to draft our corporate by-laws, issue stock certificates, and related details I failed to finalize the actual employee stock agreement. To this day, I don't understand how I neglected this. Sure I knew I did not get people to sign off on an agreement. I always intended to do that later. But how I failed to finish the actual agreement is beyond me. There was a draft, but never a finished and executed agreement. I suppose things were moving too fast, my partners trusted me and I trusted them. Yes, this would come back to haunt me.

By now we had a company name, Technology Resource Center, Inc. A company name can come about in a variety of ways. For me, I discovered that the original three or four names I wanted were already taken while conducting a name search. Out of desperation I submitted Technology Resource Center, Inc. and it came back clean – great! I would later discover that Technology Resource Center, Inc. was a terrible name. Customers, vendors, family, and even employees could not seem to keep it straight. We became Technical Resources, Technology Resources Center, The Center for Technology and so on. It was unbelievable and I'm sure you just glanced back to review the original name. We would receive school purchase orders with all variations of the three words scrambled differently. Finally, I resorted to doing business as TRC, which stuck and became the recognized industry brand I had intended from the start.

By now, I had already started producing the layout of the catalog and submitting pages to our graphic designer. I was working with publishers on the side along with Betsy to secure co-op funds to cover the cost of the catalog, and I set aside $30,000 of my money to invest in the business. Life was crazy working two jobs but deep down inside I loved it. The enjoyment, however, was quickly turning to stress as the deadline for our print date approached. I was targeting the catalog to hit the 1996 summer buying season, which was the peak buying period for higher education. The catalog would be over 100 pages which meant hundreds of high resolution images, copy, vendors to get established with, and price points to determine. Even though this was what I did at Educational Resources, I had done it with a team of eight people and an established company with existing relationships and procedures. Our graphic designer was stressing too, but she was determined to complete the project on time. She was a professional and her life was deadlines. This deadline was going to be tough.

In order to get things done, I had to get up at 4 a.m. and drive 25 miles to Betsy's house to do what work I could squeeze in prior to starting at Educational Resources at 8 a.m. After 5 p.m. I would drive back to Betsy's, thankfully only eight miles away, to do some more work. My day would end racing to our designer's house 22 miles away to drop off pages to be created and pick up completed drafts, to finally trek 20 miles home. At the time, we simply did not have the technology to electronically communicate with each other and exchange the large number of graphic files digitally. Therefore, I had some serious windshield time.

Between the hours of working my job at Educational Resources and struggling to finish the catalog by our deadline I was stressing big time. One early morning I made a reverse commute to pick up finished pages at the designer's house for editing prior to starting my regular work day. On the way back to Educational Resources, while making a turn, I struck a two-foot-high concrete median dividing the highway. I don't know how it happened, as I was either asleep or deep in thought about what needed to get done. All I remembered was the piercing sound of the collision snapping me out of my trance, finding my car immobilized and myself and others thankfully uninjured. On another occasion around midnight I was forced to call the paramedics to our house as I was certain I was having a heart attack. Stress was the culprit sitting on my chest as I was starting to physically reach the startup breaking point.

TRC was actually starting to fulfill customer orders given to us by publishers who were unwilling or unable to process orders direct from schools. I had a great relationship with the DK Publishing representative who was unable to set up direct customer accounts, ship to multiple unique addresses, or provide net 30 terms. It was far easier and cost effective to hand those orders off to a dealer, and they selected TRC for all of their direct educational orders. This was a windfall and testament to relationships. Those early orders helped us create our internal operational procedures to purchase product, package and ship. Best of all, they were high margin and provided a much needed revenue stream.

The IT industry was very small and tight knit and publishers were beginning to talk about the Jeff Weber at Educational Resources and the Jeff Weber at Technology Resource Center, Inc. or whatever they were calling it that week. One day I was called to the carpet by the Human Resource Director at Educational Resources. How do I handle this, I thought as she started to describe what she had heard about me starting a company focused on higher education and that I had enlisted the help of Betsy Horlock. Her details of my masquerade were dead on! How did they know? My initial fear was getting fired, but my subconscious fear was having to commit fully to TRC. I was still hanging on to the security of a steady job and paycheck. So I spun the story that, "yes, this company existed and Betsy was running it, and I was merely consulting her." Not quite a lie?

I am certain she saw holes in my story, but I had been and still was doing a great job at Educational Resources. Further, the company was going through some deeper issues with personnel that made my exploits look like schoolboy antics. I also had the support of two prominent executives, Pat Laystrom the Vice President of Sales who brought me in and the Vice President of Marketing to whom I reported. When I left the HR office unscathed, but ordered to cease and desist, I was immediately summoned to my VP's office. Jumping right to the chase, he expressed to me that he had independent business plans that he had been conjuring up for the past few months. Sensing I was fair and possibly game to discuss a new venture, he asked if I would be interested in his project! I gracefully declined.

What I didn't mention was by this time the founder of Educational Resources had left the company under certain coaxing and duress forced upon him by parent company Davidson & Associates. I don't know the details, but my guess is either the thrill was gone or his drive to lead and innovate ran counter to the Davidson's and all agreed it was time for him to move on. He did so by starting a new publishing company. The speed in which it launched raised questions as to what he had been doing in his spare time over the past few months. Executives were not only interested in what this new publishing company was about, they were getting ready to try and block it through non-compete agreements. With all this extracurricular activity going on I had a sense of security in my own position, but it showed how crazy things were getting in this relatively small company. Entrepreneurism was exploding, but in a very chaotic and disruptive fashion, and I was going to have to make a decision on my fate or someone else would.

CHAPTER SIXTEEN
Risk Breaking

"Don't wait until everything is just right. It will never be perfect. There will always be challenges, obstacles and less than perfect conditions. So what! Get started now. With each step you take, you will grow stronger and stronger, more and more skilled, more and more self-confident and more and more successful."
—Mark Victor Hansen, author

E ntrepreneurs seem to be synonymous with "risk taking" so it's important to understand the term. Risk is the single greatest barrier to move from the E-Formula to the startup phase. The fear associated with risk is greatest at startup and actually decreases significantly once the business is launched. Risk involves putting something of value at stake. In the startup phase, this would most likely include an existing job, savings, a home, possessions, time, and even relationships. The prospect of taking an action that is deemed risky because it may fail does not prevent us from taking action; it is the fear of losing what we put at risk.

Take, for example, the game of poker. You have to put money at risk to play the game. You absolutely cannot play the game if you don't play for money. Try it. If you don't put your own money at stake, the game becomes pointless. Poker plays directly on your mental psyche and your learned affiliation to money. With that, I'm going to tell you the one obstacle that holds every single would-be entrepreneur back from following his dreams. This is big because it applies to everyone—you included. The primary factor holding someone back from starting a business is not money but mind. Most individuals would say that money restricts their activation. But if you dig deeper, you'll find mental barriers that they themselves have erected. The individual himself is the only thing preventing him from following his dreams. So why is that?

Why do some people start businesses while others watch from the sidelines wishing they could be in their shoes? Why is it that we hear the familiar story of the immigrant who came to this country with nothing who then becomes a multi-millionaire? Or how about the story of the twenty-something billionaire genius which leaves us thinking, if she could do it, then why can't I? You are holding yourself back from being that person. It has everything to do with what's in your head and your learned fear of risking what you have accumulated in terms of possessions, wealth, and position. Immigrants continue to have a substantially higher rate of entrepreneurial activity than US-born individuals. They took their risk when they stepped foot on that plane or boat to come to America. Once that action is taken, the sky is the limit because they already made the decision to put at risk most of the aspects that feed into fear.

People are afraid to take a step backward. They don't want to give up time, money, or possessions. They fear the worst-case scenario of losing it all; even with a possibility of gaining it all back at a later date. Surprisingly, we take risks every day that arguably may be more risky than starting a business. We risk our savings by contributing to 401k plans that are invested in the stock market. We watch with joy as the principal goes up and cringe with disgust as it goes down, but with relatively little fear in comparison to perceptions of entrepreneurism.

Many put their financial security at tremendous risk through the amount of debt they take on. Credit card and home equity debt used to further individual consumerism are the greatest threats to being able to put your kids through college or to retire in a lifestyle you've grown accustomed to. People feel they are moving forward in life by collecting more possessions, allowing their outward appearance to be plentiful. However, their balance sheet is something entirely different. They fail to take into account their ability to pay down that debt or keep it manageable. They gamble personal bankruptcy—risking all they have—without really gaining much in return, and they make these decisions with far less fear or deliberation than starting a business.

Why do so many people fall into this cycle of pseudo safety? They follow what everyone else does with relatively little planning, preparation, or consideration of downside risk. Seriously, how closely do you read the prospectus on the mutual funds in your 401k or for your kids' 525 college savings? The rich are not immune; look at the Madoff scandal where mostly the affluent were robbed of an estimated $50 billion because they didn't pay attention to how their money was being invested.

It has been said that Wall Street traders only have two things that guide them—greed and fear. These two aspects are the nucleus that drives their performance. Psychologists who have studied traders and investors have discovered that although everyone who participates in investing is in it to see a profit, profiting is not the alpha influence of their behavior and decision making. Fear is actually proven to be twice as influential in one's decision making as the desire to make a profit. When bull markets occur, traders are more likely to act in a less aggressive fashion than they would during a bear market. During a bear market the prospect of losing one's gains is prevalent and pervasive. The loss of capital becomes far more vexing on the trader than the exuberance during upswings.

The reason we focus on risk, rather than fear, is because it can be measured and analyzed opposed to fear. In management, people use Key Risk Indicators (KRI) to indicate how risky an activity is. They establish risk mitigation techniques and risk management tools. Bankers assign risk premiums to loans and investment traders try to predict and calculate risk in order to abate and understand that given risk using the very complex Value at Risk formula. It is designed to take the historical variance and covariance of a basket of securities to determine a level of risk within a portfolio. It has historically provided a 99 percent probability to fund managers that their investors would not lose more than a certain amount of money.

$$VaR_\alpha = \inf\left\{ l \in \mathfrak{R} : P(L > l) \le 1-\alpha \right\} = \inf\left\{ l \in \mathfrak{R} : F_l(l) \ge \alpha \right\}$$

Most of this risk aversion psychology has to do with the prospect of "losing it all." Your upside profit is really not known when you are in the midst of that ride. You are immediately happy when you first extend into profit territory and you figure no matter what, you've made out okay and you made the right decisions—you're making a profit. There may be remorse if you sell and the investment continues to climb, but you can rest easy knowing you turned a profit and got out safe. When your investment slides, there is that same unknown as to how far it will fall and when it will recover. The fear that you could lose your entire investment is quantifiable and focus immediately shifts to dollars lost and preservation tactics. The fear of loss of a known sum is what creates a compounded reaction and stance in the investor that is proven to be twice as powerful as the profit reaction.

For most, the word risk is associated with a negative outcome because of its use in popular language as "avoiding risk" or "risk reduction." It's interesting to note that risk is derived from the 16th century Arabic word "rizk" meaning "to seek prosperity." Only through risk can one seek opportunity. No risk, no gain. The counter to risk is certainty, but you don't often go out seeking certainty, you seek opportunity. Risk has two outcomes, one is negative and the other is positive. Like the investor, we tend to put greater emphasis on the negative than the positive.

This same psychology can be applied to the entrepreneur looking to start his business. To start the business, the entrepreneur has to give up something—or put something at risk which becomes their investment. That investment can be in the form of money, time, current job or career, possessions, or relationships. Entrepreneurs are all too familiar with failure rates for new businesses and the amount of personal bankruptcy filings. Fear of a complete loss of any one of those individual investments or the dreadful prospect of bankruptcy looms in the recesses of the mind weighing down action. Where the trader's dual principle is fear and greed, the entrepreneur's is fear and success.

Hard Work Pays Off

I had one other sweat equity partner and that was my wife Lisa. Her responsibilities would include all of the administrative and accounting work. Lisa was the un-chosen entrepreneur. The one drafted by the entrepreneur based on family relationship. I could not have chosen a better partner not only for her duties but her moral support and encouragement too. Lisa was invaluable for me getting through some of the most difficult times, for encouraging me to go for it, and for being supportive of my dreams. Having a full-time job herself, Lisa would most often start her work for TRC around 10 p.m. after our daughter was put to bed and all other household duties were done.

Aside from the long hours, things at TRC were going well and pretty much on schedule. The all-encompassing goal at this point for me was to finish the catalog and far less about the details of launching the company. In fact, after crashing the car, calling the paramedics, and nearly being fired, I was actually ready to call it quits. I was going to finish the catalog, but I was running out of steam to create the business post catalog. I was exhausted, stressed, and didn't have anything really to show for all the hard work and time spent.

Printing a catalog in the mid '90s meant film had to be run since direct-to-plate technology was not available or cost effective. Thankfully, and to plan, my father-in-law's business was a service bureau that did this type of work. The business was run primarily by Lisa's brother Bob. I would work closely with him in preparing our page files for print and running the film necessary for our printer to create plates and print the job.

Bob not only provided great pricing but his services caught several costly mistakes. The catalog was a very large single computer file and Bob chose to run it after hours. The entire 100+ page file had to be run in unbroken succession due to the common image linking throughout the body of the catalog. It created a strain on the equipment and ran for over 12 hours. As fate would have it, a hose that transported chemicals in the film processor burst and flooded a portion of Bob's office. Of course it ran undetected because of the time frame we elected to do the job. I felt terrible, but Bob was a great supporter of his sister and me and he never vented his justifiable frustrations.

Eventually, with the film done, we were off to the presses. At that moment, the slate was wiped clean and all of the stress, frustration and doubt were washed away. It was such a sense of accomplishment, pride and joy to see that we had done it. We finished the catalog, raised co-op to cover most of the cost, and in a few short days it would be arriving in the mail to thousands of potential customers and TRC would truly be born.

During this phase I had developed the attitude that I would just complete the catalog, mail it, and then I would be done with it. I could say with confidence that I went for it and it just didn't work out. I would not hold any regrets. I started a company. I tried to make a go of it but, alas, it failed. All I would be out would be a few thousand dollars and my time, but life would be back to normal. I wanted to get back to normal.

Normal life would never return—thank goodness! The catalog was a hit the day it dropped. The phone rang and purchase orders arrived via mail and facsimile machine. All of our efforts to build a company bigger than start-up in our customer's eyes had paid off. We were legitimate, on the street, and people were buying from us with confidence. The orders from DK Publishing helped refine our logistics and things were going relatively smoothly. It was time to get focused on this company and start navigating it through startup.

Office Down Under

Now that the catalog had mailed, the priority shifted to providing phone coverage during our Central Time Zone business hours. Since the East Coast was an hour ahead and the West Coast was two hours behind us, we needed to be open for business from 7 a.m. to 7 p.m.

Betsy's townhouse basement was unfinished and lighted with just a few ceiling-mounted bulbs on pull strings. I brought in a couple of mismatched lamps and an old desk, while Betsy provided an additional desk and a few second-hand dining room chairs. About 25 feet away from our desks were the washer and dryer. We tried to plan outbound calls between rinse cycles

It was great having Betsy available during the day to provide our customers with a voice rather than voice mail. Occasionally, when Betsy could not do her shift, my father-in-law, Frank Rubino, would make the drive out to her townhome to answer calls. A small business owner himself, he was always willing to help since he understood the start-up struggle. He had no idea how to answer questions being asked about the technology products we sold. His purpose was to be a human voice to take a message. Frank's assistance was invaluable and helped to establish a level of customer service that I would continually demand—no voice mail. We answer the phone when our customers call.

Around 5 a.m. each weekday morning, I would arrive at Betsy's townhouse and let myself in with the key she provided. The Horlock family would still be sleeping as I silently made my way to the basement. Can you imagine that routine in your house? I knew Betsy from working with her for about a year at Educational Resources, but I met her husband only once or twice. Now I was entering their house while they slept to go work in their basement. How many spouses would put up with that? I never once heard a complaint from Betsy's husband, but I suppose she may have. Again, I selected a great partner and adjoining family too.

CHAPTER SEVENTEEN
The Risk Box

Defining Moment Number Two

"Often the difference between a successful person and a failure is not one has better abilities or ideas, but the courage that one has to bet on one's ideas, to take a calculated risk—and to act."
—Andre Malraux, author

An individual's personal and professional situation, as discussed in the E-Formula, has components which include: possessions, age, position and health. These four factors weigh heavily on motivating an entrepreneur to move forward with his idea. The E-Formula was the first defining moment of the entrepreneur and one's situation plays an even bigger role in the second determining factor: The Risk Box.

The Risk Box is just that, a box, and we all reside in one. A box has four walls which completely surround us. All decisions have a degree of risk associated with them. Risk has a cause and, if it occurs, a consequence. As individuals we start building our Risk Box at birth. Gradually, over time, we put things we value in the Risk Box for protection. The more we put in the Risk Box, the stronger our walls become. The walls become stronger because of the importance we place on the items, and it is natural that we want to guard them.

The purpose of the Risk Box is to protect, and it serves a valid and noble purpose for us. Our learned experiences reinforce the walls of the Risk Box teaching us what actions and decisions have positive or negative outcomes. The four walls sealing the Risk Box from intrusions that may take away what we put inside are represented by the situational components: possessions, age, position, and health.

Wall #1: Possessions

Face it, we are a materialistic country. We highly value our possessions and many of us have a sense of entitlement to obtain our possessions regardless of our ability to pay for them. Bigger homes and fancier cars have been put in more people's hands thanks to creative financing. Our possessions include what we put in those homes, our clothes, memberships, service plans, and our savings. The exposure to poplar media has created more want, and we seem to be successfully exporting that desire overseas addicting other nations to our materialistic values. Possessions exist not only to pacify our desires but to provide a sense of security. Certainly our home is the greatest example of this as it provides our shelter. A car is more than a status symbol, it provides required transportation, and our savings is what we'll depend upon in our golden years.

Everything you will ever want in life is just outside your comfort zone.

This phrase is universally true, but what if you in essence can get everything you want in terms of possessions? Wealth is probably the curse of the entrepreneur as it can extinguish desire. Where wealth should be the greatest catalyst to fund an entrepreneurial dream, far too often complacency sets in as the wealthy find little motivation to go through the effort to build something new. I think children born into wealth are the best example of this disease. They are born into a risk box with pre-conditioned walls, which only grow stronger over time.

How often have you seen children of privilege grow up and amount to not much of anything? They are not challenged because they don't need to be challenged, and they don't want to be challenged, nor do they feel a need to be challenged.

This is not meant to be a universal statement but one I know Warren Buffet (now worth an estimated $62 billion) agrees with. He states, "I don't believe in dynastic wealth" referring to those who grow up as "members of the lucky sperm club." Buffett donated over 85 percent of his fortune to charity and once commented, "I want to give my kids just enough so that they would feel that they could do anything, but not so much that they would feel like doing nothing." The richest man on earth practices what he preaches too. He still lives in the same house he bought in 1958, and in 2007 had a total compensation of $175,000 for running his company Berkshire Hathaway.

It is interesting to note that two-thirds of the members of The Forbes 400 have fortunes that are entirely self-made, while only 19 percent of the group inherited their fortunes. A high percentage of those inherited had done so in just the past 50 years. That number is amazing to me considering that time should be adding to the early industrialist family fortunes and the number of family members inheriting such fortunes. Certainly, estate fortunes are donated, split among many heirs, and so forth; however, proper investment should ensure family names remain on the Fortune list. A study by the Kauffman Foundation titled "The Anatomy of an Entrepreneur" wanted to find insights into what made a successful high-growth entrepreneur. Among other things, the study showed that less than one percent of their survey pool came from extremely rich families. The vast majority, 71.5 percent, came from the middle class.

This seems to demonstrate my point on human nature and of the well-funded entrepreneur who loses respect for money all too willingly.

Wall #2: Age

Entrepreneurs activate at all ages, but the vast majority tends to be younger. The reason is simple: younger people have fewer possessions, have experienced less, and are prone to take and accept risk results better than their older counterparts. Possessions and position tend to calcify the age Risk Box wall. Typically the older one gets, the more he possesses, and the greater importance his personal and professional position in life holds. Age thickens the Risk Box walls as people develop a fear of changing careers late in life. This is for good reason, as they will put a great deal at stake by making such a change.

The Risk Box walls are designed to protect our assets and relationships so we can live a safe life. Society helps shape the Risk Box walls. The news and media that deliver headlines and our own personal experiences show us how things can go wrong and how we have to be careful and protect what we have. The older one gets the stronger they hold on to what they have deposited in the Risk Box, and their assessments of opportunities tend to lean more on preserving what they have than putting it at risk for an uncertain opportunity.

Some choose to coast to the finish line of life instead of charging in completely used up. Too many look at how they feel they have to fit in the world especially when they reach a self-imposed age limit. Their experience and knowledge should allow them to dictate the rules and shape the playing field, but conservatives and popular media tell them to retire. As Buffet would agree, life doesn't pay compound interest so there is no need to save it. He's still at the helm working at age 79.

Wall #3: Position

A person's position in life consists of both personal and professional attributes that are built upon over time. An individual consciously invests in his or her position which represents the greatest investment of their most limited resource—time.

Personal position consists of a variety of things such as: marital status, children, or a caregiver role. It could represent your economic status or your involvement in groups, clubs, school, local government, charities, or religious organizations. Personal position extends to your interests: hobbies, sports, collecting, gardening, and so forth. These are the things you like to spend time on and that will be affected the most by your decision to start a business. The personal is always encroached upon by the professional, thus our desire to achieve an ideal work and life balance.

Professional position is what you do for a living. Typically, we have worked very long and hard to achieve our career position. Investments in education, relocation, time, and sacrifice are made to maximize our professional goals. Professional position is best known as the career ladder and significant achievement; wealth and respect is granted to those who climb the highest. Position is what feeds the ego. This alone may prove too powerful for some to concede in pursuit of new endeavors.

Position is an investment that is not easily parted with. It may represent the most influential aspect to Risk Box wall thickening because it attaches to and impacts possessions and wealth, and is often correlated to age. When you give up position at the top you give up more than income. You may forego stock options, bonuses, hefty vacation accrual, allowances, and other benefits designed to retain your services. Leaving a position to follow entrepreneurial endeavors can knock you off the career ladder indefinitely in your industry making it very difficult to restart where you had left off.

Wall #4: Health

Your own personal health plays a very important role in determining your ability and desire to start a business. It's vitally important if not mandatory to be both physically and mentally fit to start a business. Starting a business is extremely demanding and requires stamina, endurance, patience, and the ability to control stress. Long, fast-paced hours will press the physical and mental boundaries of the entrepreneur. Being in any type of weakened state could compromise success.

In addition, the health of close family members and friends can greatly influence the performance and resulting success of the entrepreneur. Caring for elderly parents, a sick spouse, or children will take priority over any other activities. Balancing a new business with long-term care needs of loved ones can take its toll on a new entrepreneur. Knowing such situational factors are in a negative state should cause the entrepreneur to pause and give serious consideration to moving forward. Should health issues develop unexpectedly during the entrepreneurial journey, finding supporters or new partners may be necessary to keep the business going.

Risk Box Summary

"We look at those who have accomplished great things and all we see is their success. We rarely see or hear what they did to get there; what they sacrificed, how they failed, how they feared the process and questioned success."—Jeff Weber

The possessions, age, position, and health that thicken and strengthen your Risk Box walls are independent variables in determining the outcome of a business venture. The Risk Box does not determine the likelihood of business success; rather it determines whether entrepreneurial activation will occur. The success of a business will rest in its business plan and in how well it addresses a unique customer problem or demand.

The Risk Box walls act as a filter to new experiences, and they reinforce the status quo. The thicker the walls become, the more resistant they are to new experiences. The Risk Box is not a reason why you can't start a business, it is an excuse. The content of the box is an accumulation of our life experiences. All of the contents came to us in one way or another, and we are afraid to lose them. We often don't want to part with them for a short period of time, even with the knowledge that we may get them back tenfold by following our dream. The more we accumulate in our Risk Box, the harder it is for us to break through the boundaries the box erects.

The Risk Box's intentions are to protect us, but they can become too powerful, sometimes crippling, if left unchallenged. Becoming content with your situation in life will make you less receptive to opportunity. It is opportunity which serves to challenge your situation. The Program Management Institute (PMI), the world's leading not-for-profit association for professionals who study risk, views risk as an "opportunity." Taking on risk equals taking on opportunity which means growth and not maintaining the status quo.

It takes double the energy and desire to take on opportunity because the risk concern weighs heavier on the downward potential than the upside. In a pure logic world, personal considerations of possessions, age, and position would be independent of evaluating whether to move forward with a business idea. Since we don't live in a pure logic world, it is the Risk Box that governs our situation to the assessment of a new business venture and rightfully so. But how would it be to make that logical decision confidently without the Risk Box walls' influence?

The principle of the Risk Box is reflective of the immigrant in the 1800s who came to the US with little money and impoverished means. This is not to generalize all immigrants as penniless orphans deposited on Ellis Island, but to provide the common analogy. He hit our shores with a sense of urgency and a dream to do something that he could not do in his native land. His situation in his homeland offered few prospects while America represented vast opportunity and abundance. He would pour his heart and soul into the business he started. He applied an incredible level of desire into his work to ensure success as all he had to rely upon was himself and his own efforts.

How did he do it? How did he come to a foreign land of mixed languages and succeed? Very simply, he had to. As it's said, failure is not an option. The immigrant arriving with humble means finds that just the basic services that the US provides: plumbing, water, accessible shelter, transit, trusted police protection, freedom of speech, freedom to assemble are so much more than he ever had. These are basic elements that will not be taken away, for the most part, should the business attempt fail. The immigrant has realized such an improvement in basic life that taking on risk to start a business entails virtually no risk at all.

The immigrant depicted has a Risk Box with very thin walls. His mind does not block the path with fears of losing wealth, possessions, or position in life because he is starting with basically nothing—a clean slate. It's less about entrepreneurialism as it is survival. The message is not to be misconstrued as the less you have the greater your chances of being an entrepreneur. Look at T. Boone Pickens who has accumulated much, and at age 81 is still in the investment game where he has made and lost billions over the years. I would say Pickens has relatively transparent Risk Box walls. His story is truly remarkable and certainly not one that many in this world could replicate. There is something inside him that very few of us have learned to master, but all possess. It allows him to operate without a net and as a result he achieves remarkable success.

Therefore, it is not the quantity of deposits within the Risk Box, but the value placed on them that determines the thickness and strength of the walls. Everyone's are different based on personal values and priorities. Entrepreneurial activation occurs when the idea and the importance to pursue it outweigh the value placed on the contents of the Risk Box. The entrepreneur mitigates the risk of loss by careful planning, research, and effort in launching the idea.

Escape the Risk Box – Your Career Depends on It

"A real entrepreneur is somebody who has no safety net underneath them."
—Henry Kravis, financier and investor
(Forbes 107th richest American)

Everyone can be an entrepreneur, and I would assert that today everyone needs to be an entrepreneur. Corporations that strive for their employees to develop a feeling of ownership and entrepreneurial spirit will increasingly come to expect it. Developing your entrepreneurial skill set in your present workplace will be more of a requirement than a welcomed attribute. Risk Box walls thicken over time as you reside in the comfort and security of your employer.

What has not been made clear is that the protection afforded by the Risk Box is illusionary. There are greater forces at work that can penetrate your Risk Box. Your finances and savings can be wiped out by a swindler or more likely through powerful market forces that impact valuations in seconds. Less than 18 percent of New York Stock Exchange listed stocks are traded by individuals, where well over 80 percent of equity trading is done by hedge fund dealers and other institutional investors. The individual solo investor doesn't stand a chance in today's equity markets. Your job can be eliminated due to downsizing and life threatening illness can be diagnosed without warning. These are the threats that exist to penetrate your

Risk Box security. The more you allow yourself to entrench in the status quo the greater the impact these events will have on you. The mental fallacy is that residence in the Risk Box will eliminate risk. The Risk Box limits individuals and corporations opportunities to be exposed to risk, but it also limits their opportunities to grow.

Living in the Risk Box is addictive which leads to complacency. In fact, the more things you put in the Risk Box the more habit forming the Risk Box is likely to become. Understanding and managing the enslaving properties of the Risk Box will help you move closer to living an entrepreneurial life and such a life will provide greater dexterity. The word layoff should be retired from the dictionary as it no longer exists for the most part. Recessions since 1990 have proven that companies that had layoffs in response to economic downturns did not return to pre-recession employment levels after the recovery. The term *jobless recovery* results in work being distributed to those who were left, and "laid off" workers having to find new jobs often in new industries. This development causes a shrinking of employment opportunities for a nation with an increasing labor pool. Herein is the global need and demand for the entrepreneur. It is the entrepreneur who grows employment. The entrepreneur has brought us out of the last seven recessions according to data from the Kaufmann Foundation. Don't you want to be part of the labor talent that is in the highest demand in the world?

In 2006 Daniel H. Pink wrote *A Whole New Mind: Why Right-Brainers Will Rule the Future*, which formulated a hypothesis that global demand was shifting from a left-brain-centric world to right-brain thinkers. Everything from our educational system to corporate management built processes and jobs around the analytical left-brain producer. To quote Pink, "The last few decades have belonged to a certain kind of person with a certain kind of mind—computer programmers who could crack code, lawyers who could craft contracts, and MBAs who could crunch numbers. But the keys to the kingdom are changing hands. The future belongs to a very different kind of person with a very different kind of mind—creators and empathizers, pattern recognizers and meaning makers. These people—artists, inventors, designers, storytellers, caregivers, consolers, big-picture thinkers—will now reap society's richest rewards and share its greatest joys."

Our society has been trained to be good workers rather than creative thinkers and problem solvers. The one talent I look for most in hiring individuals is an ability to think, and think creatively not mechanically. The left-brain programmers, accountants, and such are becoming a commoditized skill which can be shopped for the lowest price. Pink continues, "We are moving from an economy and a society built on the logical linear computer-like capabilities of the Information Age to an economy and a society built on the inventive, empathetic, big-picture capabilities of what's rising in its place, the Conceptual Age." Creativity and innovation will be the new skill sets in demand and those exercising their entrepreneurial gifts will be most sought after. Jack Welch, former CEO of General Electric made the statement, "control your destiny or someone else will." At heart, people want to be entrepreneurs and it is that desire to control one's own destiny which appeals to us all.

The Risk Box Kills

Arthrosclerosis of the Risk Box results in submission to the system and turning your destiny over to others. We've discussed why the Risk Box exists and how its walls get thicker the more one accumulates. The more stuff you have, the greater your position, prestige and power, the less likely you are to take chances and expose yourself to risk. Severe cases involve people equating their own personal worth to the contents of their Risk Box components.

People buy a big fancy car because it "shows the world who I am."

This point is demonstrated with profound tragedy regarding Bear Stearns research supervisor Barry Fox. Mr. Fox was a nine-year veteran of Bear Stearns when he lost his job in 2008. Like many in the financial industry, Mr. Fox was going to lose his job due to the unprecedented catastrophe in the US and world financial markets. Fox was a hard working and dedicated employee who was making a reported $250,000 salary and seemingly had his dream job. Through no fault of his own and powerless to stop his impending termination, Fox became another statistic when he was informed that there would be no position for him at J.P. Morgan Chase, the white knight of sorts who acquired Bear in their eleventh hour.

Fox turned to what history has portrayed during the Great Depression when such professional devastation befalls Wall Street: he killed himself. There were other mental health factors that presumably led to Mr. Fox's despair, but it was his removal from position that destroyed the security he had entrusted to this intangible. Powers outside of his control punched through his Risk Box and exposed his vulnerability..

It is sad that the walls of one's Risk Box can become so fortified by material matter. Careers and money can be replaced, but when someone mentally fixates on those things and establishes rigid benchmarks for them, the outcome can become deadly as we've seen during this and similar crisis. Some people snap when they fall below their mental benchmarks for money, possessions, and position. It is this same mental barrier that prevents putting some of that Risk Box wall material at risk.

Less visible is how the Risk Box kills dreams and opportunities. Impossible to tally are the countless businesses, ideas, and inventions that were blocked by Risk Box barriers. It does not take skill, intelligence, money, or strength to overcome the risk barrier. It takes courage and faith. The Risk Box is the single most substantial obstacle for entrepreneurs to activate, yet it should be the simplest to overcome.

Like the sea turtles, we humans have an instinctual drive engrained in us over generations. That drive is to live within the orderly structure of the society created around us. It tells us to get an education, find a job, work to support ourselves, our family, our home, and prepare for retirement. Stay on the sidewalk, don't walk into the forest, and don't take the path less travelled. A competing drive is entrepreneurism, which challenges how society directs us, and by so doing a life that is in waiting just beyond the Risk Box walls is revealed.

CHAPTER EIGHTEEN
Live Like You Were Dying

When Carnegie Mellon professor Randy Pausch, author of The Last Lecture *was asked if he had a list of things to do before he died, he replied with, "if they were really that important I should have done them by now."*

Death is in the cards for us all. Randy Pausch literally framed his last college lecture at Carnegie Mellon around this underlying theme. He was diagnosed with pancreatic cancer and was given three to six months to live, yet he courageously survived for almost an entire year giving us, or rather his children, a lecture intended as a guide to living. Pausch tore down Risk Box walls during his life, even prior to his diagnosis. His perspective on living and his stoicism in facing death was truly inspirational. Risk Box walls not only hold back entrepreneurial dreams, they imprison other facets of experiencing life as well.

So much of starting a business is about attitude and developing a positive mindset. I know you've heard this before and more than a fair share of "motivational" speakers have preached this message. However, attitude and having the desire to complete your vision is undeniably a prerequisite for starting a business. You have to believe and visualize yourself not only achieving your goals but exceeding them.

There is a concept called a self-fulfilling prophecy that can power entrepreneurial achievement. Sociologist Robert K. Merton has been credited with coining the phrase, which is a prediction of a future event that through the prophet's actions becomes true. The concept at first glance conjures up astrology cards or superstitious notions, but I attribute the self-fulfilling prophecy more to motivating an action, rather than creating an outcome from the chances of fate.

This concept is best described by the Thomas theorem formulated by sociologist William Isaac Thomas, which states that, "If men define situations as real, they are real in their consequences." Interpretation of one's situation results in action. The action is the result of subjective perceptions of the situation. Stating that a business will be successful, grow, and thrive is a subjective statement. If the entrepreneur perceives this as real and achievable, he will devote his actions toward its outcome. The importance is having a genuine belief and faith in the self-fulfilling prophecy.

By definition, a self-fulfilling prophecy can only be realized when the public prediction is made true. Granted, there is no objective correlation to why the interpretation of a situation came true and some self-fulfilling prophecies may not materialize. The power is in the mindset that gets established and the public prediction of the prophecy. I had spent two years writing this book prior to the final six months it took to complete it. Only in those last six months when I publicly stated that I was going to write a book did I put forth the effort and time commitment to make it happen. I could have stopped at any time and at times I wanted to. However, my public statement to family and friends was effective to force me to see it through. I mentally created a self-fulfilling prophecy that went beyond a personal goal and morphed into a public commitment that I needed to ensure would become reality. You could say to save face.

The self-fulfilling prophecy is not biased to positive or negative prophecies and either can be equally compelling. A negative perception of your potential and abilities will create negative outcomes. Randy Pausch was given three to six months to live and

I interpreted from his book that he established a positive mindset to complete various personal commitments that extended his life beyond his doctor's predictions. He had too much to complete and too many loose ends to tie up with family and three months simply was not enough time.

Unfortunately for some it takes the prospect of death to embolden us to lower our Risk Box walls to truly understand what living is about. Living is about experiencing and that can't be done standing behind a wall. Knowing death is closer than we think some set out to complete their "bucket list." They freely tackle dreams that were always put off, now lacking the fear of losing possessions or wealth because those things don't matter anymore—life is clearly number one.

I've understood this message without the prospect of death, and it drove my goal to start a company before I turned thirty. I didn't want to live with the regret of never having at least tried to start a business. Pausch said in his lecture that it was better to be a "used to be" than a "never was." I love that, and it can really help simplify your decisions. You have a list of dreams, goals, and things that you would like to accomplish and you have an equally long, if not longer, list of excuses as to why you are not accomplishing them. Which statement below is more applicable to the path you are following?

"Don't let your dreams die" or "Don't die with your dreams."

I've found the song, "Live like you were dying" by Tim McGraw to be reflective of the Risk Box topic and becoming a Risk Breaker. Like all country and western songs, it tells a story. This one is of a man diagnosed with what seems an incurable illness. When asked by a friend what would he do now with this terrible news, the response is a chorus of activities that were never attempted in the past, mending fences and focusing on relationships. Why did it take a terminal illness to start living life the way this person truly wanted to deep down inside? This person's Risk Box had a firm grip until this event arose, shattering the Risk Box walls. There's no reason to wait to pursue what you really want to do because there's not enough time to wait.

"A great deal of talent is lost to the world for want of a little courage. Every day sends to their graves obscure men whose timidity prevented them from making a first effort."—Sydney Smith

Lisa Tells Me to Call it Quits

The one element missing from this successful start- up equation was me. I was still working two jobs, still waiting for the "perfect" time to jump in with both feet. I thought that once sales were up to my current salary, I could leave my position at Educational Resources and go full time with TRC . . . a nice, smooth transition. My Risk Box was preventing me from taking that momentary financial step backward to invest in what was to come. The Risk Box was saying, "Successful people don't work in basements on old rickety chairs" and "they sure as heck make more money than what you're bringing home from this venture."

I had a mental barrier, not even a budgetary barrier. I wanted everything to be equal in my life to make my move. The same was true for entrepreneur Cookie Lee who while pursuing a side custom jewelry business simply wanted to get to $50,000 in annual sales in order to jump into her business full time. That was the amount she was making at her then full-time job. She now sells over $100 million in jewelry a year through her direct sales consultant empire.

Sales at TRC were steadily climbing, and we were continuing to gain customers, but we were not operating at full speed. A governor of sorts was on our gas pedal and Lisa and I started to realize just what it was. My split focus and commitment was holding TRC back. I was the leader, the founder, the one with the passion, and I had to be at TRC full time. The company was alive and thriving but it needed my full commitment to really succeed. I could no longer run a surrogate business through Betsy. She just didn't have the vision that I had or the personal passion to see it through. A lot of people try to "offshore" their entrepreneurial ideas to others while they wait to jump in at the most opportune moment.

Lisa and I had discussed numerous times what was needed to move TRC forward and it always came back to me leaving my job at Educational Resources. We both knew that needed to happen if TRC was going to realize the goals I had set for it. We spent our sixth wedding anniversary dinner discussing just how far we had come and the things I really wanted to accomplish in life professionally. Lisa truly is my best friend, main supporter, and constant cheerleader. She has always supported my ambitions, never requesting time for herself. Her giving is so powerful I realize daily how blessed I am to have met her. It was at that anniversary dinner that she firmly said without hesitation "go in and quit!" That was all I needed to hear to blast through my Risk Box, shattering the walls and propelling me 100 percent into TRC. I gave my notice the next day sending my life into a completely new and exciting direction.

It seemed as if all the stress and anxiety immediately lifted when I quit and started to report to Betsy's basement full time. The fact that I was fully committed to TRC would make all the difference in its growth. Most ideas don't come to fruition and businesses fail to survive past their first year because of entrepreneurial moonlighting. Instead of devoting all of one's time and effort to a new business, moonlighters keep one foot placed comfortably in their old job. I'm not encouraging anyone to rush and quit their day job. Rather, careful observation and planning is needed to know when the time is right to strike out on your own full time. The Risk Box will continually pull you back in as long as you keep a foot inside that wall. Only when you step all the way through will you realize your full potential and allow your business the greatest opportunity to thrive.

Another aspect holding TRC back was its location. Running a business out of your home makes it hard to see clients and vendors face to face. It became rather awkward when publishers who advertised in the catalog and were thrilled with the printed piece and subsequent success wanted to have a meeting at our office and to train our sales team. Sales team? I may have exaggerated the size of our workforce slightly from time to time.

I had also hired our first employee during this time: Chris Skrzypchak was a college student from nearby Judson College in Elgin. What this kid must have thought about us when he started! But he soon became intoxicated with TRC's mission and growth. He had a visible entrepreneurial passion of his own, and he really identified with what we were doing. He became a very loyal and valuable employee who stayed with us seven years after his graduation.

TRC was outgrowing its surroundings, and it was clear that it was time to legitimize this baby of ours by getting some office space. It is said that goldfish only grow to the size of their tanks. If a business is in a confined physical space, its growth is going to be stunted too. Conversely, if a business resides in an overly abundant office space it will likely grow into it. Call it psychology, parlor tricks, or the self-fulfilling prophecy at work, but I believe it's true and a growing company should acquire adequate space to expand.

CHAPTER NINETEEN
Planning and Preparation

Y ou've gotten past the fear and now the Risk Box. The E-Formula looks good as you have an I.D.E.A. that is innovative and you are ready to pour your desire and effort into all of your abilities to launch. The appropriate situation has met the right opportunity and you are ready to "go for it!" Both defining moments have been met. You are about to build a company from scratch. How cool is that! Yesterday your company did not exist, now it has a name and purpose and you are ready to show the world. Get ready because this will be one of the greatest feelings you experience while owning your business, far better than even your first million in sales. Startup represents you facing your fears and deciding to experience what you want in life and following your passion. Success or failure, you went for it and that in itself is a tremendous life accomplishment that few experience.

"Ability is what you're capable of doing. Motivation determines what you do. Attitude determines how well you do it."—Lou Holtz

People always ask me how I did it—how did I start my company? I can easily relate how my idea was generated and how I exited, but all of the details in between are too vast to deliver in an extemporaneous setting. The requester may not actually be that interested either to spend their evening listening to me relating my business startup minutia. Now that I have you as my captured audience I can share with greater details my startup phase, which is applicable to most start-ups.

Startup is more about planning and preparation and less about flipping on the lights and hanging your sign outside the door. Proper and detailed planning is the greatest insurance policy for success. Businesses that fail are often those that are ill prepared. These entrepreneurs first leap into activation with their interest and passion and fail to have a sufficient understanding of their industry, channels, competitors, or customer. Lacking in any one of these areas is considered an Entrepreneurial Success Gap or E-Success Gap which can cripple the new venture.

There are seven components in planning and preparation that directly support your idea and they are absolutely critical to complete for a start-up to avoid an E-Success Gap. Careful assessment of these components will identify holes in your business plan early. An entrepreneur has to be cognizant and on guard to these gaps all through the planning cycle. Lacking or growing deficient in any particular area should prompt corrective action or outside assistance. These components are age old principles often overlooked during the startup phase by anxious entrepreneurs. They are mentioned briefly as much has already been written on these topics, and they are presented in the order in which they should be created.

1. Mission Statement

Although a mission statement may not seem necessary for launch, it is a basic starting point. It objectively describes the business's purpose and how to guide its actions. The mission statement does not have to be set in stone and can be refined as the company grows. It takes into consideration primary stakeholders, customers, and stockholders and how your organization will be responsible toward them. The statement may include products and services offered, define what the company aspires to become, or how to differentiate the company from the competition.

A well conceived mission statement will act as a guiding and reminding force to you, your employees, and customers as to why your company exists. The statement will be your answer to strategic questions when crafting marketing material, deciding on new markets, and where and how to allocate resources.

Simple questions to ask yourself when creating your mission statement include:
- What is the purpose of my company
- What are the goals of my company
- Why does my company exist
- What are my customer's pain points and how does our product or service address them

2. S.W.O.T. (Strengths, Weaknesses, Opportunities, and Threats)

SWOT is a strategic planning method attributed to the work of Albert Humphrey of Stanford University that is used to evaluate the strengths, weaknesses, opportunities, and threats of a company. Conducting a SWOT analysis is vital at startup but can and should be repeated throughout the life of the company (yearly at a minimum) by key executives. A SWOT can be focused from an overall company perspective or as narrow as a single department, product, or marketing initiative. The goal is to get on the table the internal and external factors that are favorable and unfavorable to achieving the expected objective. The results of the initial SWOT analysis will be rolled into the business plan.

3. Business Plan

The core planning effort involves the formal business plan which encompasses all facets of what you are about to create. The plan forces you to dissect every aspect of your dream and put it on paper. Many entrepreneurs, especially those not seeking capital outside of their own self-funding sources, feel they don't need to put the time and effort into a formal plan. Many are too anxious and just jump in creating. They lack the discipline to pause and think about all the necessary startup details.

The plan is mandatory for investors; the more detailed the plan the better the chances for securing funding. Some will say a business plan can be a "build as you go" exercise. I'll agree a plan can be tweaked and changed once the business is launched.

There are dozens of resources for business plan templates on the Internet. Depending on whether you are seeking funding and from what source (angel, venture capitalist, bank), you may want to obtain a plan template that your funding source responds best to. For instance, there are favored formats for technology start-ups that venture capitalist seem to prefer. However, if you are self funded and the plan is strictly for you, a hybrid plan incorporating the pieces most applicable to you is sufficient.

Most business plan templates are thorough and there is no need to rehash them, but be sure to include the following topics which may be overlooked.

- Who will be your mentors
- What resources do you have that lend strength to the company
- What resources do you lack that weaken the company
- What experts do you have and which do you need
- What works best in this market and why
- Who has failed in this market and why
- What will be your intellectual property
- What is your lead generation system for sales
- How will you differentiate yourself from competitors
- How long will your cash last

- What will be your primary financial reports in addition to your pro forma
- What will be your Exit Strategy

4. Goal Setting

Too many business owners put all their startup efforts into establishing the physical attributes of their business to meet their "opening" date and don't make time to establish basic goals. Goals provide a completion target for all the strategic initiatives you are about to embark on. The goals should represent major milestones for moving the company forward. Goals are not exclusive to sales-oriented activities. Goals to develop every operational aspect of the business should be included in this planning. Startup is primarily concerned with creating demand for your product or service and branding. The goal is for your sales and marketing strategies to obtain a sustainable and reliable funnel of customer demand. Priority will eventually shift to demand fulfillment once the business reaches the running phase.

5. Key Performance Indicators

Key performance indicators (KPI) are financial and non-financial measures to help your company evaluate how well it is progressing toward its long-term organizational goals. KPIs serve as a dashboard to the health and performance of the company. KPIs are the metrics that you pre-determine to monitor. Like your mission statement, goals, and SWOT, KPIs need to be incorporated into your initial planning efforts.

In order to establish KPIs you need to develop business processes and the requirements for those processes. You'll then measure your results against the goals and investigate the cause of any variance. By adjusting your process and applying more or less resources, you'll work to achieve your pre-established goals.

6. GAP Analysis

After the start-up has been operational for a period of time it should conduct a GAP Analysis to compare its actual performance with its expected or desired performance. This can be a very simple or elaborate procedure depending on your style and need. At the heart of the GAP Analysis are two questions which ask, "Where are we?" and "Where do we want to be?"

Establish benchmark performance levels for each of your operational, financial, sales, and marketing areas and compare them to industry performance or goals you established for your own KPIs. GAP analysis will clearly show your performance in relation to those benchmarks. Internal goal setting will establish where you want your performance level to be and strategies will show you how to get there and what must take place to hit goal.

7. Exit Strategy

Before taking off on a flight, before your plane even leaves the ground, you are instructed to find the nearest exit. The reasons are obvious and applicable to every entrepreneur who is contemplating starting a business or currently running one. The exit strategy is for the entrepreneur—not the business. Certainly, the exit strategy directly impacts the business, but the strategy is part of the "end game" for the entrepreneur's vision, and it is very personal to the entrepreneur. Based on the strategy, the entrepreneur will run and manage the company in a very deliberate manner to attain the exit strategy. The timeframe for when the exit arrives may be irrelevant or unpredictable. However, it is generally reflective of the entrepreneur's goals and objectives for the company or his own personal ambitions.

The entrepreneur is a human being, not an entity, and he won't physically be able to manage the business he founded forever.

An exit plan is forced upon all of us whether we like it or not. Too often entrepreneurs and business owners fail to consider their exit strategy until they start thinking of retirement. An exit strategy and retirement is not the same thing; in fact, they should be irrelevant to one another. Establishing retirement as a reason to leave your business can greatly diminish the valuation of your business as I'll describe later. In a retirement scenario, the entrepreneur should manage toward succession planning or sale of the company and not have the focus on his retirement. Equally damaging can be the person who sets out to start a business solely focused on making a fortune by selling his company to the highest bidder. Why? Again, you can't start a business whose purpose is to make money for you. It must address a customer need and by successfully addressing that need you will be rewarded.

Your exit strategy should be incorporated during the formulation of your business plan. The strategy may change during the course of the business and that is perfectly acceptable as conditions change. However, it is important to understand how you, the entrepreneur, intend to exit the business you started in order to manage your efforts to that goal.

CHAPTER TWENTY
Desire and Effort

"What's desired is unobtainable without a level of corresponding effort."—Jeff Weber

P lanning and preparation takes full account of your abilities to create all of the necessary planning documents, or battle plans as I like to call them. They are built around the innovative niche that you have identified in your market which is central to your I.D.E.A. To continue the work needed to convert these documents into the physical aspects of business you need more than mere ability. There may be many times during startup that you will want to give up. The demands of your time and of your consciousness will possibly be one of the greatest professional challenges you will ever face. You will apply your talents, knowledge, and abilities, but your desire and effort will prove to be the greatest of your gifts at the startup stage. Desire and effort will help you achieve what those with greater talent, intelligence, and money could not.

Desire = Passion

Desire is the emotion needed to accomplish the I.D.E.A.

Everything we do has an emotional component. There are some things we do out of obligation or obedience and even that has an emotional component showing respect or honor. A vital component ok**

of the I.D.E.A is desire. When I talk about entrepreneurial desire, I am referring to passion.

Passion alone as an emotion is merely to have a strong feeling about your area of interest. Desire pours out of passion as an emotion and creates a sense of longing or hoping toward the area of interest. Desire creates a motivation that leads to action. Therefore, it is the desire, born out of passion that spurs the entrepreneur to act and create. I realize I'm splitting hairs with words, but each word is so powerful and equally integral to understanding the entrepreneur that it is important to dissect them.

Desire provides that extra effort that pushes you to work a 70+ hour work week. It is desire that enforces your decision to skip your weekend plans or simply to turn off the television to work on your passion. I didn't know what prime time television was while I ran TRC. My priorities were my family and our business, and having three kids just did not allow for much television time.

Many would argue that their spouse is their passion; well then, put time into your marriage. The American divorce rate is 50 percent and arguably another 10 – 15 percent of them live unfulfilled marriages. If you have a passion for someone why don't you put the effort into them? Keep in mind you don't have to correlate hours to your effort when it comes to your relationships. So instead of watching television why not walk around the block with your spouse or play a game?

Planning and preparation is just as necessary for your relationships as it is for your business. It is not silly to consider writing a mission statement, SWOT analysis, Gap analysis, and establishing goals for your relationships. Think about it. If you don't take time to plan how you want your relationships to grow then how will they?

Remember that marriage and business ownership are not mutually exclusive. You cannot have two passions under one roof and not share or include them with each other. Passions are strong emotions and one can become jealous of the other. Introducing the passion of your relationships to the passion of your business is a necessity. A spouse can develop jealousy of the business as more and more time is spent focused on it. Likewise, the business owner can start to feel resentment when he feels his spouse is not supportive of his endeavors. Both of these feelings start to cause fissures in the relationship. The key is establishing a balance and it won't be a balance measured in time but in focus. The entrepreneur needs to incorporate tending to relationships as part of his business plan—seriously. If you don't take into consideration your primary relationships and how they will be impacted by your decision to work on this business, you will be putting at risk the most valuable aspects of your life. The risk would take place solely because of your actions and your lack of planning.

Passion is a very powerful component of this entrepreneurial experience and failure to incorporate both its positive and negative effects into your plans would be a significant oversight. Passion and relationships contribute to your Risk Box. Both can thicken the walls of your Risk Box or, if managed properly, can make your walls transparent. Incorporating your relationship plans into your business plans will establish a faith in you from those you care about that includes understanding and support, and lacks jealousy.

Effort = Hard Work

Effort is the physical needed to accomplish the I.D.E.A.

You will physically work harder and longer as an entrepreneur than most of your peers. You can become cynical of acquaintances who claim they "don't have time" or feel they are being worked too hard by their employer. You'll know what hard work and sacrifice is when you are unable to make family commitments or take those free baseball tickets on the weekend. You may grow to question your decision to embark on this crazy odyssey and wonder if it is really worth it. You'll wonder why some guy is out riding his bike at 2 p.m. on a beautiful Tuesday afternoon and what the hell you're doing wrong.

Starting a business requires a level of sacrifice that you may never have encountered before. The commitment to launch will force you to concede comfort, time, money, leisure, and the opportunity to do other things. When I worked for a company I gave 100 percent of my effort assuming a typical work week. When I started TRC I seemed to be able to give 150 percent, putting in countless hours. My hours were unknown because I did not keep track of them—doing so didn't matter and served no purpose. All I can tell you is TRC's success was built on long days, weekends, and nights. Succeeding must be so important that you will sacrifice just about anything to make it happen. Typically, once the E-Formula is activated the willingness to make the necessary commitment to get off the ground comes naturally.

When you watch a goose take off for flight you'll notice that all of the hard work is at the beginning trying to gain momentum. The long neck is strained forward as both the wings and legs pump to lift the large torso into the air. Once the goose is in flight it looks effortless. Much is the same when starting a business. All of the hard work and effort is needed in the beginning just to get the enterprise off the ground. Once the processes of the business are working, the entrepreneur can start to ease up and let the business run itself so to speak.

The startup phase at TRC seemed to last for our entire ten years. I say that because I was never satisfied with where we were even though we grew to a level many would consider a tremendous success. There were always improvements that could be done in our processes, our IT, our staff development, our demand generation efforts, and our sales results. That lack of complacency drove my effort to try to best utilize my daily 86,400-second allotment. We did eventually leave the startup phase and I did curtail my hours and energy to a more reasonable level, yet still exceeding that of the ordinary worker. When vacations came around (and I did very purposely plan quarterly vacations to provide a break for me and my family), work would often accompany me. It wasn't until my later years at TRC that I would mentally and physically leave my work behind to fully be in the moment on vacation. It took me a while to realize that if I couldn't unplug from the business for one week then I must not be doing a good job of growing a sustainable business.

My focus on work was so intense that on a driving vacation out East one year I packed up my desktop computer complete with monitor, keyboard, and mouse and threw it in the back of our van. (I didn't have a laptop at the time.) My intentions of setting the PC up in our hotel room was to squeeze some work in between moments, but it more often served as a distraction robbing me and my family of my well-earned time off. Getting a laptop only made it easier to allow my work to encroach on vacations. Sitting off alone in the spring sunshine at a pool in Sarasota I could be seen with a beach towel tented over my head and shoulders to block the sun from hitting my laptop screen. How fun is that?

I would mature as an entrepreneur, and so would my business, to understand that usually the work could wait. I didn't have to be constantly connected for our doors to stay open. I would learn that my vacation was also a vacation for my employees. Proper management of my time and resources would allow me, my family, and my employees to enjoy my time off. The sign of a good manager and leader is one who can disconnect from the office for one to two weeks at a time with confidence that business won't skip a beat. It shows they have built a structure independent of the individual and dependent on the business model and its workers.

Effort – The Differentiator

The principal differentiator between levels of success and achievement is effort. What effort do you want to put into something? This applies to everything in life. Effort can vary in regards to where you are in life, what motivates you, and how important something is in relation to the effort you wish to exert. Skill separates many in various regards, especially the arts, but effort can close even that gap.

In grade school and middle school I was an average student in terms of grades. I simply was not interested in school work; I was interested in school fun. And as an elementary student I somehow knew the bare minimum that was acceptable from my teachers and school system and to keep me out of the dog house with my parents. This is not to say that I was a terrible student, but I know I did not set high expectations for myself, simply because I did not place value on the effort. Similarly my parents established expectation levels that were acceptable to them for me. They would have loved to have seen straight As but they made a mental benchmark based on my year-over-year performance and became conditioned to those results. As long as grades were at or above that benchmark minimum all would be well in the Weber household.

My expectations cemented at this average level which led to my academic confidence cementing too. Within my peer group there would be the known "smart" kids, the less admired "dumb" kids, and then those like me somewhere in the middle. What I would learn as my academic performance and confidence grew in later years is that there really were no smart kids or dumb kids; there were simply kids who applied more or less effort.

It took me until high school to develop confidence in my academic abilities. I was not superior, but I was an intelligent thinker and with effort I could obtain any grade I wanted. When I began to apply myself in high school I got As and Bs and I even earned a place on the Dean's List and was accepted into the Lambda Sigma Sophomore Honor Society in college. Was I smarter than the rest of my college class? Hell no, but I worked my tail off. I probably had to study longer and harder than other kids who got the same grades. The point is I leveled the playing field with my effort.

Entrepreneurs often get artificially characterized in a superior light. A divide is created between those who are entrepreneurs and those who are not and seemingly could never be. I believe we all have the potential to be entrepreneurs just as I believe most hold the same intelligence potential. There are those who have taken steps and exerted effort to become entrepreneurs whereas others have not. This does not mean they can't. Expectations and confidence are critical foundations to all our accomplishments, but effort seems to be the one driving measure that truly differentiates.

A Place of My Own

One of my greatest days at TRC was moving out of my partner Betsy's basement and into our modest office space. In nine months we had grown the business to the point where dedicated office space was required and, more importantly, to a point where cash flow was predictable enough to cover the monthly rent. We were responsible for our utilities, which up until now were graciously taken care of by Betsy. This was a big deal and I would sign a two-year lease. I knew we were ready, and I was confident the business would continue to succeed. In fact, I was more concerned that the business would fail if we did not make this move.

It is a great feeling—an awesome feeling—to start moving

equipment and belongings into empty office space that now is yours. Seeing your sign on the door and stepping back and looking at this business you created from scratch is an amazing experience. My dad and father-in-law were a great help on moving day. Since things were so modest, our move consisted of a single U-Haul truck that held a few desks, file cabinets, shelving units, and computers.

We took up residence in a retail strip mall in West Dundee, Illinois with a video store and dry cleaner as our neighbors. There were no office partitions to provide privacy for the four desks we started out with. It was simply a long, rectangular space that was bare of everything except the necessities to run our business. We chose the strip mall based on location convenience for me, Betsy, and Chris, and also that we would be in Kane County versus the far more expensive Cook County that was just miles away and where I lived. Since we were a mail order business and did not require a physical presence we could set up anywhere.

For me, this was the real birth of TRC. Sure, we had launched a catalog and established a meager presence in the market but operating part time out of a basement did not feel like a true business, and I did not feel like a true entrepreneur. I felt like a guy working my ass off for basically no pay and struggling to do about 50 things simultaneously; indeed, like Betsy, Lisa, and the designer, I did forego salary for more than six months. Establishing a permanent and legitimate business location was a tremendous milestone for TRC and mentally it rejuvenated my fire.

The permanent location did not last long. In less than six months my landlord asked if I would like more space. Ladi, as he liked to go by because his full Ukrainian name was difficult to pronounce, was a very colorful personality and entrepreneur who owned the entire mall. He was the largest tenant housing his own business, Century Electronics. Century Electronics was one of those original consumer electronics stores that sold stereo systems, TVs, and installed car stereos. Ladi was well known in the area for running cheesy cable television advertisements featuring him in silly scenes which always ended with him stating in his thick eastern European accent, "How can I offer such low prices? . . . Because I'm Ladi!"

I thought his proposal was nuts. We had picked up one additional employee and didn't see space issues on the horizon. Perhaps Ladi had a greater vision for me than I did at the time, as he suggested we move down four doors to a double unit that would be vacant the next month. After some deliberation, coercion, and soul searching we took the double unit, which lent itself to the phrase, "If you build it they will come." We quickly started adding employees to fill our expanded space.

The Power of Influence

It's important to have people around you that push your limits, like Ladi did for me. When you find you are the leader and everyone is continually looking to you for the next move, watch out. You need people that challenge your natural instinct to crawl back into your comfort zone. As a leader, the entrepreneur needs to foster an environment of feedback, commentary, and suggestions to disseminate thinking and decision making. Entrepreneurs get stale too. Some describe being an entrepreneur as lonely because they get isolated at the top. The danger of this isolation is stagnation of thought and falling into routine. The entrepreneur may be surrounded by people and the center of attention, yet they can be so relied and depended upon that all of the thinking gets pushed up to them. The entrepreneur can find himself in an environment that becomes far too dependent on him. Ladi was pushing me, albeit for his own reasons, but he was an entrepreneur himself and he could sense where we were going and he was confident we would grow into our extra space.

A person who I would dub as my number two man would soon join TRC and he too would serve to push and challenge me. We complimented each other well in terms of skill set and forward thinking. I could count on him to question and not always agree with me. There's a real danger to "yes men" and they don't belong in any environment, let alone an entrepreneurial one. Any entrepreneur worth his salt wouldn't stand a day with a yes man. If you see a yes man developing, challenge him to change or dump him. He'll offer nothing but simply mimic you, which is the last thing you need.

Those early years were fun as we achieved phenomenal sales growth year over year. Employees were continually being added and the office was abuzz. Customers were developing a deep loyalty to TRC for our exceptional customer service and focus that centered on their business needs and processes. Everyone at TRC understood our mission, and they were excited to be a part of a start-up. I always tried to promote TRC as an established company in order to attract customers and instill a level of confidence in them, but for new employees it was obvious we were a bootstrapped start-up.

I was always self conscious of our appearance to new hires, as we were a B to B located in a neighborhood retail consumer strip mall, and our office was certainly not lavish. Keep in mind this was the dot com age, where IT start-ups were widely publicized for having extremely trendy and "fun" offices. Employees were treated to stocked kitchens, pool tables for in-office recreation, and other silly perks provided by deep-pocketed venture capitalists. This is what I thought I had to compete with to attract and retain employees. It took a long time for me to realize that these things did not matter to my employees—they had caught our passion.

At this point, I truly learned the power of influence of the entrepreneur. I came to realize that the excitement and passion I exuded when talking about TRC was contagious. The genuine positive power and energy that an entrepreneur gives off when discussing his business can be very compelling. Whether the story is being told to vendors, customers, or employees, the entrepreneur has the ability to profoundly influence these stakeholders—and he needs to. The entrepreneur is always "selling" his company during startup and certainly beyond in an effort to promote the business.

One example of selling TRC was applied to the publishers whose products I would be selling. Most offered academic discounts to applicable institutions; however, dealers had to be authorized. Aside from Microsoft, Adobe was the dominate number two publisher I absolutely needed to gain authorization from in order to play in this market. Adobe had just recently cut thousands of academic dealers in an effort to better manage the academic channel. They were smart to realize they only needed a small percentage to respond to the market's demand; any more presented the risk of discounted academic product leaking into unintended markets.

I made a verbal commitment to the Adobe Channel Manager that I would make TRC one of their top three resellers within five years should they grant me authorization. I laid out an extensive plan on how I would market and promote the brand. Because of my relationship, reputation, and entrepreneurial passion I was given authorization. I also achieved my commitment, only in three years.

The entrepreneur has a vision for his company which extends far beyond its actual image during startup, and it is his burning desire to get to that ultimate vision as fast as possible. In doing so, he is constantly preaching his business to anyone who will listen. Many early employees of an entrepreneur act as followers of their cult-like leader and are devout in their role of achieving the vision. I discovered that I started to possess this power through my visible passion and vivid image for where TRC was going and the unique life experience it would provide. It was the charisma of the entrepreneur along with the viability of achieving a vision that helped me harness the greatest resources for TRC, which would be instrumental in realizing my vision.

The Team Rounds Out

The greatest resource, as you may have guessed, was my employees. The power of the entrepreneur's influence was at work long before we moved into our office space. It was present when I pitched the idea to my partner Betsy and to young Chris, our first employee. They both signed up for the ride because of my enthusiasm. My genuine confidence and excitement sparked something inside them which exceeded the prospect of just having a job. It wasn't a sales or elevator pitch. It came from the heart. The power was present when I drafted my designer and my right-hand man who became an equity partner.

Sam DeSoto walked into our new office space only a few weeks after our arrival in 1997. Sam was one of my product managers at Educational Resources. A few months after leaving my position to work on TRC full time, Sam left to work with our previous Vice President who had taken a post at a large corporate reseller named ElekTek. The opportunity to work for a company three times as large as Educational Resources and service more than the education segment seemed to be an exciting leap. However, the new position turned out to be far more stressful than he or his health would have imagined. The demands of the job combined with the rapidly floundering finances of ElekTek were enough to put Sam into the hospital – literally. Upon his return, he put in his resignation with no prospects of employment but the assurance that at least he would not die doing his job.

Sam knew I started TRC and silently observed our progress from basement to storefront. We exchanged a few emails, and he dropped in one day to see what we had going. As impressive as I thought we were, I know we were far less dramatic in his eyes, if not comical. We talked for a while about his plans and about my vision for TRC. Sam's a smart guy and not one to rush into things. I wanted him to lead our sales team, and I came right out and asked. He was non-committal as he was weighing his future options. Thankfully, the powers of the entrepreneur spoke and impacted Sam. Instead of seeing a half-filled office space in the strip mall he saw opportunity. He envisioned space filled with updated workstations, employees sitting at terminals taking orders, packages being picked and shipped. He saw success. Sam would take the position and ride it through to the end.

CHAPTER TWENTY-ONE
Money

M any people think money, or rather the lack of it is the greatest obstacle to launching a business—and it is a big one. Nonetheless, entrepreneurs ponder how to finance their dream.

For starters, understand that the number one source for money is going to be you. The vast majority of startup businesses will be self funded by the founder or from a small pool of relatives or close friends who dip into their personal savings. Either you are going to fund your business out of your pocket or you are going to solicit funding. If you are going to solicit funds then that means you are going to be selling and primarily what you are going to be selling is you. Your idea has to be solid, but what is going to convince someone to entrust their money with you is going to be the passion and confidence you elicit for your idea. Successful deal making is nothing more than the transfer of enthusiasm. Everything we humans do has an element of emotion in it.

People want to be a part of passion that is effectively conveyed as it is attractive and they are naturally drawn to it. Most entrepreneurs often won't even realize the kinetic power they hold until later in their entrepreneurial career. For investors, passion conveys confidence and dedication, which is expected to launch a new venture. Many entrepreneurs become the physical manifestation of the passion to their investors. It naturally exudes from the entrepreneur in an unscripted and unrehearsed manner. This is the attraction of the entrepreneur that people gravitate toward and invest in.

Charisma alone won't be enough to obtain funding. This is

when all of your careful planning and preparation comes into play. Any logical investor is going to want to see your idea on paper and this is where your business plan, SWOT, mission statement, and other documents will be scrutinized.

Next, understanding where you are going to get funding will streamline efforts. The media has burned the image into everyone's head that the first door you should knock on to get funding if you start a new business is a venture capitalist. After all, an estimated $29.7 billion went into startup firms in 2008 from this source alone. Unfortunately (or fortunately depending on your experience), a very small percentage of start-ups, traditionally consisting of a few industries, will be funded by venture capitalists. A venture capitalist is looking for early-stage, high-potential growth companies typically in the information or scientific technology sectors that retain innovative intellectual property. They look to realize their investment through an IPO, or sale of the company, coming to the table with a definitive exit strategy in mind.

Private equity firms are increasingly looking to invest in existing businesses rather than new ventures. Their investment methods may involve leveraged buyouts, mezzanine funding, or straight capital funding. The size of targeted existing business will be larger than a start-up, and these firms will be far more selective in their investments.

The next best source may be a bank loan from a community bank or possibly the Small Business Administration. A loan may not be as sexy as private equity, but you get to retain ownership and control. Often the level of capital required cannot be obtained merely by a loan. A growing source of funding now flows from angel investors who are typically wealthy individuals or small funds looking to invest amounts smaller than the minimum venture capitalist thresholds of $1-2 million. It is estimated that in 2007 angels invested $26 billion into 57,000 companies in comparison to the nearly $31 billion and 3,918 companies that venture capitalists took a stake in. Out of the more than five million businesses that start up each year, just over one percent will obtain VC or angel funding.

Understanding the investment choices of these funding sources compared to your venture will help direct you on your search for funds. Don't waste time trying to chase dollars that only have a one percent chance of coming in unless you truly have an innovative product or service that meets the stringent investment criteria of these funding sources. Likewise, don't succumb to the excuse that you don't have the money to start a business. Over 440,000 people every month figure out how to do it and so can you.

Finally, understand now how you are going to manage the funding you receive. Notice I did not say how are you going to spend the money, but how are you going to manage it. The key with funding is for the entrepreneur to maintain control of the business. When venture capitalists or private investors invest in your company, they gain ownership. When a bank loans you money, they have access to your financial performance and gain the right to question your decisions. Money comes at a price and when you dip below 51 percent ownership you no longer control the company. You are no longer the entrepreneur; you are a manager with an investment.

It is your job to act as a proper steward of the funds you receive. Being too adequately funded is just as bad as not being funded at all. Excess money can lead to wasteful and unnecessary spending. The cost of seeking additional funding can be far more expensive in the long run compared to struggling to make ends meet now. Knowing how you are going to spend and preserve the money that you have been given takes a special talent. Venture capitalists who know they have a good business cooking are far too eager to provide additional rounds of funding, of course for additional shares of ownership.

If you are the source of your funding, establish a dollar amount of how much you want to invest up front during your planning stage. Separate your dual roles of founder and financier. Your emotional passion for the business as founder can inappropriately influence your personal fiscal responsibilities. Far too many entrepreneurs have experienced their own personal money pit by throwing too many dollars after their dream jeopardizing their personal financial stability. Before you burn through the dollars that you have invested, take time to adequately reflect on how much additional funds are needed to get the business sustainable and if it makes sense for you to reinvest. This takes considerable discipline, and selling your equity may be the next best option at this point.

The best way to hit the sweet spot of funding is to do adequate planning and forecasting to determine what your absolute funding requirements include. Advances in technology have made it easier to establish virtual offices saving start-ups thousands of dollars in expenses. Obviously the type of business you start will dictate whether a physical location or presence is required. Employees represent the largest expense for just about any company. Establishing critical to non-critical roles can lead to outsourcing, temporary positions, job share, or other methods to reduce headcount, hours, and expense. Your business plan should be detailed enough to forecast expenses for 6 – 12 months, supplying predictable cash flow requirements.

The key to funding success is planning and a sense of humility. Resisting the urge to step out of the starting gate looking like a well-established company will go a long way toward cash preservation. A certain image requirement may be necessary but avoid the temptation to indulge too far in creating that façade. Pride has no place in a start-up, especially one that is bootstrap funded. TRC invested in image in our catalog and phone system, two critical core components that directly touched our customers. Behind the phones we scrimped and got by on bare necessities. Success too has a way of encroaching on your ability to remain humble and thrifty as you will be tempted to invest your valuable dollars into expenses that may be affordable but not mission critical.

Humility is seen in scripture as a position of triumph. To obtain God's grace we must humble ourselves through fasting and resisting indulgence. I like the symbolism of fasting for an entrepreneur starting a new business. You'll need to limit your spending and do without for a period of time. Your humble efforts and swallowed pride will yield rewards in due time allowing you to get that new Blackberry, copier, or just a more comfortable chair.

CHAPTER TWENTY-TWO
Frugal-preneur

M ost start-ups are self funded and underfunded. I was no different. Although I had the cash to start TRC in the sense of obtaining basic equipment and supplies, I was not able to invest enough to bring the company to a presentable level on day one. By presentable I mean having an office where you can bring a client in and have them not trip over the laundry basket. For most, starting a business is not glamorous at all; in fact, it is very humbling. That humbleness drives the entrepreneur to continue to get better, to grow, and to succeed. It is a virtue often lacking in the well-funded entrepreneur.

Being a frugal entrepreneur fosters innovation in finding new and creative ways to avoid spending a buck. Mind you, frugal and being cheap are not the same. In fact, being a cheap-preneur is bad for business. A frugal-preneur looks to spend money wisely and conservatively. He'll plop down a decent sum of money on a solution that he views as a solid investment in his business. The cheap-preneur will buy the least expensive solution that may break down, not run as efficient, or have to be replaced sooner.

As a frugal-preneur, I was notorious for finding ways to limit expenditures at TRC almost to the amazement of our outside accountant. I particularly scrimped when we attended a trade show or conference. Service fees rack up fast when you attend a conference unless you find ways to do things yourself. Schlepping is one example of cutting corners: it means hauling your stuff in by hand, by yourself, to avoid drayage fees. Those are the charges the convention center dock workers charge to receive, hold, and eventually move your material to your booth. I found numerous creative ways to avoid these types of fees. One method would be to ship my booth and material to the hotel where I was staying, much to their delight I'm sure. I would then load the material into my economy rental car, and then deliver the goods to the conference center.

The dock workers at the convention center never made my plans easy; after all they had to make a buck too. The real fear in schlepping was if the conference center were a hall that had clear-cut union rules against vendors moving in their own stuff. Many do not allow vendors to assemble their own booths or move anything that can't be carried in by hand. I'm sure people still talk about the sight of a sweaty, bald exhibitor struggling to schlep his booth to its designated position.

I am a firm believer in paying to do things right, but I'm also a firm believer in doing things for yourself when you can, provided that they make economic sense. Did the company president schlepping around make sense? In this case it did. I had the time, and I was in essence free labor. To ask an employee to run these types of hurdles would not make economic sense. For one, they would probably quit, although I did find some committed souls who were up for the challenge. But the cost if things went wrong was greater than simply cooperating with the system. My employees did not have the experience I had and to try and get them to replicate my efforts wasn't worth it. Plus, it really isn't fair to ask an employee to go through such a hassle. It is bad enough that they had to travel from family to be at an event which involved long hours of standing at a trade show booth, smiling and trying to engage people who are primarily interested in finding the coolest chotchke that vendors are doling out.

Another way to maximize the conference attendance invest-ment was by visiting customers in the surrounding area or along the way if I drove, which I often did. Since TRC was catalog driven for most of our years, I would map out which colleges and universities were on my route. Pulling off the highway to reach a college was the routine of these trips. I did not have an outside sales force and we rarely were physically on the campus of the schools we sold to, so I could easily deliver a few hundred well-targeted catalogs which saved on postage and the cost of obtaining mailing lists.

The mission was clear cut. When I would descend upon a campus, I would flood every nook and cranny with catalogs. The challenge with the college market is that the purchasing is often very decentralized across, in some cases, hundreds of individual departments. The academic departments were our primary customer, but we would also sell to individual students and faculty. The best targets on campus would be the central Informational Technology (IT) offices and central purchasing. These two controlled the global spending for what TRC was selling and they were the known buyers. The individual departments were more of a crap shoot in terms of who would be responsible for technology. To ensure I reached every potential buyer, I would attempt to scour every hallway and building on campus delivering catalogs.

Upon arriving on campus and finding a legal place to park, I would load up with catalogs. At first it was just how many I could hand carry, then I got a backpack and eventually I used a wheeled travel suitcase. Conservatively, I would start out with 80 pounds of catalogs in my bags so I could maximize my time moving from building to building.

I would look for the central staff and faculty mailboxes within the individual departments so I could place catalogs in every assigned cubby. These mailboxes as you would imagine were generally not in public locations. I would therefore sneak my way in to make the drops, more often than not escaping without notice. On occasion I would get busted by a staffer asking what I was doing.

Expecting to be tossed out on my rump, I must say about 90 percent of the time the staffer would offer to do the mail box stuffing for me. The other 10 percent of the time I would leave the campus with a sore rump.

As TRC grew in terms of employees, I was continually buying furniture. I started purchasing basic desks and chairs from various used office furniture sources. I would pay $100 for a desk in decent condition and anywhere from $25 to $40 on a chair that in its day probably cost over $200. I developed an appreciation for the cost of office furniture while managing the remodeling of the Allstate Insurance home office and installing new Steelcase panel systems. What I appreciated was that they were expensive and there was no way in hell I was going to spend that type of money.

As a frugal-preneur, I viewed furniture as non-essential equipment to the business. Sure, people need a desk to sit at, but it was not central to the mission of the company and therefore, required the minimal investment for its acquisition. Not being cheap, I didn't want to buy rusty, damaged, and non-functioning desks. Our furniture worked, looked good, and was comfortable for the user. All the desks may not have matched, but for our purposes at the time they were just fine. Entrepreneurs starting out with venture capital have the nicest offices money can buy. They seem to fail to realize that their employees are sitting and working on their equity.

I do respect the business that needs to cast an image as part of their marketing, positioning, and brand. I don't think I would feel very comfortable walking into a lawyer's office to find the type of office furniture I was setting up. The point is, every business has non-essential expenses that can be rationed. Just because you have the money doesn't mean you need to spend it. I am sure newcomers within the company would joke about how cheap I was, or possibly, they were polite and did use the term frugal. It did not matter to me, and it did not matter to my long-term employees. They got it and they accepted—no, relished—that this was our company culture. We did not retain employees who valued their workspace more than the prospect of exceeding our sales goals.

When TRC was up to 12 or 15 employees, I decided we needed modular work stations and panels to reduce noise and grant a level of personal privacy. As our employee count grew so did the value I was now starting to place on establishing an attractive work environment. My employees deserved better at this point and we could afford better. Again, I looked to the used market and scored big time. After being found guilty of criminal charges relating to the firm's handling of the auditing of Enron, Arthur Anderson LLP ceased being a viable company and voluntarily released its license to practice as certified public accountants. That resulted in the loss of 85,000 jobs and required a whole bunch of office furniture to be removed—fast. I tracked down the liquidator responsible for clearing leased office space in Chicago and bought a tractor trailer full of Steelcase workstations and chairs in great condition for $6,000. That price included breakdown and delivery to our location!

Ladi had pushed me into that additional office space at the right time as it was about to be filled from floor to ceiling with furniture. To navigate we left narrow aisles between the canyons of binder bins, work surfaces, and file cabinets. Some of our working files were in cabinets inadvertently surrounded by these stacks. Lisa was pregnant with our third child Nicholas at the time and, comically, she was unable to turn sideways in these narrow corridors of furniture towers.

It was an exciting time because it showed where we were going. I didn't get furniture for just the employees on hand; I had room for many more. Expansion in subsequent years would bring an updated furniture look with uniquely curved workstations that our sales team in particular was very excited to receive from a bank in Iowa that was remodeling. Another great deal!

CHAPTER TWENTY-THREE
Let's Do It Together

N o, the book has not taken a weird 180 degree turn to become a cheap and lusty romance novel. I'm talking about partnerships. Going into business with one or more people is a great idea if your talents, experiences, resources, or knowledge base complements each other and meets the needs of the business idea. Partners help ease the burden of running a business in terms of work load, investment, risk, and sharing the inherent mental pressures. Partnering can be one of the best decisions you make in your business or it can be very damaging.

In the heat of the moment when passion is shared, people can get intoxicated with an entrepreneur's idea. After all, entrepreneurs have that affect on people. The lure of entrepreneurialism is attractive and it can pull at anyone. An anxious entrepreneur searching for assistance can do a great job selling his idea to anyone who will listen. People may sign up for the ride but never really have any intention of getting in the car. This is particularly true of bootstrapping entrepreneurs who don't have the funds to pay salaries and are willing to exchange equity in return for labor. Partners may ride the planning wave and suddenly bail when it's commitment time. This can severely derail or set back the entrepreneur's launch plans.

I would suggest avoiding the following top partner pitfalls:

1. Don't partner with yourself

I would not advise seeking partners that mirror what you bring to the table. Although you and your buddy may be two peas in a pod, most likely that is not what your business needs. You can do what you can do. You need a partner who can do what you can't do. This disperses the work load, avoids potential clashes, and provides fresh perspectives.

2. Avoid partners whose names start with F

Partnering or even hiring Friends and Family may not be your best move and can be a recipe for disaster. Some entrepreneurs hire family out of obligation for the sake of the relationship or out of trust and familiarity with the person. You are starting a business, not an aid agency for out-of-work relatives. They may come cheap and trusted, but if they don't or can't do the work, you're screwed because they are hard to dump.

3. The poor partner

Look into the financial background as best you can of your potential partner. How long can he last without or with a limited income? He may have the best intentions or have a highly desired skill set, but if the money runs out and he is forced to bail, you'll be left with significant shoes to fill. Knowing the personal savings rate in the US is as low as it is, special consideration to partner personal finances is a must.

4. The over-committed partner

You may be attracted to a partner because you see how hard she works. She seems to be involved and working on everything. My graphic designer was like that, always volunteering and keeping multiple balls in the air. Be careful not to partner with someone who's too willing to bite off more than she can chew. I got lucky in that my partner could balance her workload by working 16 hour days. The last thing you need to hear is, "Sorry I just don't have time for this anymore."

The key to having a successful partnership is establishing methods to eliminate these problems from occurring or mitigating their effects should they occur. The only secure way of doing that is by establishing a solid partnership agreement upfront. Agreements can take all forms and I'll include my thoughts below:

Try not to give up more than 51 percent of your ownership. If it's your idea, you need to be in control of the company and this percent of ownership will allow you to do so. Even if you and your partner are considered equals in bringing this idea to life, ask for controlling interest. It would be only 1 percent more in ownership, but that could be critical down the road in terms of controlling your vision.

Document in the agreement how and when you and your partners will get paid and if bonuses will be awarded. These decisions should be based off of predetermined metrics from your financial statements. For example, you will each be paid once the company shows a net profit derived from the income statement and you will each draw a salary of 10 percent of the stated profit each month. The more detailed the better to eliminate ambiguity and to reference back to a jointly-created, factual document.

Purchase shares and put skin in the game. A clear cut way to determine ownership commitment is to put your own money into the enterprise. This may be how the company receives its original funding or it may serve to leverage individual commitment. Shares of the company can be assigned any value that the founders wish. Partners would pay the designated share price for their agreed-upon percentage.

Think long term. When partners don't put money in to obtain shares, but instead contribute their own sweat equity, careful consideration needs to be given to structuring the agreement. You don't want to give someone a percentage of your company only to see them work for six months, get tired and quit, walking away with a portion of your company. That is why stock options are usually issued so that they only become active or valuable under predetermined circumstances like the sale of the company. Those options should have language that put conditions on the partner's commitment. For instance, maybe only a portion of the options are valid after a year of service. After two years another percentage is valid, and so on. It may be agreed upon and stipulated that partners will only realize a return upon the sale of the company. Again, the more detailed the better.

Time to get out. Since people's lives change, having the ability to buy and sell granted options makes it lucrative for partners to leave when they feel it is their time. Establishing a method, like EBITDA, to determine the company valuation, allows partners to sell their options back to the company to exit with a financial gain. Further, this measurement and method serves to incentivize partners to grow the value of the company as they see that value reflective in their share price. Finally, purchasing shares is a way for the principle partner to regain shares down the road by buying partners out.

Obviously a lawyer should be consulted to create a partnership agreement that meets you and your partner's wishes. The point I'm trying to make is that partners are people, and people are unpredictable. If you are the one driving an idea and it is your passion, don't think that your partner will share that same level of passion.

Think long term and assess your partner at the very beginning of business conception. Lots of people will get caught up in the excitement of a new venture. After all, it touches internally a dream that many have—owning your own business. The entrepreneur will speak of his business prospect with excitement and energy engaging those around him. So people will want to jump on board, hitch a ride, often allowing the entrepreneur to shoulder the risk while they attach themselves to the opportunity.

The trick is to motivate your employees and partners about your venture, but always stay grounded and know that no one cares about your dream as much as you. It is in those early months or years when people fade from the excitement of what could be and retreat to the safety of what is. Be prepared to lose them. Do your best to build redundant systems and information, document procedures, and know all aspects of your business. Plan for where you can go to replace talent that walks out the door so you don't skip a beat or slip back in the momentum of your business. Above all protect your equity.

CHAPTER TWENTY-FOUR
Measure of Success

"Success is focusing the full power of all you are on what you have a burning desire to achieve."— Wilfred Peterson

Hypothetically, at this point we have achieved two successes together. We have established an idea that satisfied the requirements of the E-Formula, thus allowing us to activate as entrepreneurs. In doing so, we decided to "go for it," and adequately planned and prepared to start our company. We then assessed our desire against what we value in the Risk Box and jumped in with both feet to make the business a viable success. At this point you have done far more than most. Arguably, you have just completed the two hardest parts on the entrepreneurial journey.

Moving forward, you should get used to measuring success in accomplishments rather than in dollars. As Henry Ward Beecher said, "the ability to convert ideas into things is the secret of outward success." Money is merely a business metric, not a true measure of success. If you do things well and according to your plans your money metric should respond in kind. This perspective allows even your failures to be regarded as successes as you learn from each experience. The popular *Chicken Soup for the Soul* book and subsequent title series was reportedly rejected 77 times before HCI Books picked the title up and went on to sell over 100 million copies. The success was not the 100 million books sold, but the fact that the authors did not give up after continual rejection and failure.

Unfortunately, as many business owners grow to become

successful, they begin to lose an understanding of why their customers buy. They focus more on the revenue coming in and less on measuring their marketing efforts. They may start to remove themselves from actively soliciting customer feedback. That's the danger in the next phase, the running phase. Businesses get so focused on fulfilling demand that they do not take time to listen to the customer anymore. Startup is all about customer focus and tweaking your product or service to get it just right. That focus needs to be maintained forever.

Starting a business spans from inception to the point of consistent customer demand and then reinvention. You actually start running a business once consistent demand kicks in. That is the point when your business moves from a customer-demand-generation mode of operation to a customer-demand-response mode of operation. Danger lies for a business becoming complacent during customer-demand response. This is when businesses become reactionary instead of staying focused on customer needs, trends, and threats. When customers consistently and proactively choose your product or service, you have created a sustainable business. You are in the "running" phase. Now your talent and ability will be primarily summoned to maintain and grow what you have accomplished so far.

PHASE III: RUNNING

The fear of committing that was evident in the Idea phase turns to a fear of surviving in the Running phase of the business. Even in the most successful businesses, the entrepreneur is constantly concerned with survival. The thought may only rest in the back of his mind, but it is always present. At this point, however, fear does not freeze the entrepreneur from acting; rather it motivates him to execute. Now that he is fully engaged in the business and proven its viability, the entrepreneur will act to survive, grow, and innovate. The entrepreneur's efforts have paid off and the business is sustaining itself, and he will try to maximize every waking hour contemplating how to continually improve.

For the entrepreneur, the set of rules in the running phase of a business is completely different than the rules in the startup phase. The company is becoming more customer-demand responsive than customer-demand generating. Processes have to be developed to run the business in a consistent and predictable way. The role of the entrepreneur in the business needs to be reinvented and at this point it is all about scaling, innovating, and leading.

CHAPTER TWENTY-FIVE
The Entrepreneur's Role in Running the Company

Many laymen say being the boss is the primary attraction to starting their own business. They have some misconceived notion of sitting back, barking orders, and watching the money come in. I'm not sure you'll find many of them with the title of entrepreneur. In stark contrast, you'll find most entrepreneurs actively involved in all facets of the business and engaged in daily activity. However, that all needs to adapt once the business is up and running. The entrepreneur is the dreamer and the visionary for the business and he cannot continue to be the "doer" as well. The priority must quickly shift to hiring staff to conduct the operational tasks of the company.

Many entrepreneurs feel it is noble and necessary to be the hard worker who puts in countless hours churning out the work to be a good role model. Others are simply unfamiliar with the role of being the leader. Sometimes entrepreneurs live in the production role because they can feel a sense of immediate accomplishment. These efforts actually stifle growth crucial for the business to maintain sustainability. The entrepreneur needs to put himself in a position to observe progress, weakness, success, customer needs, strengths, opportunities, and threats. The entrepreneur's role now is to scale the company for growth.

Steer the Ship

To do so the entrepreneur needs to determine and understand his title and duties during the running phase and this will be more dependent on the organization's structure. The titles of CEO and president are often used interchangeably by entrepreneurs and they may seem redundant, where in truth they are symbiotic.

A sterile definition of roles calls for the CEO to be primarily responsible for strategy: long-range planning, company direction. The president is more tactical and operationally focused ensuring that the daily business of the company is conducted according to plan. Larger companies will have the president report to the CEO who acts as the interface between the board of directors and stockholders. Start-ups without a board of directors or shareholders will most likely not need to name a CEO and the singular title of president would suffice.

Focus

This is more than semantics because as the company grows, proper delineation of roles may become increasingly important. What is most important for the entrepreneur entering this stage of the company lifecycle is to follow some core principles which I've outlined below.

1. Work toward making the business independent of you.

A successful milestone will occur when the entrepreneur can step away from his business for prolonged periods of time and in essence not be missed. This can only happen by hiring trusted employees and establishing a culture reflective of the values the entrepreneur wants to instill. This takes talent as so much attention, dependence and guidance is directed from and toward the founder. It takes well-designed processes and people to manage those processes to allow the entrepreneur the leeway to put some space between himself and the company. This frees the founder to get ideas, innovate, and plan strategy. In a morbid sense, it also ensures the company's continuance should the founder unexpectedly die or become disabled.

2. Build controls that protect the assets of the company.

Internal or external fraud will be attempted at your business. Checks and balances around your cash and assets will help deter or detect when someone has their hand in the cookie jar. Your people are your assets too and they need to be protected. Therefore, proper screening when hiring and establishing physical building security measures are a vital consideration. You can also protect your people by providing benefits, flexible work hours, and a competitive market wage. Finally, your customers are your assets and you need to ensure you provide a safe product and internal measures to protect their data and privacy.

3. Have a solid financial understanding of your business.

Most small and even medium-size businesses will not have a chief financial officer (CFO) on staff. Likely an accountant will be hired to produce financial statements, file taxes, and perform related obligations, but the role of the CFO to manage the financial risks of the business will often fall to the entrepreneur. Regardless, the founder needs to develop a solid understanding of the basic financial statements. This transcends to a full appreciation of the cost of goods, margins, expenses, and income. This may seem obvious, but a fair amount of entrepreneurs don't want to be involved in these aspects because they are too focused on the product or service which led them into the business.

4. Hire great talent.

Your people will be your greatest asset and you should fill strategic positions with the best people you can find. They should be independent and able to grow within a rapidly changing environment. Most important, they should be able to run with your vision and effectively manage the department or division you have assigned to them. These people should challenge you as well as challenging their employees. There is tremendous temptation to just fill a seat when hiring as the process can be lengthy. Resist the urge to complete the hiring task just to move on to other matters. The time wasted on employees that don't work out is costly, disruptive, and can be demoralizing to those on board watching the revolving door. Background checks and references should be conducted on all hires, even though this is a commonly overlooked part of the process for start-ups looking to save money.

5. Create a clear market differentiating vision for your product or service.

A great deal of time and energy should be spent continually innovating your business around your customer. The intellectual property (IP) created by your company is the deciding differentiator of what you are versus what you are like. Businesses that copy other businesses typically do not sustain, as the company they copy quickly retaliates with new innovation. Innovation attracts new customers and creates new markets. Finally, the IP developed will help establish a higher valuation when it comes to selling or financing your business. Ultimately, it is innovation which defines the entrepreneur and without it he is left to compete on little more than price.

6. Develop an exit strategy designed to maximize the value of the business.

This directly relates to item five above but takes it a step further. The entrepreneur needs to plan ahead on how he will leave the business. Whether it will be retirement, a sale to employees, transfer to a family member, sale to a private equity firm or a competitor, he needs to visualize his exit plan and how to position the company for that scenario. It's not just about maximizing the pay-out to the entrepreneur; it includes strengthening the company's position so it can continue on toward its mission. How the founder manages, documents, and develops his business with the appropriate exit in mind will ensure a smooth transition for all and most likely maximize the potential valuation.

7. Manage profitably.

Understanding your financials is one thing, managing them is another. As founder you need to have a solid understanding of how your business will make and spend money. Some describe themselves as creative thinkers and idea generators and don't have an interest or desire to be involved in the money aspect. This is a dangerous route to take. You need to know exactly how your company will generate profits; not just sales and revenues, but sustainable and growing profits. Further, you need to know how to contain and control costs.

Establishing a yearly budget for every department will be your first step. The second is establishing policy and procedures on how money is to be spent and how profit is to be derived. Trust me, if you don't cap or limit spending, it can quickly spiral out of control. The same is true for establishing pricing policies that don't give away the farm. Inexperienced sales people will use price more often than not as their leverage to close a deal. Developing a strategic sales process and pricing guidelines will help protect your bottom line.

Two key areas on the operational side of the business to monitor profitability include accounts receivable and interest expenses. Letting your accounts receivable slide is a cardinal mistake in managing cash flow. Entrepreneurs who put all of their energies into attracting and winning customers are often gun-shy when it comes to collecting payment from them. The fear of hurting the relationship is paramount in their minds and it becomes easier to ignore the problem—until they find they are unable to meet payroll. The likelihood of collecting past due amounts greatly diminishes after 90 days, and often start-ups don't have the manpower dedicated to the collection process.

Increasingly, companies are turning to factoring as a method to speed their cash flow and outsource collections. A third party will purchase invoices at say 90 percent of their value and pay cash immediately. They are left with the task of collecting while you move on to the next sale. The credit worthiness of your customers will determine the rate that the factor will purchase invoices. There must be enough margin in your invoices to participate in factoring or the cost has to be built into the selling price.

Margin consideration must also be factored into interest expenses on your past due invoices, bank fees, or credit card balance. You may be able to maintain the minimum balance on your personal credit cards, but it's stupid, if not impossible, to do so using a corporate account. Credit cards can be a great source of short-term financing, but you must pay them off in full each month to preserve profits.

8. Don't copy – be copied.

Start-ups can easily get distracted by their growth and influenced from competitors and larger companies with greater resources. The business can be tempted to stray from its original mission by seeking new markets or by copying competitors. Don't compare yourself to the big, established player in your industry. It can de-motivate and deflate you. You will feel inadequate and incapable of ever being able to compete with them. The more you compare yourself to them, the more you will start to model your business after them. Copying will serve to lower what differentiates you and allow your customers to compare you on price alone. You won't win that battle. Study your competitors to see how you are or how you can become different from them. See how you can do things for your customers that your competitors can't do and learn what customers don't like about them.

You started your business to be different in the marketplace and that is how you will succeed. As a start-up, you can model your business around customer needs better than any larger competitor who will likely require customers to accept their model and way of doing business. Watch and listen to your customers and to a certain extent ignore your competitors.

9. Don't starve yourself.

Many entrepreneurs will penny pinch for years in an attempt to beef up their bottom line. The most common method is to pay themselves the lowest possible salary. This may be a necessary practice in the short run, but eventually you have to provide for your family. Pay yourself the best salary you can, when you can, and set a goal to get to that point. Failing to do so not only foregoes money you could use now or save, but upon selling your company most buyers will recognize the expense gap in salary and factor that into their evaluation—negatively affecting the amount they are willing to pay. Why? Because the buyer knows they will have to pay someone at least a current market rate to run this business. Your business is a lot more fun when you are making money!

10. Work "on" your business not "in" it.

This phrase has been used by many and most notably by author Michael Gerber who has written extensively on the topic. It is a golden rule for entrepreneurs and symbolic of all the tasks that get done daily within a business that need to be delegated to employees. Ideally the entrepreneur should have the fluidness to move in and out of the business to make observations and reflect upon its progress. Self-inflicted interruptions occur when the entrepreneur pauses too long on any one particular task and moves from studying to doing.

A company is made up of many tasks and functions, and the entrepreneur will most likely do all of them at some point. The entrepreneur will quickly remove himself from the tasks he dislikes and migrate toward those he does. This may happen intentionally or unintentionally without a conscious thought. Becoming aware of this mental association with tasks is important for two reasons, which I will cover more extensively.

CHAPTER TWENTY-SIX
Tasks

Tasks You Dislike

I t is necessary to delegate tasks, especially tasks that are "not your thing." The entrepreneur must be aware of the task and how it impacts the business so it can be monitored and managed properly. He needs to understand its function, impact, and purpose in the business to ensure policy and procedures are created to manage it. This provides clear expectations to those assigned the task, and in worst-case scenarios prevents or exposes detrimental results like embezzlement, waste, and inefficiency.

Even if a task is disliked or viewed as unimportant and has been effectively delegated, the entrepreneur still cannot turn his back on it. Far too many stories of fraud originated where the entrepreneur was not interested in the tasks of accounting. This disinterest is common, for if the entrepreneur were interested in these administrative aspects he probably would have started an accounting firm. Entrepreneurs are visionaries and seek to create businesses rather than getting involved in routine "T" accounts. I can't name one entrepreneur I know that spent a great deal of time in the accounting department.

How many headlines can you recall regarding the long-term and trusted bookkeeper who quietly stole company funds over several years of dedicated service? These people understand the accounting procedures. In many cases, the embezzler may have actually been the one that created them. That access, combined with the entrepreneur's lack of interest and/or knowledge of the tasks, leads to swindles that can cost the business thousands sometimes millions of dollars, if not bankruptcy.

What did the entrepreneur do wrong in these embezzlement cases?
- He did not understand the task
- He did not respect the task
- He did not fully understand the role the task played in supporting the overall organization
- He did not recognize or assess his own lack of knowledge of the task
- He did not put controls in place

Early in the development of TRC, I feared embezzlement and not having my eyes on the bank account. It was important for me to have a fail-safe process in place to ensure our hard-earned money would stay where it was supposed to. I had no reason for this concern from any one of my employees, but I knew it was my responsibility to ensure a process was in place that eliminated the temptation. So what did I do? I did what many start-ups do and put my wife in charge of the bank account. Like a firewall on your computer system, you need to ensure there are solid measures limiting who can access your money. The trusted family employee "should" be sufficient; however, brothers, in-laws, and nieces have gone down as company pilferers in the past. The key is having checks and balances and not allowing complete control to a single individual or individuals close to one another or who can develop a conspiring relationship. Good luck!

Tasks You Like

Naturally, an entrepreneur will focus most of his efforts on the things he likes to do. It often reflects the core competency of the business and is the primary driver of revenue, profit, and growth. This focus exploits every resource of the entrepreneur and challenges the entrepreneur to continually improve. It becomes the adrenaline fuel.

The flipside to tasks that you like is that you can become too focused on them to the point that you disregard other aspects of the business or monopolize the tasks themselves. By monopolizing, the entrepreneur may exclude valuable coworkers who can or should support the task and provide relevant input in terms of ideas, feedback, or criticism. The entrepreneur may tend to hold all the knowledge of such tasks in his head making collaboration or position succession difficult. It may also make it hard for the entrepreneur to get away from the business since he has made himself the central authority governing the task.

I had hired good people to run every aspect of TRC and managers to oversee them, yet I would still drift back into the trenches. I developed terrible habits of reviewing daily shipments going out the door and releasing Web orders that came in to our routing system. What an absolute disruption to the work flow when the president jumps in to see if orders were picked properly or he releases Web orders prior to someone's regular approval process!

During different periods of growth, I managed to acquire similar "hovering" habits in other aspects of the business. I either outgrew these on my own or by the forceful pushback of the assigned coworker or manager. I really give those employees credit for putting me in my place. The bottom line is that tasks are not what the entrepreneur should be working on at this stage of running the business. It's like our ship captain who may enjoy working the navigational controls and ends up spending too much of his time plotting the course rather than being on the bridge. He may be good at navigating, but it's not his job to be spending time on those tasks. By doing so, the entrepreneur neglects his primary duties and encroaches on the person who is assigned to the task.

Why do entrepreneurs work on tasks? They want to keep busy and see immediate results. The startup phase is a fast-paced, multi-tasking circus and it's hard to come off of that momentum. It takes a great deal of discipline for the entrepreneur to adjust his role in the company and sometimes a bit of coaxing from coworkers along the way.

First Million

Hanging the first dollar earned on the office wall is a ritual of many small businesses, but I needed to hit a much bigger milestone in order to scale to a national ambit. I needed my first million to be hung on the wall, which came in 1997. As important and exciting a milestone as it was, I had no time to celebrate. We needed to keep growing. A year later we would hit $3 million in sales in our new office location. Keep in mind the growth of TRC was completely organic without the aid of borrowing. Employees were being added based on a model that calculated their contribution and the required profit and revenue needed to bring them on.

The year we hit $3 million in sales was exhilarating. We were still very much a bootstrap operation with a modest office and a team of employees who were jazzed to be part of this daily-growing, monthly-changing environment. Our story started to get around locally, and I was introduced to someone who would turn out to be the most important contact I would make in my career.

Through a mutual relationship, the TRC story was relayed to the CFO of CDW. CDW was a Chicago entrepreneurial phenomenon that immediately became a national success under the leadership of founder Michael Krazny, who is, and was at the time, one of Forbes' richest Americans. CDW was one of the first resellers to emerge to service the IT industry in 1984. This was the beginning of personal computing and Krazny's story of founding his company at his kitchen table became legendary. A mere 14 years later, CDW had gone public and grown to a multi-billion dollar enterprise serving predominately the corporate market.

Krazny's vision for CDW went far beyond their current revenues to include new market segments, including the education vertical where I had already carved out my niche. At the time, CDW was viewed as the most aggressively priced and largest volume mover of products around. Their culture was cut throat and their sales representatives almost mythic in terms of going after business. My story was conveyed to CDW's CFO at the time, Harry Harczak, and the next thing I knew they wanted to meet with me—Harry and Michael!

A week later I was having breakfast with one of the wealthiest men in the country (the world, for that matter). I was less intimidated than I was anxious. Through our breakfast conversation I found that we were similar in our approach to our respective businesses. Our stories were so parallel that a connection was immediately made. Our companies were basically the same, only serving different markets. The mechanisms and processes were similar as were our philosophies on management, sales, and marketing.

The only thing separating us was our revenues, and that was a substantial separation. Through our subsequent interactions I saw that Michael wasn't a business god, he was a regular guy. Sure, he was a really sharp guy and shrewd businessman, but I could be him; anyone could be him by activating their own E-Formula.

CDW wanted to expand into the public sector, which included all levels of education, state and local government, federal government, and healthcare. Their growth had been dramatic but contained primarily to the corporate customer. Michael saw the growth opportunities in these niche markets. Our discussions were taking place because he was contemplating using an existing player to accelerate the learning curve into the education channel. Our talks went well and progressed quickly to the point that an offer was extended to invest $5 million in TRC to have us grow to $100 million in revenue in five years.

Wow! It was 1998 and TRC was just two years old having just passed $3 million in sales. My wife and I were invited to attend CDW's holiday party. There must have been nearly two thousand people in attendance. Hundreds of gifts ranging from televisions to kayaks were given out, and the night concluded with a performance by a celebrity comic. It was almost like a fairy tale. Michael Krazny saw the Cinderella in us and nabbing us early would certainly propel his efforts in growing the education segment. The only problem was that it didn't feel right to me.

At the time, I had no vision for what Michael was proposing. To obtain $100 million in sales in education seemed too far out of reach. The deal itself was over my head, and I failed to seek advice from experts to consult me on the opportunity. Holding back on finding experts turned out to be more deliberate than an oversight. The prospect of selling my company at this stage just didn't feel right. I dreamed about owning a company since I was a kid, and I had worked hard to get to where we were. Even though it would be considered investment capital to grow the company, I would now be accountable to someone and I wouldn't necessarily be in control. Although I was immature at such deal makings I knew in my heart it wasn't what I wanted. I knew if I took the deal I would be a millionaire, but that's not why I went into business for myself.

Michael picked up on it too, and he made it easy on me. Sensing my fear and uncertainty, he killed the deal and gracefully let me go. In 2008 CDW's education division alone had well over $700 million in revenue.

Old Models Change

TRC was dependent on cooperative advertising to generate our marketing materials. Using manufacturer dollars was like being able to market for free. Obviously, sales needed to be generated in the manufacturer's product line in order to keep getting funds and gain additional funds. When cooperative advertising started to ebb, it was a glaring sign that things were changing for TRC and the industry and adjustments in strategy were going to be necessary.

Many of our competitors did not recognize what was happening and their businesses stagnated as a result. This was not just a case of fewer advertising dollars being spent; this was signaling something much bigger. Combined with shrinking ad dollars, dealer margins were retracting. More competitors were entering the market engaged in replicative models but with few innovative attributes. Every dealer was focused on selling the same brands and the same products. They did so not necessarily out of intentional design, but through market demand; the reseller business fulfills rather than generates demand. From a mail order and Web-based perspective, resellers were the local store to pick up your IT needs. Our customers knew what they wanted and simply needed a place to buy it from. In that scenario, the only differentiator became price and quickly commoditized the products we sold.

Manufacturers who had relied on the channel of resellers to sell their products started to realize that no matter how many ad dollars were thrown at their resellers, they all sold and grew at much the same rate as they had in the past, except for a rare few like TRC. They saw that customers went to different dealers based on price, locality, customer service, delivery, or any other factor unique to the reseller. Although these factors were important to the reseller and customer, they were less influential in terms of creating demand for the manufacturer's product. The exception was when a dealer had built a particular practice around a manufacturer's solution. TRC had done just that with volume software licensing from about a dozen popular publishers.

The expanding pool of dealers entering the market was choosing to lead with price cuts that resulted in market price pressure and lower-dealer margins. The channel would push back to the manufacturer asking for greater discounts or increased cooperative dollars, but that was not going to happen. The dealer channel race to zero was on and manufacturers had their own problems to cope with. Since most IT manufacturers were public companies or were striving to issue an IPO or buyout, they faced mounting pressures to grow. The cash-flush cooperative programs of the boom years were becoming highly scrutinized and increasingly awarded based on sales benchmarks. The dollars being doled out were being cut and manufacturers were being forced to do more with fewer dealers. Marketing dollars were starting to shift from legacy dealer catalogs to the Internet and most dealers did not have programs to attract co-op dollars to support Web activity.

As cooperative ad budgets were being cut, expanding catalog distribution and any other types of direct marketing became increasingly problematic. This industry shift was loud and clear to me. We had to move away from catalog distribution to some other method of promotion and that method would be the Web. Keep in mind that in 1995 Web sites were used basically to post your company name, address, and phone number. By 1998 sites had become more sophisticated and e-commerce was evolving rapidly, but few development standards had been established.

The squeeze on cooperative advertising occurred shortly after the dot com bust. The dot com era had helped extend the life of cooperative advertising programs as manufacturers saw all forms of advertising as viable and necessary regardless of performance. Once the bubble burst, manufacturers and dealers alike had to look in the mirror and figure out who they truly were. What markets did they serve and what purpose did they bring to the channel? Many could not figure this out and dealers both big and small closed their doors. Some of the leaders in direct mail catalogs evaporated overnight too entrenched in their way of doing business to see or acknowledge the changes at hand. The ones that remained would rewrite the rules of the channel.

At TRC, we were not going to be able to generate enough profit dollars to keep adding employees and fund an expanding direct marketing budget without taking on debt to do so. More importantly was the recognition that our direct mail efforts were generating a flat response each year. Initially, when a new catalog hit the mail stream, the phone volume would pick up and orders would flood the fax machine and morning mail delivery. As TRC and the industry matured and our inside sales force grew, more of our sales were being generated from customer relationships and the Web than from direct mail efforts.

I had built a marketing group consisting of two talented product managers reflective of the structure at Educational Resources, an in-house graphic designer who replaced our founding designer, and administrators to assist the product managers. The role of the product manager had been core to the success of the reseller; however, it was increasingly clear that their role was now obsolete at TRC. The world and TRC would move to the Web and that was where we had to place our focus moving forward. TRC had to retool. We decided to completely stop producing a catalog by 2004. This was scary as we were the first to make this move and our catalog had been our lead-generation system.

The decision to cease catalog production came with a cost. Unable to re-allocate the entire staff that supported catalog operations, I had to eliminate the remaining positions. These employees had done nothing wrong and they were tremendously talented and hard working individuals, but change had greatly impacted TRC and we needed a new skill set—fast!

Ride Out the Storm

TRC's Web presence certainly was growing since our inception in '95 with early forms of online product catalogs and e-commerce. The dot com era not only ushered in a variety of Web development techniques and strategies but new business models that challenged traditional brick and mortar. TRC was caught somewhere in between, which turned out to be the best place to ride out the impending storm. New Web-based-only technology dealers entered the market selling products at or below cost. Their model was based on the newly emerging advertising revenues that could be generated on Web sites designed to capture the most "eye balls." Sales were not important in this new frontier; page clicks and new visitor counts were. Literally overnight, the race to zero became just that, and TRC was not going to win at this game.

New competitors that had never been in our channel before were emerging rapidly. Imagine waking up to a new landscape where your competitors are selling products at or below your cost and capturing headlines as a unique and innovative business model poised to disrupt the old-school providers. We couldn't figure it out and neither could our distributor partners who were supplying them. We would cry foul to both our distributors and directly to the manufacturers for granting these players pricing that we could not compete with. Their response was that there was no special pricing; they had the same structure as everyone else. Then we really scratched our heads.

How were they doing this and why? Were they buying customers only to raise prices down the road? Eventually the model surfaced that they were not in business to sell technology. They were in business to sell advertising. The low prices were used just to bring people to the Web site. So, was this truly innovative or just a new twist on an old game of race to zero? Regardless, we were feeling the pressure from customers who demanded the same pricing. Whether they understood the game or not did not matter; our customers wanted these low prices.

Scrambling to react, I had to come up with a defense. Two words in business I hate to use are *react* and *defense*. It showed I was not innovating and forcing change, I was responding to change which meant I was in a bad pole position—behind the pack. As my understanding of the model emerged, I formulated a strategy to respond. First, we would focus on what we had and that was great service and product knowledge. These players knew nothing of technology and they were merely posting SKUs for a price. They had no passion for the business, products, or customers. Their only focus was generating site traffic to promote their advertisers. Their customers were advertisers, not the consumers buying product from them.

Second, we would ride it out. Who knew how long this would last and if it would ever end? It started to become known that these guys were not making money and their end game was to go public for the really big payoff. They were not in business to support a mission of any sort. Their purpose was self serving—they wanted to get rich. That was great because I knew by having a lack of customer focus and by not addressing a customer need these guys would fail. They chose to compete strictly on price and that is rarely a winning strategy.

Customers started turning to TRC in frustration over unanswered phone calls, slow shipments, and poor customer service. Few of the new entrants were offering credit payment terms or a suitable return policy. By continuing to focus on what we did best and holding steady by not copying our competition, we would emerge from this threat. Indeed, we would continue to have record years, partially spurred on by the huge demand for technology and by maintaining a focus on our niche education audience.

The dot com bust saw new technology standards and protocols for Web development and e-commerce emerge. This would help pave the way to a greater understanding of how advertising would fit on the Web and how physical products should be marketed via the Internet. TRC would scrap its first custom built e-commerce platform to shift to new and less expensive development that allowed tremendous customization. That change would provide a marvelous opportunity to build an e-commerce platform around the unique needs of our niche audience while others built systems that aligned with the rigid needs of their own internal legacy systems.

The timing was great because we were ready to move from a basic Peachtree Accounting package to a mid-tier enterprise resource planning (ERP) software system that would manage and coordinate all the operational, information, and process functions of TRC. We invested in an ERP system with features and power we wouldn't use at the time but fully intended to grow into. We would design our e-commerce and shopping functionality to draw directly from this new ERP system in ways that were innovative to our customers' needs—something that would take our competitors years to duplicate.

Working through this period gave me a fresh vision for what TRC was truly meant to be. I realized several more changes were in order. First, we would no longer sell everything under the sun. When I started TRC, part of the pitch was "over 50,000 products at the lowest prices." I was copying what everyone else did in terms of being a one-stop shop. All we had to do was show a wide variety of products at great prices and ship fast. The catalog made it easy because the tactic was just to show a few headliner products per category to represent all that we carried. Trying to replicate the print catalog on the Web with users demanding more in-depth product representation would be taxing for our size company. Maintaining 50,000 hardware, software, consumable, audio visual, and peripheral items on our Web site and for our sales representatives proved to be impossible and cost prohibitive. Above all, we didn't sell all 50,000 products; we only sold a sliver of that.

What we did sell was software. My second decision was to put all of our resources and focus into being the most knowledgeable source for volume software licensing in the academic market. It was no accident that our strength would be software. That's where I got my training, it was my roots. As much as I wanted to grow by having customers think of TRC for all of their technology needs, our talent resided in software. Even though our sales representatives had been able to sell anything they wanted, they chose software and it was drawn from my influence whether I knew it or not.

CHAPTER TWENTY-SEVEN
Scaling For Growth

P eople take great interest in my entrepreneurial story and they want to know the deeper story of how it came to be. What they are really asking, whether they realize it or not, is "how did it scale?" Ultimately, the ability to start a business is not as captivating as the story about how the business takes off, grows, and becomes successful. Scaling is at the heart of the matter and it is one of the three primary responsibilities of the entrepreneur in the running phase.

Many equate scaling a business to franchising and although that is an easy image to visualize it is not reflective of entrepreneurship. Franchising is owning a pre-built business that someone manages. It is not being an entrepreneur, unless you are the one who developed the franchise concept. Scaling is how a business grows by economy of scale, becoming more efficient and profitable as more business is generated. Simply, the business is able to take on more orders or produce more product without adding additional resources in kind.

Scaling should be intentionally established and outlined in the original business plan and strategy. This requires an advanced capability to visualize how an idea will form a business that grows from startup into a sophisticated collection of processes and systems. The entrepreneur may not have all the answers how to scale at the planning stage; however, a general conception of the model should be formulated at this point. Generically, scaling involves establishing business systems, incorporating technology, and utilizing capital.

Tasks are subsets of processes which are components of larger systems. Systems can be viewed as the major arteries running through the organization and connecting vital functions. This infrastructure will be built with the resources on hand and will mature as budgets, experience, and technology dictate. Technology can be responsible for significant scaling efforts by replacing human efforts, increasing efficiency, and decreasing time involved within systems. All of these factors are interdependent on available capital, typically resulting in several phases of scaling evolution as systems become more sophisticated and resources more prevalent.

Below are four components of TRC's original business plan that I used to scale.

1. Know the target market and establish reproducible and expanding methods to reach that market.

Initially this focused on TRC's lead-generation methods. It started with a direct mail order catalog that brought in more results the more we mailed making scaling efficient. This expanded to a variety of other marketing methods designed to hit the target in multiple ways as frequency led to increased response.

2. Establish operational procedures to create a similar customer experience every time.

This involved creating processes and dedicating people to specific tasks to ensure quality in every operational aspect of the business that touched the customer.

3. Replicate the sales process in a predictable manner that can be forecasted.

Once a lead generation and sales process was devised that worked well, it had to be reproduced. This involved training, procedures, management, and tools. The best tool I invested in was our ERP and CRM system. I may be frugal, but I invested top dollar on the best systems for our business and the results were enormous productivity and efficiency gains. Those tools helped produce sales pipeline reports allowing us to forecast sales, review closing ratios, and zero in on significant opportunities.

4. Invest in the capacity to scale

It was measurable that each additional sales representative would bring in an average amount of revenue and profit after a 9-12 month period of training and acclimation. The benchmark served to identify under- and over-achieving individuals. Investing in people was foremost and investing in technology to serve them came in at a close second.

Expanding our office space, improving operations, buying technology all went into the effort to scale. Credit was the binding element that made all these efforts possible, which I'll come to explain in detail.

Go Backward to Move Forward

Eliminating our catalog and cutting back on the variety of products TRC sold felt like I was going backward. In one sense I was reacting to the changing environment that made it increasingly difficult to keep up with the product maintenance and management of 50,000 products. Direct mail was less effective and TRC had to embrace the Web. Based on our cash flow we couldn't maintain both models.

The decisions made would not take TRC backward, but propel it forward. My methods to scale were constrained by our original business model. Specializing in software licensing would allow us to zero in on the specific subset of customers responsible for volume licensing decisions and all marketing would be directed toward their attention. Operational procedures and sales processes would be tooled to reflect the requirements of licensing alone. TRC's technology sales had included projectors, desktop and laptop computers, servers, network equipment, printers, audio visual equipment, and more. Each of these categories required unique and individual approaches to be successful. With TRC's structure and resources, we were mediocre at best in representing them all.

I never wanted to say no to a sale during startup, but now I saw reason too. TRC could not be everything to everybody and we were going to have to turn down opportunities to focus on what we could do best. The company had matured and I suppose I did as well. It's funny because my sales team was telling me to go this direction for some time but I didn't want to listen to them. They did not want to respond to bids or quote customers for categories that they had low chances of winning. They had started to niche themselves before I actually pulled the trigger. It was at this turning point that another more significant revelation became clear to me.

Things happen because of a decided course of action. I am confident that the success of TRC and the advancements we made would not have occurred if I had followed a different course through startup. By bootstrapping the company, I was involved in the creation of virtually every process in every facet of the company. I was thrust into sales and marketing and saw firsthand what worked, what didn't, how customers responded, and what their pain was. I've stated that as a reseller we didn't create demand. Selling products was not resolving a problem for the customer other than answering the question of where to obtain the needed product. Even though selling products was what we did, I discovered it wasn't why we were in business.

TRC was in business to consult on volume software licensing, to develop an easier method to procure licensing, to establish a process that ensured the compliancy requirements our customers needed to adhere to, and provide reporting and other administrative requirements. It was clear my original purpose for TRC was rather different than our purpose now. What seems like a clear focus and strategy going in can be radically altered after a series of customer engagements and trials. I think the well-funded entrepreneur who has the luxury to hire layers of staff to execute on the processes and tasks of the company robs himself of the direct feedback that only he can be receptive to based on his original design.

My change came when the company changed. When I stepped into the visionary role and out of the daily activity, I was able to assimilate what I had been exposed to and learned. The experience helped me reinvent the company to address a genuine customer need that I alone was uniquely positioned to deliver at the time.

Credit and Scaling

The bootstrap model of funding is taking a limited sum of money to launch a business. Typically it is only enough to buy the basic necessities to become operational or to support the effort for a designated period of time. My personal investment was the only source of funding and most of it went to front the catalog and pay for our phone system. That's why I had to bring partners like Betsy on with equity and no pay.

The bulk of TRC's cost would always be in personnel. Adding an employee not only included a salary but insurance and other benefits. The recurring costs of phone charges, utilities, rent, and other operational expenses were monitored under a microscope to ensure cash flow continued uninterrupted. The bootstrap model worked for TRC because we experienced rapid and continual growth that funded the business.

Monthly cash flow came strictly from our monthly net income and cash received from outstanding accounts receivable from customers. With a certain sum of cash received, Lisa would do her juggling act of deciding what bills to pay by closely reviewing our current accounts payable outstanding. Every single month for ten years this dance went on and Lisa was the lead.

TRC kept a modest product inventory on site to fulfill the most popular selling items rapidly. The vast majority of our orders were custom volume licenses which had to be drop shipped directly from the software publisher or distributor to the customer. The drop-ship process worked well as TRC never had to physically touch the product, which reduced operational expense. The inventory we did carry turned at an incredible rate based on our just-in-time process. Three primary distributors were located in our home state of Illinois or just over the border making UPS shipments a next-day activity. We had the luxury of using them as our warehouse. Orders over a certain dollar amount shipped for free from our distributors and when shipments arrived at TRC we used every packing peanut and sometimes the box itself for our outgoing shipments.

The art of juggling accounts payable is nothing new, but Lisa's skill was truly something to marvel at. Approximately 92 percent of our customers were given credit to pay their invoices in 30 days. This was customary and a requirement in our market selling to schools. Often invoices required approval at monthly board meetings then were routed through the school's own operational process. That made it difficult to get an invoice paid within 30 days. The normal float would be more around 35 days but some would take even longer.

What further strained our float capability was the growth TRC was experiencing. Each month larger orders were being placed with our suppliers. The average order size was rapidly growing and significantly increased once we focused on volume software licensing. The anomaly orders of $100k, $300k and $500k were starting to become routine and they hampered our credit. Add to that the costs of adding new employees, the six-month ramp-up time until they were profitable, plus ongoing payroll concerns, and you have a lot of balls in the air.

TRC always made payroll, although Lisa can confess to several sleepless nights as to how that was going to happen. Thankfully, deposits always seemed to come through in the final hour before the 15th and 30th. However, cash flow alone would not sustain TRC. Credit would be the sustaining life blood; without it we would shut down.

As you work to grow your business bigger to gain a sense of stability and security, other factors can make it even more vulnerable and credit is one of them. With sales exceeding $10 million and then $20 million, a predictable flow of business was generated monthly; however, any interruption in our credit capacity to fulfill those orders would trigger an immediate backup of orders which could result in a shutdown of business. Even though your suppliers are saying no more orders until you pay down your balance, your customers keep on buying based on the lead-generation system you've created. The orders start to pile up, complaints rise due to late fulfillment, orders get cancelled, and it becomes a tumultuous time.

TRC's credit foundation was formed by net 30 terms granted by our suppliers. Modest credit limits would steadily increase after every annual review, but our receivables generally would lag behind our commitments. Instead of obtaining debt to provide a cushion of operating cash flow, TRC would utilize credit, which if managed properly would cost us nothing. The pace of TRC would rapidly outstrip any credit amount provided and I increasingly turned to personal credit cards to supplement payment for supplier purchases. Most of our suppliers accepted credit cards and did so out of their own necessity to extend credit risk without interrupting continual customer orders.

We had twelve different credit cards with varying levels of credit, all in either my or Lisa's name. All would be paid in full on a monthly basis. I was adamant about not incurring finance charges as that would have lowered our profit margins. I was a hawk monitoring our earned profit dollars and literally fought any internal or external influences that eroded them. There is no such thing as a small expense when you bootstrap.

I quickly learned I could artificially increase my credit by finding more creditors—suppliers willing to provide credit— although that could only take you so far based on outstanding payables on your balance sheet. The trick was to continually give more business to a supplier and pay them on time or as reasonably close to on time as possible. We would continually work with our distributors to increase our credit limits throughout the life of TRC. We could source much of the same product from multiple distributors and take advantage of various credit lines in that respect. At times we would pay more for a product depending on the source simply because credit was available at the time. Growth pressured the process as a balance would be paid in full on one day and then completely used up again the next. The only relief came from the seasonality of our business, allowing our credit time to catch up during the slow months from November through February.

Requesting exceptions to increase credit lines during peak season became routine with our top suppliers. Suppliers had seen growth like ours in other resellers and they wanted to ride those horses. Reviewing our financials, suppliers would understand our need to reinvest earnings into the business but closely followed key metrics to monitor and ensure things were not getting too out of control. Ultimately it came down to trust. It was everyone's job in the company to ensure we maintained a good partnership with our suppliers, and it was my job to lead by example and establish the highest levels of personal and business integrity. That's an important piece of the puzzle in growing any business. The entrepreneur cannot be so focused on himself and his business that he disregards or takes advantage of those he partners with. Remaining outwardly humble is paramount.

To fuel our growth and the increasing size of our transactions, we still needed additional forms of credit. We had one more major weapon at our disposal that was fairly unique to our industry. A credit vehicle called "flooring" provided a revolving line of credit on purchases made through our major distributors. A term born out of financing in the automotive industry, flooring was a separate and much larger line of credit that would grant 30-45 day on IT purchases made at participating distributors. Where a distributor granted $100,000 in credit, flooring may provide $400,000.

Flooring credit was provided through a large financial institution like Bank of America or Deutsche Financial. The distributor would pay a fee to the bank in order to have the additional credit available to their customers. In essence, they shifted the accounts receivable risk to these institutions which then allowed merchants like TRC to buy more from them: a bit like factoring.

Flooring was great for TRC, but not such an attractive business for the banks. It was extremely low margin for the banks, and we found ourselves regularly having to find a new flooring source as institutions would abandon the market in search of higher-margin opportunities. In spite of the upheaval and administrative work to establish a new flooring company, we were always able to do so, and that kept our business humming at a very low expense.

Suppliers who did not use flooring had to have terms and credit lines negotiated individually. Usually, we would have to balloon our credit lines during our peak season of May through September. K-12 schools would ramp purchases prior to their fiscal yearend in June and colleges would have a similar peak in August and September. These periods coincided with new semester enrollments and that is when schools would receive an influx of cash from tuition.

Suppliers liked that TRC was growing, but all profits were immediately reinvested back into the business. Company assets were not growing at nearly the same pace as our top line, aside from what was sitting in accounts receivable. Bootstrapped meant we did not have a bunch of investor's cash sitting in the bank providing a nice cushion to cover expenses. There were no retained earnings growing silently in an account. The pro was we were debt free and growing but there's always a yin to a yang. My yang was the comfort level of our vendors to continually extend additional credit with minimal collateral.

To supplement their increased risk exposure, suppliers would employ additional measures of collateral, which would include my own personal guarantee. That guarantee was a legal document stating that I would be personally responsible and bound to meet the debt obligations of TRC. If I wanted TRC to continue to grow, this was the risk I had to take. By taking out personal credit cards and personal guarantees, everything I and Lisa owned personally was exposed to TRC's obligations. Further, some suppliers wanted TRC to have an open bank line of credit that we could draw upon to meet payments in addition to any personal guarantees. In order to obtain the line of credit desired at our local bank I would have to use my house as collateral, which I did.

Through the success of my company I had just formulated the perfect storm for personal bankruptcy should something go terribly wrong. I could lose everything. To an outsider I would be the picture of the classic entrepreneurial risk taker—betting the farm on his venture. Those statements are true; however, I never had a concern of losing my house. I never gave it a thought. Was I just gutsy and fearless, risking everything I had along with being married with three kids? Although that perception is perhaps more admirable as courageous the truth is far more academic.

In reality, I simply managed risk. I understood how my customers paid; I knew how not to overextend myself and where I could cut back if needed to reduce expenses. I carried no debt, other than credit balances. I never paid interest fees to erode profit margins. I calculated every expense. I studied my financials to know my monthly income and expense and how to manage my cash float. I added employees and other expenses within a prescribed formula, never exceeding my benchmarks. The bottom line was that I was confident in my business and the control I had of it. External forces would not bankrupt me as I controlled the structure and level of risk. I knew if my doors had to close on any given day I could release my employees and pay all of my obligations based on my accounts receivable which I knew I could collect.

There were three primary factors that kept the credit flowing and growing for TRC: our balance sheet, my integrity, and TRC's relationship with suppliers. Flat out, our balance sheet had to be sound in order for our partners to continue taking our orders. I wouldn't say it was stellar as we were in a low-margin business, but it was respectable.

TRC's growth rate required even our distributors who had flooring options to increase their own credit lines with us. The financial guys at these outfits would pour through our financial statements using a time-tested method that would calculate ratios to determine the amount of credit they could supply based on our cash flow, outstanding accounts receivable, pending obligations, and assets. Our accounts receivable balance would stay fairly consistent and our customer base held a very low risk of default. However, we were now coming to them with larger and larger orders, some topping a million dollars. Because there was no credit limit set for us to do those types of orders, our vendors had to get creative and I had to sell—sell them.

Business and life is about relationships. If you can't communicate well with the people you are in business with or if you don't like that aspect of working with your vendors then get out or get someone in who can. To obtain additional credit and maintain the credit we had required selling and solid ethics. I had many conversations to explain to our partners our financial outlook and provide them with the certainty to extend additional credit. Selling involved addressing the individual with confidence and looking him straight in the eye so that he walked away feeling he was making the right decision.

It came down to trust and honesty. You can't fool people you work with over the long haul. Any deception no matter how small rises to the surface and will only come to bite you down the road. As the leader of the company, your actions are transparent and scrutinized and that should always be remembered. Whether it is with your vendors, customers, or your employees, you always have to instill a sense of confidence and model ethical behavior.

CHAPTER TWENTY-EIGHT
Ethics and Honesty

The topic of honesty and ethics may seem trite. Most new entrants to entrepreneurism don't give it a thought in their business development process because at the moment it is not a functional component. It is not a visible aspect of the company that has to be created in order to begin business. However, it is an important bullet point to detail in your own personal business plan. Introspection gives you time to pause and think of what type of person you are going to be when you are faced with ethical decisions. When you take a dry run in your mind and contemplate what could become defining moments in your journey, you will be better prepared when you abruptly face them.

You can find plenty of stories of CEOs, founders, and politicians going to jail over fraudulent business practices. Hopefully, your thought is that would never happen to you as that is certainly my mindset. What you don't anticipate is that temptation may come right to your doorstep in the form of a familiar face, as it did to me. A past associate from Educational Resources called me one day asking if I would be interested in a cooperative advertising deal. What was instantly confusing was that he was now with a competing reseller. I agreed to meet with him at my office to hear his proposal.

His proposition was for TRC to include his company's advertisements in our daily customer shipments as a box stuffer. We would "stuff" a paper flyer in the box going to our customer and in exchange his company would pay us. This was a common practice; however, you never stuffed a competitor's flyer in your own boxes—it doesn't make sense. The caveat was that instead of paying TRC cash his company would pay us in product, which again was somewhat customary. He suggested that I select around $10,000 worth of computers, printers, or whatever I wanted that his company sold in exchange for this service. This marketing method was legal and prevalent in the industry, but it made no sense to do it with a competitor. I didn't get it.

To his dismay, my past coworker had to be blunt and explain that I didn't have to actually put the flyers in the boxes. I could throw them in the trash as far as he was concerned. In fact, the flyers never needed to be printed. His plan, as he explained, was for me to take $10,000 worth of his company's product for this bogus service but to send him an invoice for $20,000. Guess who was getting the additional $10,000 worth of product? This guy was starting a business of his own on the side, and he wanted computer equipment for his own enterprise. Since he was an executive with this reseller, he could submit the paperwork without anyone ever questioning. Now I got it!

This scheme would be easy to pull off, and no one would ever find out. His company was very large, and they were doing deals like this all the time. In addition, he was the one in charge of the program. Nothing could point back to me because I could just say I put the fliers in our customer's boxes per the agreement. If this guy skimmed product off the top, it wasn't my problem. Well, I could have gone through with it and received a windfall of much needed computer equipment. Instead, I threw him out, and told him to stay the hell away from my company.

Consideration of ethics is not exclusively self reflective; you need to consider how you will address and prevent these potential issues with employees, vendors, and customers. Most likely, you will be faced with some type of fraud or theft during the term of your business—in fact, I guarantee it. Attacks on your company may come from outside sources such as the Internet, but most fraud develops from within. The best prevention is to remove temptation and install checks and balances into the processes surrounding your most sensitive assets: your cash and your merchandise. Pay special attention to areas such as check processing, petty cash, payroll processing, expense reimbursements, and invoicing. Thinking through policies and procedures and understanding those tasks upfront will decrease opportunities for fraudulent behavior.

Oftentimes the thief is a long-term, trusted employee. During my time at Educational Resources two major incidents of theft emerged. One was from a woman in accounting who was writing checks to herself rather than vendors and another was an actual criminal ring of thieves working in the warehouse. They would create false customer orders and ship product to acquaintances. At TRC, we lost more than $40,000 to a fraudulent customer operating out of Miami and Puerto Rico who was using quick mail shops to receive product under granted credit terms leaving no traceable address. Even though we found the guy's real name and a business he actively promoted on the Internet, I could not get the FBI to take any action. They were too overloaded with other fraud cases. There were things I wanted to do on my own, but the prospect of ending up in a Puerto Rican jail was not that enticing.

Do not be naive in believing fraud will not intrude your business, and do not be foolish by neglecting to establish preventive measures to detract and detect it. I recall a school teacher coming to a conference where TRC was an exhibitor. This woman, along with her 10-year-old child, selected several items and was ready to pay by check. My first concern was raised in reviewing her check. Her check was drawn on an out-of-state bank and contained no address or phone number. For identification she provided a state ID card rather than a driver's license. All of these are glaring signs of a check ready to bounce up in your face. When I made the decision not to accept her check and deny the sale, she simply walked away without saying a word. It made a lasting impression on me. Here was an educator with her young daughter and she was knowingly and deliberately committing premeditated fraud.

As most of you know, fraud grows deeper and more sophisticated as you move to the Web. In the early days of TRC, which were the early days of the Internet, we were getting weekly attempts at online fraud through our e-commerce mechanisms. Today, those attacks are hourly in most big online firms. Such prevalence reinforces the need to incorporate ethical practices into the business plan and culture of your company and review them regularly.

CHAPTER TWENTY-NINE
Selling

"I wanted to be an editor or a journalist, I wasn't really interested in being an entrepreneur, but I soon found I had to become an entrepreneur in order to keep my magazine going."
—Sir Richard Branson

I never set out to be in sales; in fact, I was rather deliberate in my career to avoid it. There was some sort of preconceived notion in my head that I would be in management and that somehow was the superior position to hold in business. It turns out we're all in sales from the day we go on our first interview selling ourselves. What greater product is there to represent? Regardless of your position, you are, or should be, continually selling yourself to your boss, your peers, and your stakeholders. A bit opposite of Sir Richard Branson's statement above is that I wanted to be an entrepreneur. My desire early on was entrepreneurship and that somehow did not equate to sales in my head— someone else would do that. However, from the beginning of formulating TRC all the way through to my exit, I found I had to sell, and I discovered that I really liked it. It turns out selling and entrepreneurship is practically synonymous.

Selling is not just about ringing up a product sale at the register. At its highest form sales is about strategy, influencing, and positioning. It requires some of the greatest abilities of an individual to sell effectively. We've learned that in the idea phase the entrepreneur sells his idea to those who will listen to gain feedback and validity. At startup he then sells potential investors, creditors, employees, vendors, and prospective customers on the virtues of the company. All the while these stakeholders are taking stock of the entrepreneur for validation and confirmation of the enterprise's value. As running is the longest duration of the entrepreneurial journey, the entrepreneur will have the greatest opportunity to sell himself, his product, and his firm to his ever-expanding base of stakeholders. Everything the entrepreneur does from idea to exit involves selling skills that strategize, influence, and position the company.

A sales career is one of the greatest professions one can pursue in business. Not job, but career. Professional salesmen and women utilize some of the greatest and widest skill sets that include reading comprehension, writing, speaking, listening, observing, presenting, organization, mathematics, body language, and psychology. The simultaneous application of these talents into a well-positioned strategy can provide great professional rewards both financially and in accomplishment.

For all this distinction, Sales can often be the most under-appreciated department in a company. It most certainly has to be one of the most important components in almost any organization as sales representatives are the closest link to the customer. Yet, all too often I hear departments providing operational support complain, "Sales is bunch of prima donnas," "Sales gets this…Sales gets that." Well you're damn right! In my book, Sales is on the top of the pyramid and all other aspects of the company, including the executive branch, exist to support the efforts of Sales.

Sales is the group that intimately delivers the company's mission to the customer. Sales fuels R&D and all other aspects of the organization. If not appreciated, the sales effort can be strained and lack efficiency. The sales staff can easily get distracted and pulled off task. How often do you hear, "give it back to the account manager, after all, he's getting paid on it"? This mindset can permeate, create a condoning culture of push-back and ultimately departmental silos which further clogs and slows the system. The organization may seem to be running great at 10 percent annual growth but perhaps it could be at 15 percent if Sales were fully appreciated and understood. I'm a great protector of sales teams, as all too often I've seen organizations unconsciously erect barriers to sales efforts and ignore the front-line reconnaissance that only sales representatives can deliver.

I've practiced sales for many years and studied various methodologies of best practice. Scaling involves sales and I've talked about methods to scale. But what about a method to sell? Volumes have been written on selling, but I learned something about sales in training my sales teams that breaks down selling to its most basic principle.

I'm going to introduce my Sales Maxim, which explains the nucleus of any type of sale. Like the E-Formula, the Sales Maxim practically serves as a mathematical formula to represent the lowest common denominator for success in all sales-related situations. When I studied sales representatives who performed well to those who were struggling, I could always identify the root of their success or failure to this maxim.

The Sales Maxim

The Sales Maxim is a simple structure by design because it serves as the rudimentary formula for success valid for any sales situation. It does not matter what you sell, be it product or service, this maxim holds true. The maxim plays a role beyond physical selling as it applies to any type of strategy, influence, or positioning which can include negotiations, promotions, barter, and conflict resolution.

Purpose of the Maxim – Why use it?

Remember, just about everything the entrepreneur does involves selling. By understanding that fact and applying the Sales Maxim to each situation, the entrepreneur will improve successful outcomes. The Sales Maxim is not just for entrepreneurs; it was originally formulated to assist in training new account managers. The focus is on the individual as opposed to the organization and its purpose is relevant to all. Companies spend a great deal of effort crafting techniques for account management, territory planning, and compensation, which takes into consideration the Sales Maxim. However, time and again I have seen a percentage of account managers at small and large corporations fail at the fundamentals of selling—this includes supposed top performers too.

In all types and levels of sports, training is centered on fundamentals. Everything else can be built off of that foundation. The same is true of sales. Companies may do a great job on boarding, training, and development of new account managers. Yet new hires are quickly inundated with information when they start with a company. The fundamentals get lost in the sea of information being presented around CRM and ERP systems, internal procedures, communication tools, and methodologies. Seasoned account managers, often those with assigned and mature accounts, can become complacent in practicing their skills and fundamentals.

When a new account manager is turned over to the sales manager there is a sense of urgency to get the recruit into the field selling. This is when one of three things happens; they either do well, they take time to ramp up, or they struggle. My goal of understanding the Sales Maxim was to improve on the later two outcomes. I found hires that were new to sales were accustomed to classroom learning for the most part and applying selling skills was a new world. Seasoned sales professionals who ramped slow or struggled often had forgotten the fundamentals.

New account managers typically won't tell their manager why they are not successful because they either don't understand the underlying reason or they are embarrassed feeling pressure that "they should know this by now" based on the training received. Their struggle can often be pinned to their confidence to engage a customer and represent the product. Management equates this as a bad hire—the person should not be in sales. That may be true, but it also may be that they lack understanding of the maxim and the sales manager does not necessarily keep this fundamental top of mind either. I am convinced more account managers can ramp faster, be more effective, and improve attrition by incorporating the Sales Maxim on a daily basis. So let's take a look at it.

> **Sales = Confidence**
> **Confidence = Knowledge**
> **Knowledge = Customer and Product**

Sales = Confidence

Every book and every manager will tell a salesman that he has to be confident when selling, but what does that mean? What is confidence to a salesman? It means he or she can pick up the phone to make the cold calls, knock on doors, or network to establish relationships. It entails pushing oneself into uncomfortable and unpredictable situations. It involves talking in detail about a specific topic to a specific person. It means taking chances.

Will purchase orders then shower the salesman with the most confidence? Confidence in one's self is important, but is irrelevant alone in the sales process. Confidence may conjure images of the stereotypical slick-haired salesman that talks loud, swaggers when he walks, and wears an open shirt, and gold neck chain. Confidence has nothing to do with having an attitude or a false personification of one's abilities.

Having a belief in one's ability to respond to the outcomes of a situation demonstrates self confidence and yields a greater likelihood to succeed in those situations. How does one achieve this type of confidence? It's simple: confidence in just about anything is derived from knowledge. By achieving a level of superior knowledge and understanding, a salesman can enter any related situation with conviction to address all potential outcomes.

Confidence = Knowledge

Knowledge instills confidence. So much focus is applied to being confident with little direction given on how to gain it. A well-trained salesman that is knowledgeable will gain confidence. He does not have to pump himself up to be confident because he will be naturally through the mastery of his content. Confidence is the number one performance accelerator or the primary performance killer of any salesman, or employee for that matter. The costs related to turnover and poor performance of account managers can often be traced back to knowledge gaps.

The key to creating a great salesman is not to fixate on confidence building but in knowledge building. We've recognized this for some time and that is why companies invest so much in training and development. But I'm not sure many have threaded together the psychological correlation and affect that knowledge has to confidence in the sales maxim, and then manage with that in mind.

Knowledge is gained through experience and education. The Wikipedia entry on knowledge states, "The term knowledge is also used to mean the confident understanding of a subject with the ability to use it for a specific purpose if appropriate." That really describes sales to a tee.

Knowledge itself is rather broad and framing a definition in the context of sales is required to complete our understanding of the Sales Maxim.

Knowledge = Customer and Product

Knowledge has two universal components related to the Sales Maxim and they are customer and product knowledge. This may seem unusually simple, but I like to think of it as simply elegant. When a salesman understands to a great depth the product that he is selling and the customer who is buying it, only then will he be confident to walk into any situation and be able to sell effectively. He will be able to face any situation without breaking a sweat and do it successfully with his own style and personality.

I hired many sales representatives at TRC and subsequently had to let some of them go. The process of training, mentoring, and managing my sales team and the sales process I developed is how I established the Sales Maxim. I learned that most often when sales representatives were not working out it could rapidly be boiled down to a debilitating lack of product and/or customer knowledge.

The Sales Maxim is important to understand for both management and the sales representative as it serves to direct self assessment and improvement. Often a struggling sales representative will not be able to articulate why he is failing and the reasons may not be apparent to management either. Understanding that most performance gaps or deficiencies can be linked to either the product or the customer component will expedite corrective action for both. People naturally want to succeed in their position. When their confidence is eroded they are likely to spiral downward or out of the organization if management is not acutely able to dissect the cause. Identifying product or customer deficiencies is like a revelation that provides direction and focus. Senior account managers who either start losing deals or have flat performance may need to be reminded of the fundamentals as well. Too much latitude can be given to the "proven" representative but, like all things, even the pros need refresher courses.

The depth and focus of product and customer knowledge will vary and is customized to every company; however, the following are some illustrative points for consideration.

Product Knowledge

Features & Function
- Understand what problem the product solves
- Understand what need the product answers

Comparison/Differentiation
- Understand the product's strengths and weaknesses alone and in relation to competitors
- Understand the competition's strengths and how to minimize them in the eyes of the customer
- Understand the competition's weaknesses and how to exploit them in the eyes of the customer

Production & Support
- Understand how the product is it made, delivered, and supported by the company
- Understand how the customer is involved with your product from purchase to delivery, to deployment, and through its life cycle

Position
- Understand what opportunities your product provides the customer

- Understand the threats your product removes for the customer
- Understand why customers don't buy your product or service

Benefits

- Understand the pain points your product resolves or may create for the customer
- Understand how your product helps your customer make or save money, or if it is an expense

Customer Knowledge

Position

- Understand your customer's influencers and decision makers
- Understand what motivates the buyer
- Understand what their job is and how they do it
- Understand who the ultimate end user is
- Understand the type of customer you are engaging

A sterile method of customer profiling is to divide customers into quadrants ranging from high-profit and low-resource usage to low-profit and high-resource usage, with high-profit, low-resource customers being the best. This ideal model allows managers to focus on their best customers while potentially firing their worst. The component least considered in this model is the degree of influence exerted by any given customer. The definition of influence is unique to each firm and how they view their customers. A customer can have a degree of influence within their organization, community, or industry.

Influence is when a customer can be beneficial in promoting or advocating for the firm that they purchase goods and services from. They may recommend new customers to the firm, encourage vendors to partner with the firm, direct funding to the firm, or serve as a promotional platform for the firm. When a customer is viewed as influential they tend to draw more resources from the firm. The entrepreneur must be acutely aware of this gravitational pull of resources to the influential customer to determine the return on investment for those resources. He must also assess if the customer is truly influential or is simply perceived as such by the firm.

A false sense of influence is created within the firm by its management who also controls resource allocation. The title of influencer may be granted simply through the notion that the "customer is always right," regardless if the customer is low-profit, low-revenue, and extremely demanding in the amount of resources required to service it. They may yield no influence in terms of attracting new customers, suppliers, partners, or funding. However, management may adopt a one-size-fits-all mentality and fear losing even the worst customer. As a result, limited firm resources are pulled from the entire customer pool, improperly allocating more to the false influencer and less to true influencers and high-profit customers.

High profile customers like Fortune 500 companies are often coveted as influential to smaller firms because of their utility as being named as a customer or the large revenue they may bring to the firm. However, they may be low-profit customers and require an inordinate amount of resources to satisfy. If their influential power as a customer does not bring in other favorable results in proportion to the resources they exert then they may not be as valuable an influencer as the firm perceived.

Resources throughout the firm are devoted to all customers. Ideally, resources are allocated based on the systematic nature of the firm. As a simple example, if one account manager can handle one million worth of revenue or profit then you can scale additional representatives according to that model. The degree of influence of the customer is irrelevant in this quantitative comparison. However, business is not so simple. Customers have the ability to skew resources. Ever hear of the squeaky wheel? Most often the squeaky wheel is a low-volume, low-profit customer that demands high maintenance, thus pulling firm resources from all other customers. This inappropriate leaching of resources can go on undetected and unappreciated by management for some time and may get progressively worse. Entrepreneurs and managers need to be aware of the makeup of their customers and their effective degree of influence and corresponding allocation of resources. Failure to appropriate resources to the best and truly influential customer segments will result in profitable customers leaving your firm, often unnoticed until it is too late to recover them.

Function
- Understand the purpose your customer serves to their customers
- Understand why your customer exists
- Understand the nuances of your customer's market segment

Utility
- Understand why your customer would want your product
- Understand how the customer will use your product
- Understand why your customer uses competitive products

Structure
- Understand the customer's decision and authorization process

- Understand the customer's buying procedures
- Understand the customer's financing
- Understand the closing cycle and how to influence it

Information about the product and the customer may change over time and should be continually monitored. This is not only to breed successful sales representatives but to maintain product development, positioning, and further innovation. This knowledge assessment forms the basis of launching a new business as well as maintaining an existing one. Use the Sales Maxim when writing your business plan, pitching your company for funding, negotiating terms with suppliers, hiring employees, or securing a lease. It can be used for anything by thoughtfully putting yourself in the customer's shoes and mastering the role of buyer and seller. The maxim helps to differentiate your firm and ultimately how to maximize its value.

Try the Impossible Again

Shortly before the dot com bubble burst, I was trying to come up with a way to sell Microsoft Select licensing. I obtained this software license authorization for my former employer, now competitor, and that gave them along with the other 19 Microsoft-designated Large Account Resellers (LAR) in the country a significant competitive advantage. TRC needed to sell this product, and I was eventually able to discover a back door to make that happen. I partnered with an existing LAR who had no focus on education. Basically, TRC would sell the Select licenses to our customers as a broker at a marked-up price. The schools would make their purchase orders out to the LAR, in care of TRC, and the LAR would fulfill the order. Aside from a variety of operational issues on the LAR's side, this worked well. The ability to sell Select created incremental revenue and the offering was getting us exposed to a completely different level of sales traditionally reserved for the biggest dealers in the country who were LAR authorized.

Since our pricing to the customer was higher due to the markup, we had to be able to provide more value to our customers than anyone else. This led to a series of innovations in how TRC addressed procurement, fulfillment, compliancy, and the administration of volume software licensing for our customer. We exposed all of the weaknesses and pain points associated with those four key components of software licensing that the other LARs tended to ignore. Value-added services and features were developed on our Web site and in our sales and customer service processes, which resonated with the licensing administrator who was our customer.

As I architected TRC's new Web site, I incorporated these customer needs and our unique answers into a functional response. Integrating the Web site into our ERP system allowed us to do some pretty amazing things related to enterprise software licensing. Volume software licensing was and still is complicated as every publisher has a different methodology for providing volume discounts on their licenses, license maintenance, and license upgrades—not to mention the variations of licensing options like annuity, perpetual, and concurrent.

What compounded confusion was the different part numbers or SKUs established for corporate, government, and education pricing. All of our competitors built systems that were essentially non-dynamic catalogs. In short, the SKUs were input into the ERP system and that's what was shown on the Web site. If a customer searched for Adobe Photoshop in licensing they would get hundreds of SKUs back as search results. This made buying volume software online virtually impossible. Our competitors viewed this as the way it had to be and it was the customer's problem not theirs. They were right; it was the customer's problem.

The system I designed at TRC started at the SKU and customer experience level. The publisher SKUs would be categorized by TRC in a hierarchical fashion that the user could make increasingly more granular decisions based on their criteria. Further, the system was intuitive by recognizing a user at login and immediately showing them the applicable SKUs based on past purchase history which was tied to a specific software agreement or customer type. Our system would know, for instance, that a customer was an academic Adobe CLP, level-C customer and we would only show them those applicable SKUs. If they searched for Adobe Photoshop we would return only the SKUs related to their academic CLP level C contract, not government or commercial. Not only did this help our customers but it improved the speed and accuracy of our own sales team to generate quotes and process orders.

The system went even further by delivering the assigned serial number to the end user automatically and generated the correct CLP level-C contract number on the TRC purchase order to the distributor, which was an operational requirement. TRC had not only automated the complicated volume software license process but greatly enhanced the user experience and made online volume software license purchasing a reality. All the critics saying that allowing customers to buy volume software licensing online was a recipe for disaster because of the amount of possible errors drove me to create our system.

Customers wanted to buy online, but the dealer channel just wasn't making it easy for them. The problem didn't fit into the dealer's established system which was working fine for them. All of my developments were created from user feedback and by studying the common recurring errors caused by this inefficient system. I listened to the complaints from our sales team, reviewed the return reports, and spoke to our customers for the answers.

Our system reduced errors by 90 percent and decreased the time to process an order by more than 70 percent. I went on to make further enhancements, constantly refining and adding new features based on the user experience.

This innovation became our competitive advantage in the marketplace. The focus was not on price, but on how our system could eliminate the host of headaches caused by the complicated and changing world of volume software licensing. Complaints are to be celebrated as they are the windows to new opportunities. By adding Microsoft licensing to our new Web engine, we were attracting an entirely new type of customer. The large public research institutions, which we rarely did business with, were now awarding TRC their request for proposals (RFP) for volume software licensing. To our humble satisfaction, we won the University of California System's RFP for not only their Microsoft, but five other popular publishers as well. We were the clear underdog, but I was confident our proposal was far superior to anyone else responding and a smart customer would choose TRC. The contract would be a multi-million dollar award that locked us in for two years serving all nine campus locations.

It was now time for me to make a case to Microsoft to become a LAR. I had done the impossible once with Educational Resources, could it really be done again with another reseller?

CHAPTER THIRTY
Innovation

"INNOVATION is the specific tool of entrepreneurs, the means by which they exploit change as an opportunity for a different business or a different service. It is capable of being presented as a discipline, capable of being learned, capable of being practiced. Entrepreneurs need to search purposefully for the sources of innovation, the changes and their symptoms that indicate opportunities for successful innovation. And they need to know and to apply the principles of successful innovation."
—Peter F. Drucker

It should be clear by now that innovation is the core nuclei of the entrepreneur. It is what differentiates him from all others. Innovation is the first key element in the original business I.D.E.A. that is accompanied by desire, effort, and ability. Entrepreneurs start up businesses based on that innovation and must rapidly turn their focus to running the business and scaling its growth. It is at this period of running the business where a focus must remain on innovation, and it must transcend from being solely the entrepreneur's responsibility. Maintaining and fostering an innovative environment becomes a primary responsibility of the entrepreneur during this phase of business. Peter Drucker says, "Entrepreneurs need to search purposefully for the sources of innovation" and in most cases those sources will be his employees.

The Role of the Entrepreneur is to Innovate

Innovation defines an entrepreneur. Steve Jobs said, "Innovation is what distinguishes between a leader and a follower" and this statement has profound organizational significance. The workplace structure creates jobs, which are a series of tasks. The organization enforces and rewards employees to complete their tasks because the tasks make up the sum of the whole, which creates the predictable outcome. Organizations are built to preserve the predictability of the task completed by the worker. The challenge for the entrepreneur in the running stage of his business is to create an environment that preserves the tasks, but also encourages creative thinking for improvement and to challenge the established process to exploit improvement.

As the organization grows, the entrepreneur needs to understand that new sources of innovation are lying dormant within the company. The need to innovate is now becoming a responsibility to foster innovation from employees at all levels of the company. Too many organizations fail to recognize their primary source of innovation or how to harness it. The tool used to mine innovation is listening. The entrepreneur and trained receivers of innovation must be good listeners who actively listen for problems, pain points, concerns, requests, and reasons for satisfaction from both customers and employees. An employee may not hand you the blueprint of the next innovation, but he will purposely or inadvertently discuss it and it is your job and the job of trained receivers within your company to pick up on these opportunities to innovate.

Types of Innovation

Somewhat correlated to the two types of entrepreneurs—innovative and replicative—there are two types of innovations dubbed blue-sky and integrative/transformative. Blue-sky innovations closely align with the innovative type of entrepreneur in that they are revolutionary or radical in scope. These innovations transform and create industries and extend the economy's efficiency to produce more with the same or fewer resources. Such innovations literally come from the test tube. High technology discoveries created by scientists or inventors and supported by the research community are responsible for most blue-sky innovations.

The majority of innovations great and small are the integrative/transformative type created primarily from a replicative entrepreneur. These are not exclusive relationships between entrepreneur type and innovation type as entrepreneurs are not limited to single innovative breakthroughs. Integrative innovations meld into existing technologies, companies, processes, and products. A term coined by Henry Chesbrough, a professor at the University of California at Berkeley, is Open Innovation. The concept draws on input and participation of innovation development from sources outside of the company. To expedite a means, firms may want to license existing technologies, patents, and form joint ventures or create spin-offs to foster new innovation. In a simple form of open innovation, User innovation relies on end user inspired innovation—feedback, comments, and suggestions—to adapt or improve an existing innovation.

What's great about innovation is that it does not necessarily have to be derived as a novel idea or start out as its final iteration. Many successful businesses and innovations are derivatives of existing products, services, or models. The innovation of these businesses is in altering the way they address their consumer's needs. Great examples of this are Southwest Airlines, Jet Blue Airlines, Starbucks, and Google.

Transformative innovations become successful after they morph into their final form. The innovator may have had a completely different plan for his product, but he was forced to alter it after the target market rejected his offering. The story of Federal Express founded by Fred Smith is such an example. While attending Yale University in 1962 Smith wrote an economics paper outlining a new concept in overnight delivery. It wasn't until after his service in the Marine Corp that Smith started Federal Express in 1971. His original intention was to provide overnight delivery for the Federal Reserve System. However, the Federal Reserve was not interested, and Smith had to find a new market for his concept. He decided to think bigger and expanded his focus to the entire business market.

You don't have to invent the next light bulb to be a great innovator; you just need to spark an idea that serves an undeveloped need. Innovation seems easier and more achievable when looked at from this perspective. You can still hit a home run just by keeping the ball in the park. Innovation can be taught—it's in all of us. Psychology studies show how humans as well as animals innovate to solve problems. Many of us do it every day, only in small measurements and outcomes.

Entrepreneurs excel and seek out innovation as a means to differentiate. They innovate not only in the initial conception of their business, but more importantly throughout their control and direction of the company. The entrepreneur has to continually improve on what are mostly new and untested processes. He has created something new and he must frequently assess, measure, evaluate, and adjust.

I loved to innovate and change at TRC. I always preached to my team our need to regularly change to grow and survive. People that worked for me either got excited about the prospect of continual change or were immobilized by it. If you are immobilized then you are ineffective; if you are ineffective you are a drain on resources and progress— you had to go. Working directly for or in an entrepreneur's company is not a walk in the park. You either fit or you don't. There is not much middle ground unless you are in a non-critical role. Even in those seemingly low-profile positions, the entrepreneur will uncover ways to enhance your responsibility and improve your ROI.

The amount of change involved in a start-up is the primary cause for some to become immobilized. Seasoned corporate workers are used to environments where the business is sustainable and the job requirement is to complete tasks in a prescribed manner. However, start-ups require constant self reflection and critique to improve. The environment changes rapidly and the individual needs to change with it. Some just don't like to be on that type of rollercoaster. They are too fixed on ensuring things happen the same way rather than how they can be changed for the better.

Likewise, it can be difficult for an employer to recognize an innovator, and in some cases know how to use that resource to the firm's benefit. In the eyes of a manager, the innovator is there to do a job. Jobs are predefined and have descriptions. They limit innovation, because in theory, the job has been defined and needs no further refinement. This runs counter to quality programs that preach continual improvement I know, but it is true. The entrepreneur who brings up ideas and suggestions can be viewed as wandering, unable to stay on task like a child with attention deficit.

Innovators can get lost in an organization that does not provide the structure to organically grow innovation. Because job descriptions are well-defined, they condition employees to focus on the task at hand. Managers unconsciously don't come to expect "thinking" from their employees; they want repetitive and predictable performance. The organization itself resists innovation unwittingly.

To compensate for this organizational deficiency, managers will hold off-site seminars and breakaways to innovate. These are well intentioned and in many cases productive meetings. However, innovation is timely and perishable. If ideas are not harnessed, reviewed, and acted upon quickly they fade away. A delicate balance of innovative requirements and encouragement needs to be incorporated into job descriptions, manager's objectives, and top executives' receptiveness. It can't wait for an annual planning meeting—the competition won't allow it.

The Need for Innovation

Innovative firms are valuable to our economy because they often grow rapidly in order to support their innovation and the consumer demand requesting it. These firms help expand economies because they hire more, thus generating more output and supporting a higher standard of living for their employees and the customers buying their product or service.

The need for innovation should be obvious to business owners and managers alike, yet it can easily slip out of focus when daily life involves customer concerns, employee matters, cash flow, production schedules, and just keeping up with email. It is the entrepreneur's responsibility to ensure innovation stays near the top of the organization's priority list. Innovation will be the primary driver of the company's success and growth. It will differentiate from competitors, create intellectual property, establish closer customer relationships, improve efficiencies, eliminate stakeholder pain points, and enrich employee satisfaction. I never asked myself how I could get our sales to increase. Instead I strained to think how I could; do things differently, do things better, cut costs, speed delivery, enhance the customer experience. All of these things led to innovation, which resulted in increased sales.

Possibly the most important purpose for innovation is in driving change. Change is the one constant companion to the entrepreneur. Understanding change and its significance is a vital aspect to the study of innovation.

A Rare Opportunity

"When written in Chinese, the word "crisis" is composed of two characters-one represents danger, and the other represents opportunity."—John Fitzgerald Kennedy

In 2001 and 2002, TRC earned a rank on *INC 500* magazine's fastest growing company list for achieving 1356 percent and 582 percent growth in those respective reporting years. What a thrill it was to make the listing that first year, being ranked 210 out of 500 and seeing our company named in the magazine. Coincidentally this represented the end of the dot com era, which spanned from TRC's inception in 1995 through 2001. It was sort of sweet vindication that real business models prevailed over the upside down ones that seemed to have threatened us.

Things were going great in 2001 as we continued to enjoy year over year double digit growth and expansion. We moved into more office space in "Ladi Land" and had more than tripled our square footage since we signed the lease in 1997. Our employee head count was rising and TRC became well established as one of the dominant educational resellers in the nation. We had come to be respected and feared by our competition, loved by our customers, and embraced by our suppliers.

I was on my way to work unusually late one morning in the early fall of 2001, and as usual was listening to national public radio (NPR) when they reported that a plane had hit the World Trade Center in New York. Few details were available. Thoughts of a stray Cessna came to mind and I really did not give it too much thought, other than anticipated interesting viewing on the evening news later that night.

As my brief commute drew to an end, the reports were

becoming more detailed and utterly unbelievable. Surprisingly, no one had heard about what was unfolding on the East coast. . As a company, we all moved to huddle around the company television to understand exactly what was taking place.

It was a surreal experience watching what would be one of the most ghastly human activated events in American history unfolding before us. Our minds were lagging grossly behind in comprehension of the severity and depth of impact this action would have. As the second plane hit and the towers burned, reports of additional hijackings surfaced and I felt I had to play manager and control the situation, at least within TRC. I asked people to return to their desks and take alternating shifts watching the news so that we could remain somewhat productive. I regret that decision. I should have allowed everyone to watch or even to go home if they wished. I just didn't grasp what was happening and what to do at TRC.

By the time it was over I think we all felt as if we were hit in the gut and left aching for air. Realizing this was a terrorist action oddly did not terrorize me or frighten me.. I had more of a sense of tragic and wasteful loss and anger. By day's end, I had time to reflect and that's when I felt a strange sense of optimism. I felt America just received a new-found power that would manifest itself in how we would respond to this horrific event.

America was now the victim displayed on screens across the globe. Where some nations may have historically viewed the US superpower as an aggressor and possibly even a bully, exerting influence and doctrines around the world, now we were unjustifiably attacked in a horrible and inhumane manner which touched all. Certainly we had been assailed before in our embassies, the Trade Center in 1993, and the U.S.S. Cole, but profoundly this was different. On this day everyone in the world watching personally experienced this violent aggression and it was moving. The result of the event would demonstrate how violence was not effective in rallying a cause. As successful and celebrated the 911 attacks may have been in the jihadist community, they backfired by immediately serving to polarize world support behind the US. Sympathy from some of our most contentious protagonist nations came pouring in immediately.

The balance and support the US had always sought to counter this growing movement of hatred was now at an all-time high and nearly universal. In the days and weeks following September 11, the U.S. was given the opportunity to request the action and support of virtually any and all nations in the world to combine to take global action against terrorism.

I will not question the response and actions of the US administration following 911. I respect everyone who had to serve during that time and make difficult and unprecedented decisions. It would not be respectful of the victims of 911 and the many brave servicemen, journalists, contractors, and civilians who have died in subsequent wars and actions taken in response. Further, there is a tremendous amount of information that is not disclosed to the public, for very good reasons, which may explain the reasoning for the direction that the US took in the proceeding weeks, months, and years after that dreadful day. However, I personally believe that the US failed to harness the full potential of the opportunity that the 911 situation provided. The possibility of unprecedented world collaboration that the terrorists inadvertently provided would be a pinnacle moment in human history.

An optimist sees an opportunity in every calamity; a pessimist sees a calamity in every opportunity.—Winston Churchill

I saw an America being handed an opportunity that could dwarf in comparison the brutal act that was forced upon it. I saw an opportunity where for the first time America could rally the entire world behind it. I think we failed to recognize that this was not an attack on New York but an attack on the world. The US gained world sentiment and support lining up to fight global terrorism. They needed leadership, an idea, and a plan.

The *Season of Life* by Jeffrey Marx, the story of former NFL defensive lineman Joe Ehrmann who founded Building Men and Women for Others, had an interesting passage on 911. Marx discusses how Joe Ehrmann recites his checklist in response to 911 that is applicable for anyone in hard times. It asks in such challenging times how will we respond. What will we do? How will we act? And in making those decisions will we lose our integrity? Will we lose our faith? Will we lose our humanity? We know our leaders asked "how will we respond," but did they ask the later questions?

Did we need entrepreneurs in the government after 911? Could new innovative tactics been used that would have: been more effective, would have captured Bin Laden, would have toppled evil regimes, and would have done so with less violence? What we did learn was that violence was not effective against the US and, therefore, why would we think it would be effective against our enemies? Sure I wanted bullets to fly at the bad guys, but that was an emotional response. Innovation means a new way of doing something. It is innovation which fuels the creative actions of entrepreneurs to see opportunity where others do not and to activate a response when both the situation and opportunity presents itself. The E-Formula can be applied to anything. Recognizing the formula exists and having the right resources available to respond to it, is the sign of truly great leadership.

CHAPTER THIRTY-ONE
Cha- Cha- Changes

Change is the only constant with a new business and it should be a purposeful constant factor for a mature business as well. A new business will change at a far greater rate than an existing business, and that change will take place across all segments of the business. It's only logical that as a company grows from nothing to something it will outgrow many of its original policies and procedures. Children are the perfect analogy to a growing business. As they grow, children need new clothes and shoes. Their bed and other furniture change. Their toys change, their food, the games they play; their independence grows, their interests evolve, their speech improves—you get the point.

The same holds true with your business as it grows. Many entrepreneurs start their companies like parents: highly involved in all aspects of the operation, knowing every aspect intimately, involved in each component's conception and creation. Then, by necessity, they let go more and more, trusting aspects of its growth to others—employees—all the while adapting, changing, and reinventing the business in response to environmental cues. These cues stem from suppliers, customers, the economy, employees, partners, personal aspects, funding, good fortune, bad fortune.

Change is best when it is the result of strategy that involves interpreting environmental factors and making decisions. A fundamental pillar of an entrepreneur that separates him from a manager is that a higher proportion of an entrepreneur's strategies become innovations for the enterprise, while manager's strategies tend to be more operational or logistically oriented within their span of control. Managers execute strategy while entrepreneurs create strategy. Both are equally important and necessary and both define the roles each individual plays within the enterprise.

If an entrepreneur's strategies become overtly or exclusively focused on the managerial, he runs the risk of sustaining a business rather than growing it. He takes on the role his management team should be tasked with. This starts to define the overbearing and suffocating entrepreneur. This is the one who fails to grow because he cannot delegate.

The entrepreneur whose strategies become weighted toward managerial aspects also inadvertently devalues his company by failing to innovate. Often without any awareness, an entrepreneur can get polarized in supervising business components. The lack of innovation equates to fewer value adds, fewer intellectual property offerings, and other differentiating elements forcing the firm to respond to change rather than drive change.

What Drives Change?

"Without change there is no innovation, creativity, or incentive for improvement. Those who initiate change will have a better opportunity to manage the change that is inevitable."—William Pollard

In business you drive change or change drives you. William Pollard's quote sums it up nicely. Pollard was twice CEO of The ServiceMaster Company and is currently Chairman of the Board. He has authored *The Soul of the Firm* and has contributed to several other publications. His statement demonstrates the significance of innovation in firms of all shapes and sizes, and how he who controls change holds the upper hand to the competition. The key is in positioning change.

Is change driving you or are you driving change? Change is a variable that at times you will control and at other times it will control you. Inevitably, most firms will be on both sides of the sword and can use each to their advantage, only if they are prepared to do so.

Change Drives You

Change that drives you creates what I call "scramble innovation," which is responsive and reactionary to the change at hand. Immediately you are a step behind the driver of change, which may be a competitor, customer, regulation, supplier, or any other stakeholder or environmental cue. You find that you have to scramble to respond or catch up. This is not entirely negative in that you have the opportunity to learn from the leader's mistakes or other's iterations. You have the opportunity to respond in an even wiser manner. The change may force your organization to perform better, cut costs, or improve efficiencies.

However, as this change is reactionary, it is often unplanned and can become a subsequent drain on resources. You don't want to be the guy looking over his shoulder all the time. It has been said that when faced with change, people either fight it, ignore it, or embrace it (that is, if they even recognize it). You'll notice that all of these are reactionary responses. Company size has often been an Achilles heel to change response and I have found larger companies in particular fall into the following change traps:

1. Helloooo. Is anybody there?

The rank and file on the front lines is one of the greatest assets to a company in being receptive to potential change. They hear and see what works well and what needs improvement. They can see change early on but they may fail to have a voice within the company to get people to listen, or they may get so fed up with trying to sound an alarm that they remain silent. If people are not measured, incentivized, or given recognition to innovate, they won't; they'll just stay quiet.

2. This is the way we do things.

Let's call this item ignorance or arrogance. Companies can develop a tendency to be too inwardly focused and too stubborn to change processes already in place. They develop a mentality that the customer needs to develop a process to work within their structure, rather than the other way around. Everything is working just fine for us and now you want us to change? Hey, this is how we do business, if you don't like it go somewhere else. Certainly, one has to be selective in what gets changed and why, but letting internal operations trump the voice of the market can be a risky practice.

3. Help! I can't move.

What may be worse than stubbornness to change is an inability to change. Companies can create a layered structure so complex that it immobilizes them from enacting changes. A sort of corporate paralysis develops. They know they need to do something about the changes taking place, yet they can't get their arms or legs to move. Look at General Motors with their legacy repetitive divisions building basically the same cars with different name plates. Imagine all of the internal politics and bureaucracy to reform that structure to compete with firms like Toyota and Hyundai. It took bankruptcy to turn them around, and now they have their chance.

4. We are too big for change to affect us.

Some companies adopt the attitude that they are too big for change to affect them. They have the mindset that they can dictate the pace to respond to change and in some cases they can. However, they run the risk of lost market share or added cost to respond to change. Others may feel their company is too small to worry about watching for change. They feel they'll do just fine in their little niche flying under the radar. The local town pharmacy certainly is an example of how trying to fly under the radar found that either a CVS or Walgreens had popped up overnight on prime corner locations in their backyard.

Change can be swift or gradual and small companies are just as vulnerable as the big guys. Internal change is usually the top concern for small, growing firms. They quickly outgrow original processes, people, methodologies, and technologies. The change traps that I find most in small growing companies include the following:

1. Don't get left behind

It may be difficult for some employees to adapt to the changes taking place in a growing company. You may have a solid team player who's been a great employee for a long time and then the business jumps to its next level and that employee does not jump with you. Loyalty tugs at you to accommodate this person and work around their deficiencies; however, accommodation can be detrimental to your business growth and survival.

2. Step by step versus one giant leap

Either due to constrained budgets or constrained thinking, small businesses can tend to think small. When faced with change, they may make multiple little step-by-step changes which consume valuable time and resources. If possible, small companies should take the time to fully think through the change at hand and leap frog one giant step forward. The upfront cost may be greater, but the return will come swifter and ultimately cheaper in the long run.

3. Don't cry over spilled milk

Any new business invests a great deal in getting established in terms of raw dollars or time spent to develop specific processes, procedures, or products. Regardless, change may come knocking and require you to adapt and morph. Original plans won't work as intended. Getting upset about the need to change or focusing too much on your original investment is futile: change is a necessary part of growth. If the changes are needed for the right reasons, incorporate them and move on.

You Drive Change

Change drives innovation or change is forced upon others by innovation. Being the one who proactively drives change is a much more enviable position to be in. Apple Computer is a great example of a company that leads driving change by innovation. So many of their product innovations over the years: the floppy disk drive for PCs, graphical user interfaces, Newton, iMac, multi-colored computer casings, iPod, iPhone, iMovie, iTunes, and the MacBook Air have forced their competitors to react while Apple took market share and preserved healthy margins.

Drivers of change are intentional. They do not operate by accident or by scrambling. They are planned and calculated. To grow sales, these companies lead with innovation creating change rather than innovating to react to it. They invest time and resources to strategize how to create change to become the creative destructors of their industries.

If you keep doing what you've always done, you'll get what you've always gotten. That statement is about change. If I want to be successful or improve my financial life, personal relationships, physical health, or spiritual grounding, I need to do something different. I need to take action to create change, otherwise I stay the same. Every business and every person must change over time, and for each, that change becomes their innovation. Knowing that change is inevitable and constant and that innovation is the response to change means that companies need to establish a process and culture of fostering innovation to become the drivers of change.

Lightening Strikes Twice

I had started down this same path years earlier with Microsoft by making a request at Educational Resources to become a LAR. At the time the program was closed and there was heavy resistance to even discussing the prospect of adding additional LARs. Nothing had changed since my original success and I probably helped cement the topic by adding Educational Resources to the LAR mix. Regardless, I was determined to get LAR status for TRC and I started to build my strategy using what had worked well the first time.

TRC needed to have LAR status to be a contender with the major players, but my pitch would have nothing to do with TRC's needs. Rather I focused my thesis on customer need, the poor service of existing LARs, and the subsequent impact on Microsoft.

I was laying the groundwork for this debate for some time. My assigned Microsoft account manager was great for bouncing ideas off and gleaning inside information. His charter was to grow TRC sales and he had no inhibitions of protecting the holy grail of LAR status. Although he told me on numerous occasions my efforts were probably more than futile, he played along. Microsoft is a great organization and people just don't do things to serve their own needs; they have to make business sense. My account manager wanted TRC to grow and he saw merit in my case. Through his efforts and connections he was able to grant me an audience with the primary decision maker of the LAR program.

Demonstrating the deficiencies and difficulty of volume software licensing, I showed how TRC built systems that resolved customer pain points and that high-profile customers like the University of California were migrating to TRC for our service. Existing LARs were part of the customer's pain and Microsoft was sensitive to this fact. The pervasive LAR mentality was how to make the process best fit their needs versus how the process affected the customer. The LARs had done nothing to innovate and expand the LAR program; they simply filled orders and complained to Microsoft about how difficult the program was operationally. The existing LARs had grown complacent and seemed entitled to be LARs.

My argument centered on how making license acquisition difficult would drive customers to easier alternatives. I disclosed program deficiencies and how TRC alleviated them. I detailed the education customer's unique needs and how the existing LARs had ignored them. I closed my argument by showcasing the value-added services and functionality that would address the customer pain points and expand their Microsoft purchasing as a result. I had utilized the Sales Maxim by mastering the customer knowledge, who in this case was both Microsoft and the end user, and the product knowledge of volume software licensing.

After nearly nine months of presentations, conferences, and interrogations, TRC became a Microsoft LAR to the shock and concern of our closest competitors. I became the only person in the world to obtain LAR authorization for two separate dealers. Many dealers have tried over the years to obtain LAR authorization and failed. They tailor their pitch to their needs which falls on deaf ears at Microsoft. My approach was on the customer experience and how that ultimately impacted Microsoft. With that message I got through. It wasn't lip service either. It was genuine, and TRC went on to fill a tremendous gap in the market which customers rewarded with their purchase orders.

In the dot com era, I was reacting to being blindsided by an unexpected competitor. Thankfully, the competition's strategies died off before they had a chance to impact TRC. That experience made it perfectly clear that I had to drive change moving forward, and that change had to be centered on the customer. Through this focus, I would be able to develop intellectual property that was difficult to replicate, and this would be the driver to scale our future growth. TRC went from $3 million in sales in 1998 to $8.5 million in 2000. By 2004, the year we killed print catalog, we would be at $21 million, all fueled through our focus on volume software licensing.

CHAPTER THIRTY-TWO
What Blocks Innovation?

"Business has only two functions - marketing and innovation."
—Milan Kundera, writer

I n chemistry, a polyepoxide (epoxy) is a bonding result created through a thermosetting chemical reaction between two separated elements. They are separate by design because once they meet they set off a reaction that bonds the elements together into an incredibly strong adhesive. The process polymerizes a single oxygen atom with a catalyzing agent of two joined carbon atoms, known as the hardener. To spur employee-generated innovation in a company, you need a similar type of chemistry equivalent. I equate the single oxygen element to any employee who generates an idea, and I name him the Idea Agent. The combined carbon atoms, the catalyzing agent, are represented by management and an Activation Agent. Combined they become an epoxy to foster and trigger innovation. However, this is all dependent upon the company having a deliberate system that allows these agents to meet.

There can be any number of idea agents, and I typically find them in the front-line workers and managers. They are constantly generating ideas and thoughts around policy, procedure, customer service, production, presentation, implementation, and efficiency. They genuinely want to do things better and seek improvement. The second element, the activation agent, is in place to listen to the idea agent, filter the idea, prioritize the idea, and assign action to the idea. The activation agent has authority to cut through departmental silos and bureaucracy. The idea agent formulates innovative ideas based on their intimate customer and product knowledge while the activation agent is in a position to assess and implement the innovation. In the running stage, the entrepreneur's role is to innovate and to scale innovation through trained receivers. The activation agents are those trained receivers of innovation.

The problem with most companies is that the best idea agents get their ideas stifled by the organization. The organization pushes directives down and out toward them. They are trained to work in a prescribed manner, which limits their innovative autonomy. Management does this to standardize and have predictable outcomes. Other reasons may be due to lack of trust. Management is not accustomed to bottom-up creative thinking, as they are the creators of policy, procedure, and objectives. They are poorly trained to solicit and receive creative input that in essence challenges the orderly structure they themselves created and manage. They want their front-line workers to deliver predictable results and free thinking encroaches on measured performance. These divisions between idea agent and activation agent occur when a process for innovation is missing.

The downside to stifled creativity is that idea agents begin to say, "What's the point…why should I bring up ideas that won't go anywhere?" Most companies don't provide an effective process for ideas to be heard. Unfortunately, many companies don't have expectations to harness this home-grown intellectual property. In many organizations, creativity and innovation are granted to a narrow, trusted subset of employees where innovation is produced via committee and task force versus experience, intuition, and instinct.

Those companies that do establish trained receivers as activation agents listen to the trials and tribulations of their front lines, and they tend to outperform their industry counterparts. They react quicker to their customers and design services around their specific needs. Companies with the founder still at the helm tend to appreciate and expect employee feedback more than others. Either consciously or unconsciously, founders understand and know how to harness the power of their coworker's experiences. They know how to listen, assess, contribute resources and execute on ideas. They also have the span of control to make it happen quickly and effectively.

This is true of The Home Depot whose founders, Bernie Marcus and Arthur Blank, describe their organization as an upside down pyramid where the executives are servants of the front-line staff who are closest to the customer. They respect the front-line worker as an idea agent providing invaluable intelligence to management who are the activation agents. The Home Depot has built an innovation system that listens to the front line, filters, and aggressively acts on their feedback.

Bureaucratic corporations have many layers of filters between the idea agents and the potential activation agents. Often those filters work hard to keep information from the idea agents permeating to the top. They work especially hard at keeping the bad information from filtering to the top and allowing only the good. The good is almost always useless data. It supports the existing structure and marching orders. Good news serves as confirmation, not correction. I insist on hearing the bad news as every executive should. The bad news is what spurs solutions to problems. Part of regular management briefings should include a list of the top bad things happening within the company. Learn to celebrate bad news. Don't find blame in it. Don't fix it and move on. Find innovators to improve it and turn it into an asset.

Many companies recognize the need and purpose for employee-generated innovation, yet they struggle with how to make it happen within the organization. The primary cork to employee innovation development comes from management failing to develop a process for it. Since organizations operate based on processes, there must be a process for innovation. Correlated to the process is establishing a culture of innovation whereby management endorses the process and employee innovation development is an expectation. Top management has to establish an environment that makes the effort and risk worth it to the employee. Even an employee nestled in the safety and security of a company has a Risk Box which prevents him from sharing his creativity.

The employee's Risk Box prevents him from stepping out of the task to challenge the established process. Corporate cultures are too quick to criticize, and those perceived wrist slaps stifle employee's courage to challenge. It's easier and safer to work within the status quo. Managers are the logical destination for employee innovation announcements and they can be poor activation agents as they are often not trained to respond, recognize, or implement innovation. Managers are typically more risk averse to innovation than their subordinates by tending to make career-focused decisions versus innovation-based decisions.

A *Harvard Business School Journal* studying the process of innovation in corporations by Professor Clayton Christensen gave a case study of a toy manufacturer that was straining to obtain imaginative new ideas. Christensen stated that "inside the large manufacturers you've got middle managers who want to put forward only those products that look like what's been approved in the past." A real or perceived fear is present that the product idea may get rejected or, even worse, fail and possibly damage the manager's career. "As a consequence of this natural process of deciding what to carry forward, the ideas that get developed into business plans are the ones that look a lot like the ideas that got funded before." Do what you've always done; get what you've always gotten.

This fear of damaging a career thickens the Risk Box walls and adds to the next blockage point—reward and recognition. Employees who see no reward in innovation wonder what the point is in trying. The organization, without a process for innovation, establishes too much personal risk for either too little reward or too unlikely an acceptance of their innovation.

The Devil's Advocate

One naysayer can kill a good idea, and continual exposure to that ritual is enough for anyone to clam up and keep quiet. In *The 10 Faces of Innovation,* author Tom Kelley focuses on innovation and its arch enemy "the devil's advocate," the abortionist of ideas and innovation. As Kelley explains, the devil's advocate kills ideas at conception in the meeting room when they are first introduced. Quickly someone in the crowd inevitably takes on the role of the devil's advocate and throws out the worst scenarios that could occur should this idea be allowed to see the light of day. Kelley's research has shown that if the devil's advocate is given the floor, he can be effective in forever silencing great ideas as there is a psychological safety in residing in the not-doing-something-new camp as opposed to trying something new.

Entrepreneurs are faced with devil's advocates whenever they open their mouths to share their ideas. There's always a devil in the crowd. He's just waiting to shoot your idea down, tell you how absurd it is, how counter it is to the way things get done in that business or industry. "You can't do that, because that's not the way it works in our business." It can be human nature to side with the devil's advocate, feeling it is safer than taking the chance with the individual with the new idea.

Entrepreneurs actively seek out people to share their ideas because they want to gain validity to their assumptions. They too can be easily discouraged and defeated by that single devil's advocate in the crowd. They may talk to five different people on five different occasions and all those people give them encouragement and validation that they're going in the right direction and that they really have something, but that sixth conversation with the devil may be all they need to hear to close the books on their idea.

Perhaps subconsciously, we continually ask people their opinions to find that negative response to end our quest? We like having ideas, but we fear putting them into action because we fear the level of commitment required of us to make it happen. We fear having to take that next step when we really have to roll up our sleeves and get to work and commit our resources. Not that we fear work, but we fear the investment we need to put into that work without a guarantee that it is going to pay off.

The other reason for entrepreneurs allowing the devil's advocates to torpedo their ideas is that they may be lacking the strong vision and passion they need to have. I've been there with one of the many business ideas I've shared with family and friends. It's easy for me to share a great idea with a level of exuberance and excitement with those who will listen and validate my plans, and it is just as easy to allow the devil's advocate in the crowd to tear apart those ideas. Why do I allow him to destroy my will to move forward with these great ideas? Because deep down my will is not strong enough to move them forward, or I'm searching for someone to jump in with me to share the heavy lifting.

For the most part, the individual employee can't accomplish innovation alone. The short cut that companies take is in discussing innovation in a seminar and then telling employees to "go do it." Weekend retreats, one-day workshops, or statements that the employee is empowered to make it happen is not enough to overcome the inherent personal corporate Risk Box barriers. Innovation is fostered over time, through experience and interaction. To be successful, innovation must be part of the daily and weekly agenda of all. It must become a business process and part of a standing agenda.

Employees certainly can apply innovative methods to their "desk" and things under their direct span of control which is beneficial. However, to unleash inter-departmental and far-reaching innovation that creates dramatic results, collaboration is required. Collaboration on innovation is difficult if a culture is not present to welcome the participants as equals focused on a mutually beneficial purpose.

Some companies think they'll find their innovation out of the Idea Box. Providing an anonymous process may reduce the Risk Box but it does little to foster innovation. The idea box is a suggestion box. Not an innovation box. Suggestion boxes are more often viewed as a method to appease worker gripes in an anonymous setting versus providing a forum for innovation. It is not a conduit for the front line to communicate accurate, relevant data and experience to those who can put it to use. Truly relevant and practical good ideas cannot be scribbled on a piece of paper and submitted. They need to be discussed and white boarded. Further, the person or persons tasked with reading and filtering ideas are typically not trained activation agents. They may not identify with the front line or recognize an innovative idea if it bit them on the nose.

Catch the Spirit

Innovation is vital to any business, and yet it has the least structure, understanding, delegation, or empowerment—aside from companies with devoted research and development. CEOs in large corporations are challenged with how to incubate an entrepreneurial spirit within their staff, but equally challenged as to why it just doesn't happen organically. Many a formal appeal delivered by a CEO, director, or line manager has been made practically begging the troops to adopt an entrepreneurial spirit and innovative mindset. What they fail to recognize is that the environment they have confined their people to chokes the desired outcomes.

While the entrepreneur seeks to escape the formalized life, the established protocols and guidelines, the large corporation gravitates toward these as a means of structure and survival. As negative a connotation as bureaucracy may resonate, it is a necessary ingredient for the organized and fluid nature of the large corporation. Therefore, executives need to first understand the bureaucratic foundation of their organization before they introduce this polar opposite aspect of entrepreneurial spirit in order to breed innovation.

Judith Cone of the Ewing Marion Kauffman Foundation wrote an essay titled "Entrepreneurship on Campus: Why the Real Mission is Culture Change" where she states that "One of the greatest challenges of our society is to keep our large organizations from falling prey to bureaucratic sclerosis. We must learn to keep them entrepreneurial from within, adaptive, and creative." This statement is so profound and yet so poorly addressed.

It is by nature that a company grows and matures to a level where controls and bureaucracy are necessary for the orderly facilitation of processes, services, and procedures. However, like plaque in one's arteries, the bureaucracy can harden and thicken the walls of the organization to the point that its life blood—its workers—are conditioned to completing tasks often in a thoughtless, unimaginative, and noncritical manner, void of seeking opportunity in the tasks that they are responsible for.

Cone continues, "Entrepreneurship is about opportunity recognition; agility, constant response to the market, quality products, and innovative practices. Entrepreneurship and bureaucracy cannot co-exist." How often have you seen prominent corporations slowly fade in stature or close altogether? Can you think of large companies that seem to be the same exact company today that they were 10, 15, or even 20 years ago? Possibly that's hard to do since 70 percent of the companies listed on the Fortune 500 had been replaced since 1975. Why? Perhaps they did not innovate.

Continual Innovation

I was proud of the innovations created at TRC around volume software licensing, which attributed to our LAR authorization. Automated key code and serial number delivery was revolutionary, as was our method to display software licensing online in a fashion that was easy to search and discern. A remaining nuance and aggravation of software licensing was that the pricelists provided by publishers contained lengthy abbreviated titles that required an advance degree to translate. Our competitors would take the publisher's price list and post it verbatim on their Web catalog. At TRC, we took the time to create product titles that any end user could find, decipher, and order without assistance.

For instance, a publisher would provide a title description which read, "ACLP3 PhotoCS4WNCONCLC" and that is exactly what dealers would post on their Web site. The translation of this title was that this was an academic market only Photoshop version CS4, CLP volume discount level 3, Windows computer type, concurrent license. I won't bother to dissect the acronyms further—you got the point. TRC provided a title that was easy to read and understand: "Photoshop CS4 Windows Concurrent License." The other portions of the description were not needed because they were incorporated into our hierarchical product search engine. This may seem trivial but imagine having to sift through dozens even hundreds of SKUs from a search return using the original publisher descriptions and trying to decipher the correct product. Since licenses were non-returnable, if you made a mistake you were stuck or had to go through a lengthy appeal process. The market applauded our careful attention to detail as did our publishers.

When TRC's attention became dedicated to volume licensing a flurry of innovation erupted. We learned that our customers had the authority to grant TRC the ability to replicate Microsoft CD media on their behalf as opposed to buying the manufactured media sets, which often took a lengthy time to deliver. By burning our own media, our cost of goods were in the neighborhood of a couple dollars and we were able to sell the disk sets just below $20 which undercut our competitor's cost on the pre-manufactured sets. Now we controlled production and could deliver media faster and cheaper than anyone in the market.

Microsoft had a college student and faculty purchase program under the Select licensing agreement too, which afforded drastically discounted prices on products like Microsoft Office and the Windows Operating System upgrade. The process to order and the product itself was cumbersome to the end users and LARs who were selling it, as it had two components. One part was the physical CD media and the other was a virtual license. I say virtual because there was no physical license shipped, only an online registration to prove ownership. The product was restricted to the academic audience only and the LAR had to authenticate each customer's eligibility.

The student/faculty licensing product was not available in a retail package, making it impossible to market through traditional student outlets like college bookstores. To respond, I created an inexpensive bundle of the CD media with a physical printed copy of the end user license stuffed in a plain white 9 x 12 mailing envelope. A four-color product cover sleeve was designed that was shrink wrapped to the sealed envelope. We sold the finished pieces to college bookstores whose campus was licensed to offer the product. We sold a ton of them through this new channel and we were the only company in the country doing it.

A later innovation developed after our new site launched was an electronic software download service of selected products directly from our Web site and integrated into our e-commerce platform. The software could be sold as a transaction or enabled as a benefit to allow the customer to download the software already purchased when and where they needed. Again, TRC appeared to be the only LAR with this capability in the volume software license field. The power of this capability became evident when one of our key customers relied on this service in the aftermath of hurricane Katrina in 2005.

Tulane University had recently become a TRC customer in 2005 after a long courting process. Being the crown jewel of the independent colleges in Louisiana, Tulane was a big-volume license customer who was drawn to our value-added capabilities. Their decision to work with TRC would pay dividends when they were faced with having to quickly set up a remote IT command center in Houston immediately following the levee breaks around New Orleans where the main campus resides. The Tulane IT team had all of the hardware set-up established, but they needed to load software and all of their disks and key codes were in New Orleans irretrievable due to the flooding and evacuation order. Because of TRC's functionality, Tulane requested the software on a Saturday morning and within minutes they were able to download the required products along with their applicable license key codes. Thank goodness I was working that Saturday!

This was truly a rewarding experience to see our innovation put to use during such a critical time of need for our customer. This event helped entrench our presence within Tulane, and we used that story to tell other customers about the unique capabilities of TRC. We were no longer selling a commoditized item based solely on price. We were selling a service. Our singular focus into software licensing brought even more success stories and new relationships with school consortiums representing numerous colleges who endorsed TRC's services.

TRC's approach to the market was based on establishing customer relationships with a proprietary service offering. That formula earned TRC numerous industry awards and peer recognition as being one of the best, if not the best, in software licensing in the education market. TRC became one of the top education-focused dealers in the US for Microsoft, Adobe, Symantec, and several other name brand publishers. Our foremost intent was to find ways to better serve our customers and eliminate their pain points, and the rewards came as validation of our execution.

CHAPTER THIRTY-THREE
The Innovation Garden

"Innovation is the specific instrument of entrepreneurship. The act that endows resources with a new capacity to create wealth."
—Peter F. Drucker

A t the time, the motivation at TRC was to differentiate more so than innovate. The word innovate really was not part of our vocabulary even though that was what we were doing. Organically, the company was structured and responsive to this innovation allowing rapid deployment of approved ideas. Internally, operational processes could be scrapped or reinvented to serve the needs of each new innovation. We were practicing what Ken Blanchard in *The One Minute Entrepreneur* calls "interpreneurship." The concept of interpreneurship is where employees take ownership of new initiatives and get others to buy in.

I had become the primary activation agent and all of TRC's employees were idea agents, including myself. I was actively receptive to customer feedback provided to our staff as well as listening to their own concerns over internal bottlenecks and barriers. Employees were encouraged to participate because they saw their feedback being reviewed and often put into action. Their opinion and input mattered and recognition was aptly provided to those who brought forward ideas. There was no fear of embarrassment or ridicule; even rejected ideas received praise for originality and effort.

Without consciously knowing, a process had been created to pull customer and product knowledge from all available sources, formulate a response, and deploy it in a short timeframe. Like the Six Sigma process of quality business management created by Motorola, innovation needs to be a strategy incorporated into a business process. Since every business is run by processes then innovation must follow a process if there is any hope of it having success and ability to scale within an organization.

Employee-driven innovation in any established organization can only come about when a commitment to foster innovation is developed from the highest levels of leadership. To assist in that process, I suggest planting an "innovation garden."

The innovation garden is a conceptual process to foster employee-driven innovation in six steps.

Step 1: Prepare to plant the garden

For innovation to become organically generated from all levels of the employee population, it has to become part of the company culture. Executive management can show their endorsement by establishing public goals for the outcomes of employee-driven innovation. These are some of the goals I like to promote in my innovation garden.

- Obtain great ideas from the best source of innovation— employees
- Nurture a culture of innovation that reduces costs and increases productivity
- Promote a genuine feeling of ownership and empowerment to innovate
- Become competitively superior through innovation
- Exceed customer expectations through innovation

Executive management needs to define, create, and nurture the innovation process and culture to prepare the company for innovation. To make it happen four things should be put in place.

A budget

This budget won't cover the cost of implementing an innovation, as that amount would be unpredictable. Rather it establishes a budget for creating a dedicated workplace, material, and training. This may also include employee recognition.

Defined employee roles

Employees will be classified as idea agents or activation agents.

Employee training

Staff development needs to inform and define innovation to the staff, explaining its strategic importance in differentiating the company. The role of agents and the process of selecting an innovation to implement is a requirement to get everyone on the same page.

Rules and procedures

This involves creating an environment of trust, blocking the devil's advocate, and removing bureaucracy from the innovation garden.

A heavy emphasis on encouragement and trust is vital since innovation comes from ideas, which are highly personal. There is always a risk in sharing ideas as they may be rejected, challenged, and debated. An individual may feel embarrassment, humiliation, or even degradation in stature. Innovation should be challenged by a process not by an individual, and when innovations are adopted, the success or failure is shared by all in the team. This ensures an environment that is free of rebuke, judgment, and fear.

Phrases like "Would you bet your job on it?" have to be eliminated. At one point this may have served to ensure one's decisions were well thought out and researched, but it matured into a fear-inducing mantra that froze middle managers into replicating the status quo just like Professor Christensen's toy manufacturer case study. The magic of the innovation garden is that its environment is cocooned from the status quo of the business. All ideas can sprout without critique or repercussion.

The entrepreneurial mindset is a natural resource. Economic studies have discovered that stifling entrepreneurial expression either through political, economic or educational restrictions will have dramatic consequences on the long-term economic well being of a country imposing such restrictions. Entrepreneurs who are enticed with more fertile and open environments will tend to develop their innovations where they are free to do so benefiting those countries. We're seeing a loss of scientists and students to foreign lands due to restrictive immigration policy, and it has the potential to have a dramatic impact on our innovative output. The same principle is true of companies who do not harness the innovative power and desire of their employees to express creativity. Their employees may not go abroad, but they will go down the street.

Step 2: Establish a place for the garden

A physical location to innovate is required for the innovation garden. This fixed location is a permanent reminder that shows the commitment of executive management to make innovation happen. The location creates a dedicated space to innovate so that active brainstorming does not spill over into all hours of the day causing disruption of work. Time should be scheduled by idea agents to meet with activation agents in the garden.

Scheduling a recurring time for innovation is in conjunction with establishing the place to innovate. Innovation needs to get on everyone's calendar as a recurring routine that designates the day, time, duration, and location. Scheduling time for innovation is vital for establishing the longevity and commitment of the process. When everyone in the company is required to attend a quarterly or monthly innovation session, it establishes a habit and a culture of innovation that is practiced. The process is then expected and seen as important at all levels of the organization.

As innovation is practiced over time, people get better at it and develop an awareness to innovate. This is when the garden bears fruit. Too many companies want their employees to think like an owner or an entrepreneur, but they don't engrain their employees with the habits of the entrepreneur. The only way to develop habits is to practice on a routine basis. The byproduct of establishing a culture and practice of innovation is increased ownership of the process, goals, and mission of the company. The fulfillment and satisfaction of being creative and making a difference resonates with everyone.

A key element to scheduling time in the garden is duration. I suggest monthly meetings that do not exceed one hour. Innovation sessions are not brainstorming sessions. Participants come to the session with ideas and spend time on refining them for harvest. The innovation garden should be equipped with whiteboards, flip charts, audio visual projector, and other aids to convey the ideas to the activation agents. Leaving ideas on the presentation aids for others to see may help refine ideas or spur new ones.

Have white boards posted publically in every department to serve as innovation parking lots. During the day as employees get a great idea they can write it (park it) on the white board. This creates a culture that is surrounded by innovation. Ideas are encouraged and shared for collaborative feedback. The obvious exception to this type of sharing would be sensitive research and development that needs a greater level of security.

Step 3: Plant the seeds

The seeds of innovation are the idea agents who will be the majority, if not all, of the employees in the company. Innovation is the result of an idea put into action. Innovation will surface within a company through individual "ah-ha" moments and group collaboration. Both methods need to be encouraged in the garden to yield the greatest results.

Individual ideas and "ah-ha" moments

Ideas will strike an individual at any moment of the day, and the individual will want to discuss them right away. That's why the departmental innovation parking lot white boards are an important part of the process. They act as placeholders until time can be scheduled in the innovation garden. Companies can create "innovation intra-net" sites that bring individuals into a virtual innovation parking lot 24/7 in order to park their ideas. The point is to grab ideas when they are ripe and place them into a forum where they can be reviewed and acted upon in a scheduled and consistent manner.

Group innovation

Sometimes it makes sense to establish groups who have ideas or are assigned a topic to focus their efforts. This engages more people in the innovation process and spreads the culture of innovation. The topics for focus group innovation could relate to departmental or corporate S.W.O.T., KPIs, processes or stakeholder pain points. These become the most structured ideas to bring through the innovation process and they may take longer to launch as there often lacks a single idea originator. Activation agents need to take a greater role in facilitating the group through the process and keeping all on track.

Step 4: Water and weed

Essentially the gardener who waters the idea agent is the activation agent. The activation agents will be specially trained employees who do not necessarily have to be managers. Activation agents need to pass specialized training that allows them to be keen receivers of ideas, selective in processing ideas, sensitive in rejecting ideas, and to recognize when refinement of ideas is necessary. The activation agents should have a firm understanding of company goals, customers, processes, and related stakeholders. Part of their training is to be able to weed out ideas that don't fit pre-established criteria in terms of likelihood of activation, scope, or funding requirements. They must be trained in delivering rejection to Idea Agents as not to hurt feelings or dissuade future participation.

By weeding innovation ideas so they are clearly focused provides room for the best ideas to flourish. The activation agent will listen, encourage, filter, guide, and coach idea thinking and will use a process to accept or reject ideas rather than a subjective perspective. That process is the "idea selection process".

Idea Selection Process

   a. Define the innovation clearly in a statement or as briefly as possible.

   b. Define the stakeholder(s) primarily involved.

   c. Define what the innovation will do.
   • Save money
   • Produce greater efficiency
   • Ensure greater customer satisfaction
   • Differentiate the company
   • Add intellectual property
   • Address a stakeholder pain point

d. Define what the innovation will cost in terms
   of resources.
   - Is there a budget for this?
   - Can a budget be created for this?
   - Does the innovation exceed the group's authority?
   - Does the innovation exceed the group's abilities?
   - Does the innovation exceed the company's
     abilities?

e. Calculate an ROI (based on dollars or KPI).
   - Based on the ROI is it worth pursuing or are other
     innovations more worthwhile at this time?

f. Provide a final analysis.
   - Are other innovations better suited for the same
     resources or ROI?
   - Is this a viable innovation or are we forcing it?
   - Does the innovation require involvement of senior
     management or other stakeholders?
   - Should the innovation be parked, killed, or pursued?

Step 5: Harvest

Once the innovation has passed through the scrutiny of the idea selection process, it should be prepared for presentation to the ultimate decision makers. Depending on the scope of the innovation, the decision makers can be represented at the departmental level or by an executive committee consisting of a broad representation of the company.

- Is the innovation clearly defined for the decision maker?
- Are all possible questions addressed that may be posed by
  the decision maker?

- Can proof of concept be tested for the innovation?
- What expectations does the idea agent/activation agent have of the decision maker in the presentation?
- Are all benefits of the innovation clearly detailed for the decision maker?
- Are all known costs associated with the innovation reported?

Step 6: Reward and acknowledge

Innovation needs to be incorporated into annual appraisals and goal settings. Participation over performance is to be measured and reviewed. In other words, don't just reward the successfully executed innovations, reward the failures too. Public review and appreciation of innovation should be encouraged as it happens. Appreciation and acknowledgement are consistently listed as the things employees want most from their superiors and peers. It ranks higher than money! It is also an area where many companies perform poorly. Creative, consistent, and reliable ways of sincerely acknowledging good work is what humans crave. People generally spend over eight hours a day, five days a week at work, and they need to feel appreciated.

Be innovative in how you reward. You'll be surprised that it does not always mean cash. Ask your employees for ideas on how to acknowledge innovation. In fact send them to the innovation garden as their first assignment to come up with an innovative response.

A wonderful example of an innovation garden using group innovation existed at Circuit City in the early '90s. To find new business opportunities unrelated to their core consumer electronics business, a team was formed to study industries that were yet to be dominated by any major players. Project X, as it was known, eventually settled on the used-car market. By developing a fresh model from scratch that was built around consumer need, a new concept in used-car purchasing was born. That innovation became CarMax.

Competitive Advantage

All of TRC's sales and marketing innovations served to help the company stand out in the crowd. The industry was filled with "me too" competitors who were selling the same commoditized product we were. Our innovations took the focus off price and placed it on how TRC could address the pain points and concerns of our customers. The running phase added maturity to both my customer and product knowledge which helped me continue to differentiate TRC from the competition.

In our startup days, TRC competed on price since we had low overhead. Originally, I saw TRC as being the low-price leader, the Wal-Mart of software. However, I found that going to market on price alone diminished the value we provided to our customers and made it increasingly difficult to run the business on cash flow alone based on such low margins. Over time our innovations helped maintain acceptable price points and established brand loyalty to TRC. Due to the substantial operational and IT investment that would be necessary for our competitors to match our functionality, we stood alone in the advancements we brought to market. All of our developments were serving us well, but we still needed to do more to differentiate the products we were selling.

The flag ship software lines in education were Adobe and Microsoft. Each had high-volume license programs that could encompass the entire licensing needs of a campus, and they afforded both student and faculty purchase options. Since we were not the manufacturers of these products, physically changing them to differentiate ourselves would be impossible. We eventually would disrupt the dealer channel by blocking competitor access to sell these product lines to large pools of academic customers.

I discovered that just about any K-12 school or college in the country could be associated with an independent, often non-profit, consortium or cooperative organization. These consortia existed to support, lobby, or extend the purchasing power of all their member schools. Their focus had long been on establishing things like group insurance rates, state funding, or discounts on furniture. TRC was one of the early leaders who introduced these groups to cooperative purchasing on technology, specifically software licensing.

Volume software licensing is constructed on the principle of the more you buy the lower your price. By stretching the boundaries of the publishers' intentions of their volume licensing agreements, we were able to get individual member schools to consolidate their orders to achieve higher discount levels. After establishing a relationship with a consortium, we would propose the value-added benefits that license consolidation would provide to their member schools. Schools would save money on licensing, and the consortium would be recognized for providing the opportunity.

The consortium would promote and communicate the offer to the member schools, often at the president's level. Combined with the influence and long-standing relationship the consortium had with its members, our offer came with an endorsement that no competitor could rival. This would provide TRC access to regular consortium meetings allowing a forum to present the benefits our proposal afforded. Schools who had not worked with TRC in the past were now enticed to participate, which effectively added new customers to TRC's portfolio.

Due to the considerable logistical work required by TRC to make a multi-school consolidated order happen, TRC was afforded exclusivity. By combining all of the individual school orders together, TRC would be able to provide a price that most individual schools would not be able to achieve on their own. This allowed schools to avoid having to go out to bid as was customary with public schools. For individual schools who determined they still needed to bid, our competitors could only quote on a single requesting school's quantity, which would put them at a higher priced volume level. Often even bidding at cost, our competition couldn't touch the group pricing afforded through the consortium.

TRC would not have to discount the volume tier we were provided because we were the only ones who could offer it to the designated consortium member schools. TRC established the relationship with the consortium and the policy and procedures to promote, communicate, and process the combined order. The member school's affiliation with their consortium was strong, and they welcomed this new benefit and the cost savings it provided. This tactic allowed TRC to gain access to new schools that traditionally channeled their software through other dealers. Our offer was irresistible, and we were able to easily take market share especially when our other value-added services were communicated.

The consortium, being a trusted partner of the school, was doing the marketing for TRC and reaching sometimes hundreds of schools at once. The tactic to use consortia and to consolidate multiple school orders was unique to the marketplace and allowed TRC to scale in ways unimaginable to our competitors. Certainly some caught on, but others were completely in the dark or operationally incapable of replicating. This strategy became a game changer, and many of our competitors were blindsided and unable to respond.

This innovative move provided higher margins for TRC and a lower price to our customer. It attracted new customers, allowed TRC to scale by servicing several customers with one process, created tremendous customer satisfaction, and left our competition scratching their heads. It was all good. Now we just had to lock in as many consortium relationships as possible before the smart competitors caught on.

CHAPTER THIRTY-FOUR
Leadership

A great leader's courage to fulfill his vision comes from passion, not position.—John Maxwell

L eadership has been such a popular subject of research and study that many have developed careers spinning variations of leadership theories like Trait, Behavioral and Style; Participative, Situational and Contingency; Functional, Transactional and Transformational. The prevailing focus of leadership study has been on the corporate manager, whereas the entrepreneur displays a significantly different impetus. In addition to scaling and innovation, leadership becomes the third primary function of the entrepreneur during the running phase.

Entrepreneurial leadership is a natural instinctive behavior that surfaces when one is placed in a position that is either granted to him, or that he creates himself, and one where he is passionate about leading. The key to this type of leadership is having the passion to lead for a specific purpose that the entrepreneur and his followers believe in and support. It energizes everyone involved and creates a catalyst for leading. Even individuals who may not have shown a particular interest or aptitude in leadership seem to naturally fill the role once they adopt a passion to pursue.

Situational theory states that situations are responsible for leadership decisions and actions, which I associate most with entrepreneurial leadership. Research from Professors Victor Vroom, Arthur Jago, and psychologist Fred Fiedler all support the popular theory that the best type of leadership is driven by situational variables. Situational theory asserts that effective leaders actually change their leadership style in response to the situation they are facing. This is descriptive of an entrepreneur who is faced with constant change in creating a company from the ground up. If change is constant in an organization, and the organization must respond to or drive change then the same must be true of the leader's style.

"The times produce the person and not the other way around."
—Herbert Spencer (1884)

Vroom and Jago stated that "Situations shape how leaders behave and influence the consequences of a leader's behavior." Depending on the situation at hand, the leader's decisions and style may prove to be effective or actually ineffective if their assertions are incorrect. No single style of leadership can be static to all business situations, and the truly effective leader will change his style to best address the challenge.

I subscribe to the situational theory because the leadership is focused on the situation as the point of motivation for the leader. The macro situational focus is growing the business to sustainability while dozens of mini areas of situational focus need to be addressed in order to achieve that larger goal. Understanding the focus of entrepreneurial leadership is central to comprehending the type of leader and his motivation to lead.

The core motive of most corporate leaders is self fulfillment. They want to accomplish a task or assigned goal, yet they ultimately do so for self positioning, recognition, accomplishment, influence, promotion, or some other form of self gratification. This is not to be construed to mean that they are not team or company focused, but, ultimately, when you peel away the layers, at the center is self motivation. After all, people choose to work for a particular company for their own personal reasons, and they make contributions during their career ultimately for their own personal reasons as well.

An entrepreneur's core motivation is company-mission centered. His focus is on growth, vision attainment, and preservation. True, being the founder, he has personal motivations as well, but they are practically congruent with the company's interests. This creates a completely different leader than the corporate counterpart. In fact, because of these motivational drivers, you can't ever purely replicate the entrepreneurial leader within a corporate environment. A primary reason for this differentiation is that the entrepreneur has a high internal locus of control. That is, he believes he is in control of his own future, success, and failures, whereas the corporate leader believes someone else, the company he works for, is in control of his future. The corporate leader has self preservation needs that are tied to his personal performance in the eyes of his employer; the entrepreneur's self preservation is tied directly to the preservation of the company—a relationship that tends to be exclusive to the entrepreneur.

Leadership is not management. Managers administer while leaders innovate, develop, motivate, persuade, and create. Leadership is not about giving orders, it is about influencing. The influence must be genuine, transparent, and built on trust. Followers agree to be influenced because they believe in the cause, goal, or outcome. Business leader Alan Keith said, "Leadership is ultimately about creating a way for people to contribute to making something extraordinary happen." People get excited about being a part of something extraordinary like starting a business. The leader shares a vision that people see as achievable and worthy of effort.

This is how the situation serves as the motivation. It is the focus for the entrepreneur. The entrepreneurial leader assigns a goal or reward to the situation which the followers visualize, understand, and agree to pursue. The leader's style can be charismatic or dictatorial, but the promise of accomplishment overrides everything.

Often for entrepreneurs, the situation goal is grand and that alone is captivating, enticing, and engaging for followers. The followers understand the enormity of the goal and they respect the leader for the risk assumed, while they fill a support role to make it happen. Working toward the goal is exhilarating to the followers and their job becomes more than work but a contribution to a mission. The entrepreneur recognizes and fosters this, which is how a great leader can get followers to achieve remarkable things.

The entrepreneurial leader's role is to influence, direct, and keep the mission prominent and focused. He will accomplish this through effective communication, which has four components: communicating expectations, listening, delegating, and providing feedback. A strong characteristic of entrepreneurs' communication skills is the ability to filter incoming information effectively. This serves not only to discard useless and time-wasting information but to screen for opportunities that often are missed by managerial counterparts. Entrepreneurs develop an ear to listen and an eye to spot growth or innovation opportunities through all forms of feedback. They are able to pick out the tiny nuggets of information that can be used to exploit a competitor's weakness or enhance an existing strength of the firm.

"Leaders are made, they are not born. They are made by hard effort, which is the price which all of us must pay to achieve any goal that is worthwhile."—Vince Lombardi

Entrepreneurs often are created into leaders by necessity. The effort from the idea to achieving the goal of viability and sustainability is thrust upon the entrepreneur by the situation at hand. He learns quickly what he needs to do to survive and he becomes a passionate leader. Most followers of entrepreneurial leadership are enticed out of an admiration of the entrepreneur. This may sound egotistical, but it goes back to the earlier message that everyone has an entrepreneurial passion in his heart. Martin Chemers, a social psychologist with interests in leadership, team, and organizational effectiveness, has described leadership as the "process of social influence in which one person is able to enlist the aid and support of others in the accomplishment of a common task." More than anyone, entrepreneurs have this tremendous ability to enlist people in support of their goals.

Leadership Lost, Then Found

Leadership at TRC was like climbing stairs. Each landing was a new goal and achievement to strive toward. My job was to continually put these small goals out for the company to attain and then to recognize and reward everyone for their efforts upon completion. This provided continual positive reinforcement on targets we could reach while moving us closer to our ultimate goal. That goal was our mission statement, "To be the most recognized provider of volume software licensing in the education market."

The vision I provided to my team was crystal clear. Everyone could see it, and they knew what would be required of them to make it happen. The reward of accomplishment was communicated to the individual but was universal in comprehension. We would continually grow the company to a point where we would be acquired by a company that shared our mission and would provide the capital to scale TRC even further. Individuals, for their effort, would receive the additional benefits and opportunities of this larger parent organization. I wanted to build careers for my employees, and this strategy would provide numerous avenues for personal development that were not present at TRC.

Aptly motivated, TRC employees did extraordinary things to move the company toward that goal. On several occasions, employees took it upon themselves to work all night, literally sleeping in the office to meet deadlines. What a surprise to arrive at the office around 6 a.m. to find employees crashed at their workstations and realize they never left from the day before. This is not to convey the image of a sweat shop or that I condoned all-nighters. I encouraged people to get home to family, but we also fostered a culture that when things needed to get done, extraordinary efforts were required. These employees went well beyond extraordinary and they established a bond and attitude that permeated the office.

There was a time when I thought I had taken TRC as far as I could under my leadership. We hit a dry spell in terms of creativity and growth, and I considered hiring a new president to run the company while I migrated to chairman of the board. My thought was to find someone with executive experience that could introduce new concepts, processes, or expertise. I felt that someone else could do a better job in the CEO position and that someone else may have been better qualified. Thankfully, I quickly realized that I was the best qualified and that my team needed me.

Feelings of isolation can happen with entrepreneurs, as it did with me, which can lead to a sense of tunnel vision. Lack of exposure to peers, mentors, board members or forums can lead to stale views and a sense of entrapment within your own company. I got my grounding by talking to other entrepreneurs about the dry spell I seemed to be in. They helped me realize I still had much to offer, and that I probably needed to shake things up a bit to revitalize the spark. By establishing new goals in all facets of the company and placing expectations on the managers of those areas, I was able to pull my leadership out of the doldrums.

One of the sparks generated from this self reflection process was a vision to obtain $100 million in sales. We were approaching $30 million and now the $100 million mark didn't seem as ridiculous as it had when Michael Krazny first shared it with me in 1998. In fact, the more I thought about it, the more arduous the idea of not being closer to that milestone became. Now energy had to be shifted toward how we could make this goal happen, and what I would have to do to make it a reality. I was refocused and revitalized. I was back at the helm!

"Entrepreneurs don't need motivation, they need to motivate. Their motivation is manifested already in their internal desire to accomplish their mission through the work of others."
—Jeff Weber

PHASE IV: EXIT

It's a mild June morning. I've just arrived at the Radisson Hotel in Rosemont, Illinois, the hotel and convention center Mecca surrounding Chicago's O'Hare International. I find my meeting room with the typical continental breakfast set-up and mingle with a variety of fellow participants. The audience is a peculiar mix of young and old, mostly white men dressed in a wide range of formal and informal attire. Our hosts are clearly discernable: three well-dressed men who look like high-priced lawyers or Wall Street barons. The trio includes a senior executive in his late 50s, a similar gentleman in his 40s, and a young 20-something apprentice.

I had finally responded to one of the many advertisements I receive regularly from this and comparable companies. The advertisement's pitch was to come and learn the strange and mysterious world of mergers and acquisitions for only $50. If you've ever considered selling your business, the timing is perfect—it's now! Even if you don't want to sell, you owe it to yourself to have this valuable information. Foreign companies are lining up to buy American companies—your American company—in all sectors, in all shapes and sizes, regardless of profitability—they want you, and they will pay top dollar! Because of the dollar's value, now is the best time for these foreign companies to invest in you. Act fast because this perfect storm in the M&A market will not last!

Okay, I'll stop. If you own or have ever owned a business, you have been hit with these direct mail pieces. Redundancy and recency marketing principles do work, and they finally got their hold on me. I paid my $50 online and registered for the course, class, seminar—or whatever they called it. Yes, I paid to attend an infomercial. Why can't I be the genius who charges people to listen to my advertisements and sales pitches? It is a lesson right out of Marketing 101: attach a value to what you do and it will carry more weight. It also weeds out those who are not quite baked enough and need to stay in the oven to receive a few more of those direct mail pieces.

Anyway, I settled in for what was a fabulous sales presentation. Some of you might be asking why is he telling me this story; can't I just skip ahead a few pages? What if I told you that these may be some of the most valuable pages you read in your career as an entrepreneur? What if by reading these next few pages you might be able to save $20,000 or $30,000 or even far more?—perhaps millions! It's true.

These guys are sharks; in fact, sharks would/should be afraid of these guys. They are some of the slickest, polished, and scripted— now I have to think really hard about this next word—salesmen, I have ever come across. It was hard for me to say salesmen and not something more profane. I have great respect for the sales industry and the art and skill of selling. Selling matches buyers with sellers by addressing needs, requirements, and wants. You could say these guys were doing the same thing, but instead of relying on skill, they resort to deceit, lies, and the classic bait and switch.

The sales pitch centers around all of the raw emotions the business owner has absorbed into his psyche and ego over years of dedication and engagement in his business. The pitch starts with the climate for merger and acquisition activity, which as you would guess, is ripe and at its all-time peak. Then it moves to the seemingly endless list of likely buyers and why they would presumably want your business. They paint scenarios for roll-up strategies, Fortune 100s seeking niche plays, foreign companies desiring a foothold in the US market and a list of wealthy private investors looking for a place to park their abundant cash.

You might say I'm being overly harsh and critical by claiming they were deceitful and lied. Well, they did and they do. They do so by knowingly presenting information that less than one percent of any given audience would qualify for. They are deceitful in how they position their minimum fees, which would erode a sizable percentage of the gross sale from the typical business owner.

The lead salesman (or actor) orates on his impressive biography supporting his knowledge and experience for you to entrust your life's work with him. His counterpart, the purposely chosen elder spokesman has a well-rehearsed role to fill by providing a level of confidence and to identify with the gray-haired demographic in attendance. The middle-aged lead player does most of the talking and is a very polished pitchman. The team play off each other in perfect choreography as the audience is increasingly drawn in by building up the supposed market demand and the sharing of success stories. The youngest member is tasked with handing out brochures and observing to learn the trade.

The dessert is served up with a final cherry on top: a formula showing how the business owner can actually make more money after selling his company compared to what he was making as an owner. All of this foreplay arouses everyone in the room to a near frenzy. Now comes the hard close.

The attendees who are interested in taking the next step are interviewed on the spot to assess whose business is worthy of going through this process with this prestigious firm. After all, there are a lot of businesses out there in a variety of industries and not all would meet the stringent criteria of such a scrupulous and discerning market maker. Sitting with one of the representatives, I share the details on my technology-centered business catering to the education market. Well, jackpot, I was the proverbial holy grail of ideal businesses that the M&A market were clamoring for. Now if I would just sign a multi-page agreement and write a check for $20,000, I would be guaranteed to be a client of this firm for the next year.

The agreement grants exclusive rights for a period of one year to this firm to sell my company. The $20,000 is a good faith payment to ensure my intent and to cover the vast amount of upfront expenses required to properly prepare my firm for market. If my company is sold (which it certainly would be without question), that $20,000 would be reduced from their customary fee. If there were to be no sale, the company would happily return the $20,000 after the one-year period.

Amazingly, there were several jackpots for the crew that morning. In fact, everyone that sat down at the table was a winner. The full court press was on in this final stage of the sale. Any sales pro knows that when you let a prospect walk or give them time to think about their actions, the close rate dramatically falls below 20 percent. They wanted me right then and there. Not surprisingly, they wanted every other person that chose to sit down with them too. It was remarkable that every business seemed to fit their highly selective screening process.

My intention of attending this gathering was to learn about the process and what was behind all of those glossy direct mail flyers that I had been receiving—and that is exactly what I got. I politely walked from the conference room out to my car and eventually was able to shake the last one off of my leg before closing the door. I had learned a great deal.

CHAPTER THIRTY-FIVE
Why a Business is Sold

Why do businesses get sold? We've just spent most of the book talking about how entrepreneurship is the dream of so many, and how these individuals overcome enormous obstacles to create their business. Why would they want to sell it?

I found that when friends and relatives are first told that a business was sold, their reaction is one of concern that something went wrong, forcing the owner to sell. Fewer people have an immediate reaction to congratulate the owner. I have not invested in psychological studies to obtain conclusive findings why this happens, but it is my strong assumption that it is reflective of the individual's Risk Box.

Those who draw negative conclusions from "I sold my business" view entrepreneurship as a job, a source of income, something they are dependent upon. They only associate how they would be if they "lost" their job and how that would destabilize life in their Risk Box. Those with celebratory reactions have a greater closeness and understanding of the entrepreneur and view selling the business as reward for years of hard effort.

Certainly there are a host of reasons why an entrepreneur sells his business. Businesses can be sold due to financial strains, divorce, death, differences between partners, lost contracts and agreements, family disputes, disasters such as fire or flooding, just to name a few of the more negative outcomes. People who are not entrepreneurs often think of these scenarios as forcing the sale of a business.

My immediate reaction is quite the opposite. I view the sale of a business as positive and the result of the direction and control of the entrepreneur driving change. Reasons to sell may include a desired lifestyle change, a sale to merge the business for future growth, an opportunity to raise capital to start another business, or simply to realize a profit.

The most common and understood reason to sell occurs when an entrepreneur is ready to retire. That is also the most vulnerable time for the entrepreneur to not fully realize the full value of his business, which I'll come to explain. Investment banker Bob Contaldo of Corporate Finance Associates, a mergers and acquisition firm, has outlined ten points that he has seen entrepreneurs consider when deciding whether or not to sell their business.

1. The thrill is gone

I think every entrepreneur goes through one or more phases wondering what the heck he got himself into by going into business. Frustrations develop with customers, credit, employees, regulations, and a hundred other factors. I've certainly experienced the thrill is gone a few times at TRC. Struggling with shrinking margins and customers who are obligated by state regulation to buy on price rather than value become an increasingly disheartening prospect.

The thrill is gone is often a brief period of exasperation which more beckons for vacation than a complete sale of the company. I don't think many entrepreneurs sell on the emotion of the moment as they usually can regroup and get re-energized to tackle the frustration they are faced with. When the thrill is truly gone and there is no hope of reconciliation, the entrepreneur has to realize the emotional state he is in and logically make a decision on how to proceed.

Selling on emotion is dangerous and can be costly. If the entrepreneur does not come to balance the emotional situation he is in with the business situation he is putting himself in, he runs the risk of selling his company for a price below its true market value. Acting on emotion in any facet of business should be avoided.

The time may come when the business no longer fuels the passion that led the entrepreneur to start it, and to a certain degree that's okay. This may be an opportunity to pass the business on to a family member or trusted and deserved partner. It may usher in a new role for the entrepreneur as board member versus CEO. Hiring a replacement to run the daily aspects of the business may allow the entrepreneur to look at the business more as an investment than a job, or it may simply be time to cash out.

2. The marketplace is changing

"When it comes to the future, there are three kinds of people: those who let it happen, those who make it happen, and those who wonder what happened."—John M. Richardson, Jr.

Every business and entrepreneur needs to embrace and seek out change. Change is what moves them forward. Eventually, the business environment that was present when the entrepreneur entered his chosen market will change and often the entrepreneur is responsible for that change. However, having to respond to significant and unexpected change may prove to be too much for the entrepreneur.

There are all sorts of market changes which include competitors, regulations, customer qualifications, labor requirements, patents, technological advancements, and supply constraints. Some market changes can be easily met; however, others can be very costly and disruptive to complacent businesses that have not foreseen such changes. Investment in capital or regulatory compliance to carry on may exceed a company's credit limitations.

Failure to adapt to market changes can be costly. Those who respond or react too slowly may eventually close their doors without an opportunity to find a market to sell their company. An entrepreneur who gets into this predicament has failed to manage and lead his company. Entrepreneurs who are on their game are able to look to the horizon and adapt accordingly. It is the complacent entrepreneur who allows his business to exist in the today rather than planning for the tomorrow. These entrepreneurs have essentially stuck their heads in the sand and, as Bob Contaldo says, "their emotions are simply not willing to embrace change."

3. Risk becomes a four-letter word

Risk seems synonymous with being an entrepreneur. However, time and routine can entrench an entrepreneur and discourage him from taking risks, thereby causing him to miss market changes. The Risk Box is constant and can hold an entrepreneur back from getting to the next level. It is said that fear is a great servant, but a terrible master. Most entrepreneurs are financed by personal guarantees on bank loans and lines of credit. Taking the company to the next level may not be realistic using traditional financing vehicles, and the entrepreneur may not have the stomach or knowledge to obtain more elaborate methods of funding. If the entrepreneur is unwilling to work with these new methods to grow his business or he simply has run out of gas in juggling the cash flow against obligations, then as Contaldo says, "there comes a time when it makes sense to take some chips off the table."

4. A change would be good for the family

Here's our workaholic entrepreneur who invests all of his effort and abilities into his business leaving little for his family. It is worth repeating that business ownership and marriage are not mutually exclusive relationships. Businesses don't require physical and emotional nurturing and neither may the entrepreneur, but the entrepreneur's family most certainly does. Temporary neglect may be acceptable to the family but it can't be a long-term situation. Some entrepreneurs simply don't know how to make the shift, and selling may be their only option. Not many business plans include an exit strategy to grow your business to the point to where your family is about to leave you and then sell.

There are plenty of paid services, experts, coaches, and friends who could help the entrepreneur balance his commitments and I would stress those options foremost before opting to sell.

5. Unprecedented seller's market

Bob Contaldo's fifth consideration for an entrepreneur to sell is valid, yet more a bit of self promotion to the business broker world. I don't prescribe to there being unprecedented seller or buyer markets. I suppose there are cycles where low interest rates, tax considerations, foreign interest, or other factors cause unusual spikes in merger and acquisition activity. Conversely, during the economic slump of 2008/2009 M&A activity virtually ceased as credit markets went into a deep hibernation. Anyone hoping to sell during this time undoubtedly found fewer buyers and experienced more deals falling apart forcing many to postpone selling. For the average entrepreneur, the time to sell a business is probably less influenced by the "perfect storm" scenarios as business brokers like to espouse.

6. Unusual financial gain

Contaldo describes this consideration to sell as every business owner's dream. The buyer who wants your company is much larger than your company and has deep pockets of cash just aching to be spent on your company. A cash deal is attractive because about 80 percent or more of all businesses sold are financed in some fashion. Financing a sale increases the cost, lengthens the time to close, and poses risk of the deal faltering due to complications related to the financing. Therefore, the cash buyer is the dream buyer for most sellers. Contaldo describes this buyer as willing to overspend because of their burning desire to own your company. As Contaldo says, "We can dream, can't we?"

For the typical small-to-medium business, this buyer scenario happens probably less than one percent of the time, but it is the scenario brokers paint most vibrantly. It pulls at the emotional heartstrings of the entrepreneur. The entrepreneur who does not plan or have a vision for this type of exit plan has virtually no chance of making it happen. However, the entrepreneur who does plan for it can greatly increase the odds of this long shot.

7. *The business is growing*

Scaling for growth is one of the entrepreneur's obligations, and in some cases, he may be too good at it. Fast growth is exciting and rewarding, but it comes at a price and has unique demands. As the business grows, the entrepreneur may not know how to let it go to the next level. He may be holding it back as he is stymied on how to properly manage risk and debt. The business can buckle under the strain of wanting to grow.

We've seen businesses that rise up fast and evaporate just as quickly. Steve & Barry's grew at an envious pace to its retail competitors as it consumed premium mall space at lease rates far below market because of its desirable anchor status. Steve & Barry's sales grew as they aggressively scaled growth by opening store after store. However, the business and profits could not keep up with the real estate obligations it was making. When bargain long-term lease agreements expired and were renewed at current market rates, cash subsidies provided by past eager mall owners slowed, and sales were not enough to add black to financial statements.

Even if cash flow is not the concern, experienced management may be. Entrepreneurs who recognize when to turn over the reins to an experienced management staff that can run the business at this high-growth stage are truly visionary. We've seen Michael Dell, Bill Gates, and Steve Jobs all hand over the keys to the next generation of leadership.

8. The business is flat

Whoops, too late. You don't want to be in a position of having to sell or wanting to sell when your business has gone flat or is in decline. Just like taking a new car off the lot, the value of your business is going to be worth far less when you go to market with flat or declining revenues or earnings.

Unfortunately, many entrepreneurs do sell at this point. Often this occurs after the peak of their career, when they have less fire in their belly to continue with change and innovation. They start to let things slide, relax on oversight, or become complacent. As a result, growth stalls. Business may get flat due to the particular industry, geographic area, or other outside factors. This is reflective of what I have been saying all along: most entrepreneurs do not have an exit plan. If they did, they would not let things get to this point before deciding to sell. The unplanned entrepreneur gets into a jam and then wants to unload damaged goods.

In researching this book I conducted a survey on what title resonated best with individuals. It was interesting to note the novice suggested I take *Exit* out of the title. They stated some entrepreneurs don't want to exit and that would turn them off from buying the book. Well guess what? Entrepreneurs don't have a choice in whether they will exit or not. The ultimate exit is death and I haven't found one entrepreneur able to prevent that change from occurring.

9. *Managing people has worn you out*

This is very similar to the thrill is gone. In fact, employees may be exactly why the thrill is gone. Most entrepreneurs of small-to-medium size businesses cite employee issues as one of their greatest headaches. Some of this may be self inflicted in that they have not inserted enough managerial levels between them and their workforce. It is critical to establish such boundaries to keep the entrepreneur working on the business rather than working in the business.

Employee issues may be more elaborate if unions are involved or if your workforce requires things like work visas. Employee-related costs such as medical insurance, profit sharing, taxes, and retirement plans are often not factors enough to wear out the entrepreneur. More often it is simply the day-to-day management of people that consumes too much time from the entrepreneur's true interests and keeps him from what he should be doing: innovating, scaling, and leading.

10. *Personal compelling reasons*

Selling for personal reasons can encompass a whole array of concerns. Hopefully, the entrepreneur who finds himself in this position is considering a sale as a positive lifestyle transition. Many successful entrepreneurs develop a compelling need to give back after they sell. They find themselves with both the time and money to focus on more philanthropic concerns, and that's where they want to be and how they want to round out their legacy. There may be a whole host of negative reasons as well that compel an entrepreneur to sell and "get out."

Where next?

The entrepreneur's vision is not a dream but a glimpse at a reality that can be achieved. There is confidence in knowing it can be obtained and then a longing to make it happen. I could clearly see that TRC was capable of $100 million in sales and figured it would take us seven years to get there. Now the only question was how. The bootstrap model was working fine, but it seemed unrealistic that cash flow alone would be able to propel 20 percent year-over-year growth for the seven consecutive years required to obtain this goal. Our facility likely would not be equipped for such growth requirements and neither would our credit vehicles. Staffing would have to ramp at an unprecedented rate and for the sanity of all involved, we would need a staff development manager to train an ongoing procession of new hires. Everything from our IT infrastructure to our lead generation system would have to be upgraded in order to move TRC into this heightened growth mode.

It was clear to me, as clear as my vision for $100 million, that all of this was not going to happen the same way we had done things in the past. I needed capital to fund and support this growth. My options would be a bank loan, private equity, or a wealthy investor. For those of you shouting IPO, the answer is no. TRC was not the type of company that would have made an attractive public company and would more than likely fail to find an underwriter. (Not to mention the costs and headaches involved with being a public company.)

I had secured bank lines of credit in the past as a safety net in case we needed extra capital, and I knew they wouldn't be sufficient. With margins being what they were, the cost to take on debt was concerning and my desire to grow could cripple the company by over extending ourselves. My Risk Box was trying to protect me. The other options of private investors or private equity either didn't appeal to me or didn't seem realistic. I sought professional advice which led me back to the options I had already arrived at on my own. So what did I want?

The recurring vision I had looking five years out was a dramatically altered marketplace for enterprise software sales. Although I could not pinpoint it, I sensed creative destructionism would be at play in the reseller channel during this timeframe, and technology would produce a radically different model that would quantum leap distribution and all related service aspects of software sales. The changes would be dramatic and require significant capital to build and replicate. I saw this innovation coming from outside of the traditional channel taking most existing players off guard and leaving them improperly tooled to respond.

As for TRC's innovations, they would be replicated or outdated within this timeframe replaced by better methods to meet customer needs. Certainly I could continue to innovate, but did I want to? Were the margins of this business attractive enough to make these investments and would there be a way to boost margins in the future? The immediate answer to these questions came in supplementing human services along with the software sale. Consulting and installation services were nothing new to the channel and value-added resellers were typically responsible for providing them. Along with the higher margins that services would provide, higher paid and technically skilled staff would necessitate a new selling process to attach services to the product sale.

How would I differentiate my services from everyone else? How could I scale a services model nationally? What trumped those questions was whether I wanted to even be in that business—and the answer was no. Services provided little passion for me. TRC had grown to an impressive $30 million in sales, became one of the most respected resellers in the nation, and was at its peak. Now we were stuck.

CHAPTER THIRTY-SIX
Why a Business Should be Sold

You've now seen reasons why a business is sold, but that does not answer why a business should be sold. When an entrepreneur is asked why he sold his company, seldom does he reply that it was a part of his business plan to do so. Establishing an exit strategy early should be viewed as a fiduciary obligation of the entrepreneur. Benjamin Franklin said, "By failing to prepare you are preparing to fail." Shockingly, over 75 percent of owners of private companies fail to establish an exit plan for themselves according to a study by PriceWaterhouseCoopers.

Based on 2008 census data, it was conceivable that half of the then current US business owners would plan to sell their business in the next ten years. It is fairly typical to assume that a third would sell to an independent third party buyer, another 30 percent would sell or transfer ownership to a family member, around 18 percent would consider employee purchase options, and the balance would most likely liquidate and close their doors. That's nearly 20 percent that close their business failing to realize a profit in their exit! Selling a business is not like putting a Business For Sale sign in the window. A business should be sold because a plan to do so exists.

Selling a company is a soul-searching prospect. After all, this venture has exacted most of your energy, emotion, money, and time. The thought of selling can be prompted by the constant advertisements from M&A brokers hitting the founder's desk. It may be brought on by watching competitors consolidate or worse— watching them go out of business. Sometimes a really lousy day may have the entrepreneur wishing he could just pitch it and walk away. Hopefully, those thoughts are lost after returning home and getting a good night's rest. There is also excitement in wondering just how much the business is worth, which is occasionally on an entrepreneur's mind.

Typically, the most important and valuable tangible asset an entrepreneur will have in his life is the business he has started. Most likely he has taken few steps to understand how to turn that asset into cash and transition out of the business. Most entrepreneurs don't start businesses for this end game and they likewise don't plan appropriately for the process of selling.

When it comes down to one of the most important decisions and processes of the company, most entrepreneurs are negligent because they are ill-informed and ill-prepared. I say negligent because by not being fully educated in the selling process, they are not mindful of their shareholders, even if the entrepreneur is the sole shareholder. The failure to comprehend and study the process can be costly, and many entrepreneurs who sell their business pay the price. They either spend too much in consulting, broker, legal, and other related expenses or they end up leaving money on the table.

Several valid explanatory reasons for selling a business have been provided, but there is one ideal reason why a business should be sold: The business is in a position to maximize shareholder value by virtue of a sale. The entrepreneur may be the single shareholder or there may be hundreds. Intentionally, this view is generic in scope in order to take into account personal, environmental, competitive, legal, economic, and other factors to weigh when selling. For instance, a business may foresee considerable losses in upcoming years or severe regulations that the owner is not capable of addressing and therefore moves to sell now to realize the current maximum value of the business.

Once a plan is established and it is understood why the business is to be sold, the entrepreneur must prepare himself and the company for the selling process.

It Feels Like the Right Thing to Do

The one option I did not explore to grow TRC to $100 million was an outright sale of the company. Perhaps I could sell the company to a firm that shared my vision of where TRC could grow and who had the capital and resources to make it happen. I intended to sell the company when I started it and created a benchmark goal to sell at this very time frame. Why not now? TRC was at the top of its game, showing consistent year-over-year revenue growth and a realistic capability to grow to our targeted levels.

I briefly considered merging with another large educational re-seller, Journey Education Marketing (JEM), who was a comparable competitor of TRC. They had been in business longer than TRC and carved out an enviable position selling software to students and faculty, making their model more of a consumer focus than business to business as TRC was known for. Publishers provided academic discounts to qualified individuals and schools on software, but the software could only be sold by authorized dealers such as TRC and JEM.

This, in essence, protected us from competing with retail outlets or online shops. The only competition for student business would be the mostly unsophisticated college bookstores, and JEM had obtained an exclusive relationship with the two major players (Barnes & Noble and Follett). JEM acted as their sole e-commerce and fulfillment platform. Bookstores wanted to sell technology but they were turned off by the rapid change in product versions. Partnering with a company like JEM removed all of that exposure. Blending our companies had significant benefits for each and would likely put our combined revenues very close to the $100-million mark.

I had a very informal conversation with JEM's founder and president. He had been entertaining similar thoughts, although for a variety of reasons, he planned to take action at a much later date. That took JEM off the table for consideration and gave me more time to review my long-held belief that competitor mergers don't work or don't yield the benefits intended. Whether the move involved debt, investment, or merger, I would be giving up a certain degree of control. That would be a significant change for me and one I wasn't entirely comfortable with.

A deal that would provide partial ownership for me while being dependent upon a combined interest was vexing since I would not have complete control in setting the course. Would I be able to grow the value of my interest in a combined entity or would I be better off selling TRC at once based on its own merits at the present time?

This deliberation caused me to reflect on three personal goals I set for myself many years earlier. One was to start a business before the age of 30, one was to sell that same business in ten years, and one was to sell to a Fortune 500 company. The first is not all that unusual but the second two deserve more attention. Why would I attach a timeframe to sell before the company ever opened its doors?

The answer is unique to the business I started and its industry. The one constant I could rely on was that technology would always be rapidly changing. Being the seller of technology meant that I would continually have something new to sell, but technology would be changing my business as well. While writing the TRC business plan, I knew that in ten years we would either be an established company ready to achieve our mission of being the most recognized provider of software licensing into education or market advancements would have eclipsed our growth. In either scenario, we would be in a position to sell based on the course of action I had seen other technology companies take during my career.

I was not steadfast about selling in ten years; it was a benchmark to ensure I was reviewing my progress at this significant milestone.

I formulated my goal of selling to a Fortune 500 company when I first started TRC. My vision was not so much to build a company that sold software to schools, but to build a company that penetrated a niche market that a Fortune 500 would want to tap. The education market represents over 15 million students and it refreshes every year. Factoring in the community college market, the demographic expands dramatically.

If I was going to take on the risk and investment of starting my own business, I wanted it to count and count big. I envisioned a business that would build in value and be able to achieve a sales multiple that would provide a significant pay-out. This may seem contrary to everything I've said about following your heart rather than your pocketbook when starting a business, but there is no fault in creating a business you are passionate about and devising a way to make a lot of money from it as well. The idea and the passion came first and formulated the mission statement. The goal to sell to a Fortune 500 came second. My passion and focus were on being the best provider to our customer base and to continually differentiate from the competition. I knew that if I achieved this the rest would come naturally.

I decided to sell TRC outright. This conclusion was based on my concerns with the industry outlook and investment needed to reach our seven-year target, but more on an incredible optimism that this was the best time to realize both of my goals for TRC. Now was an opportunity to maximize shareholder value. It felt right, and I had learned to listen to my gut. If TRC were to grow to $100 million, it would do so by putting the heavy lifting and risk on the acquirer.

I was starting to feel a profound obligation to achieve the goal that I had pitched to just about everyone we hired. Almost every interview I conducted included sharing my goal to sell TRC to a Fortune 500 company. I did this purposely to let potential employees know what I intended to do with this company should they come to work for me. The prospect and uncertainty of being sold was not for everyone, and I didn't want someone to make a career change only to be dismayed to find their employer was being sold. In my eyes, the goal served to be motivational and a testament of our ambitions. I wanted to make that rhetoric a reality and, in doing so, live up to the promise of expanded career growth.

CHAPTER THIRTY-SEVEN
Selling Your Business

There are two parts of consideration to a successful exit—transition and wealth maximization. Transition is when the owner moves to a new role as a result of the sale. Wealth maximization is tied to shareholders receiving the best value for their ownership interest. The two may not happen at the same time. If the decision to sell has been made then careful preparation must be conducted to ensure the goals of transition and wealth maximization are both achieved.

Owner Preparation and Transition

An owner may transition from CEO to an advisory role and allow a family member to succeed. An owner may transition to monitor an employee-ownership plan. These scenarios account for 48 percent of owner-exit plans and often delay wealth maximization. To simplify the topic of exiting, I will postulate that exiting equates to outright selling the company.

The question to ask is, once you sell your business— essentially your job—what are you going to do? Depending on the duration of being in your business exiting will be a life-altering experience. Your routine and energy has been centered on your business and depending on your exit you may no longer be involved. In preparation of this event you should be able to answer the following questions without vacillation.

1. Why do you want to sell?

Not only is it important for you to soul search the answer,

this will be the first question every potential buyer is going to ask you. As such, you may have an answer for yourself and an answer you want to tell the rest of the world. Personally, you need to be clear as to why you are selling so you will rest easy after the sale is done. Are you doing it for the right reasons? Are there alternatives to selling? Have you considered all the worst-case scenarios and lowest returns acceptable to selling?

Assuming your personal considerations are addressed then the public reason you want to relate should be spun into an engaging elevator pitch that you will recite with confidence. Buyers will probe an owner for their true motivation for selling. They want to find skeletons in the closet that are not being disclosed that may expose them to risk or overpayment. The buyer will also want to find a nerve that may help them negotiate a lower price if they perceived the desire to sell as a weakness during negotiations.

2. What do you want to happen from selling?

When you sell you are not merely turning the keys over to someone new, there are often a variety of outcomes you want to realize as a result. An owner may stay on in a transition role temporarily or permanently. They may be asked to leave the day the deal is done or they may want to. The business may become part of a conglomerate used to go public several years down the road. The firm may be broken up or infused with cash to expand. The answer to these questions will address the owner transition considerations, which leaves the issue of wealth maximization.

Undoubtedly, an owner will have a predisposed notion of what the business is worth and that will serve as a minimum accepted bid. However, the financial outcome of a sale can be very complicated with a wide variety of methods to pay out the eventual agreed-upon sum. The owner needs to consider ahead of time what will be acceptable. Some deals are paid in stock, options, over time, paid as an earn-out or any variation thereof. The vast majority is financed and may involve a degree of risk and extended time to complete. Do you desire an asset sale or a stock sale? What are the tax and legal implications of the sale and how are they unique to your type of incorporation?

Selling a business is far more complicated than just receiving a check and heading to the golf course. The outcome you desire needs to be incorporated into the offering when your company goes to market and related when you are asked why you want to sell.

3. What can go wrong by deciding to sell?

Owners can inadvertently become self-centered when it comes to selling their business. It is a very personal process, but it involves far more people than may initially be considered. Stakeholders, friends, and family interpret a company for sale in different ways. Regardless of stated reasons, each will likely draw their own conclusions. Customers are of primary concern and most will see little upside in the news that their vendor is being sold. Similarly, employees will have very real concerns about job security and new management. Suppliers will fear losing you as a customer and competitors may take the news as a sign of weakness or an opportunity to obtain what had been confidential information. Considering these concerns, it is best to keep news of a potential sale confidential.

That being said, you may go to market to find there are no buyers or none meeting your reserve requirements. Further, you may get an offer and due to a variety of reasons the deal may not go through. This will represent a loss in time commitment, resources, money, and energy. When you go to sell there is a natural adrenalin rush that lasts during the entire process which can result in a dramatic let down if nothing comes to fruition. Think about it. Mentally you are prepared to sell your business and transition to your next passion and then it fails to happen. It is difficult to regroup and direct your energies back to scaling, innovating, and leading the business you thought you were going to sell.

Company Preparation and Wealth Maximization

Once you've established how you want to transition as the owner, attention must be directed toward how to maximize the value of the company. Selling your company is not a task to accomplish; it is the ultimate strategic sale. Be prepared to start putting in long hours like you did during the startup phase. The Sales Maxim tells us that you need to have confidence when you go to sell and that is gained by having as much knowledge as possible about your product, which, in this case, is your company, and the potential customers who are your acquirers.

Representation from a variety of experts will be required and researching who you will want to use well in advance will be beneficial. Certainly the services of an attorney with merger and acquisition experience and an expert on applicable tax consequences is a must. Optional services may include a broker and a professional negotiator which I'll later discuss in greater detail. As you've seen in the idea, startup, and running phase, preparation is the first order of business in the exit phase. If you intend to maximize the value of your business then you need to get your ducks in a row starting with the following areas of focus.

House in Order

Just like putting a house up for sale, a business owner needs to put his business house in order prior to a sale. This won't be conducted over a weekend and optimally will be in process over the course of possibly several years. Foremost, all legal affairs must be in order before any consideration of selling is to be attempted. Any type of personal or business litigation needs to be concluded prior to a sale. That includes divorce proceedings. The last thing you want is an ex-spouse making a claim against your business while you are at the negotiations table.

Cleaning house includes touching up what I call bruises and blemishes, and the list can be rather lengthy. As an example, consider reviewing your accounts receivable and value of bad debt. Old receivables are going to be a point of contention and will likely be taken off the valuation after an offer is made. Anything over 90 days will be considered a write-off. You'll either want to work really hard at collecting, hire an agency to collect for you, or consider selling off your old receivables. Depending on how inventory is managed, it may be wise to draw down to a just-in-time level. If there are persistent or recurring customer service issues, particularly with high-profile customers, get them corrected. Certainly, this should be a priority regardless of a sale.

Documentation

Careful review of internal documents and financial records should be assessed well in advance of going to market. The due diligence process that will take place once an offer is made is incredibly thorough and involved. Legal contracts as minuscule as copier leases and telecommunications contracts will be reviewed, and quick access to these records will make the process go smoother. Any type of agreement between suppliers, customers, employees, partners, service providers, and landlords will be requested. This includes bids awarded by customers. Taking a dry run with an expert may be beneficial to know where your documentation deficiencies are so they can be corrected prior to the chaos and frenzy of due diligence.

Run through the various financial valuation models to get an estimated worth on your own. Ensure that you have been following proper accounting principles, procedures, and documentation. Don't create work or go through expense unless you are advised to do so by professionals. For example, don't rush out and conduct an audit if you've never done one just because it's optimal to have been audited. Audits are expensive and in many cases won't be necessary depending on the size of your organization.

Now is a good time to update and document your S.W.O.T. analysis. This, along with cataloging your intellectual property and differentiating features, will serve as content that will go into your company profile that will be used as a marketing tool when you go on the market. Patents, trademarks, and copyrights will lead the list but any other nuance, procedure, process, messaging, or methodology that makes your company unique needs to get on that list. The sale will consist of a valuation of your financial model and your intrinsic/IP factors and the later will provide the greatest leverage in boosting the offeror's multiple. There's a lot stored in an entrepreneur's head and that needs to get down on paper, not only for marketing purposes but eventual transition as well.

Presentation

Just like any sale, you will need to develop an effective sales presentation by learning acquirer needs and how your company can address those needs. A prospectus of sorts should be compiled that gives a high-level overview of financials, market niche, product and service features, and intellectual property. A broker will either produce or assist in creating such a document along with a one-page sell sheet for initial mass release designed to garner interest. Subsequent presentations will be tailored to the specific company expressing interest and tailoring your profile to their needs.

Ready to Go

Even though margins were eroding in the market, TRC remained successful by winning business based on the value-added features and innovations we had developed. We continued to grow, specifically in the academic consumer segment and with consortia partnerships. Our direct academic reseller competitors were not faring as well. Reliant upon strictly academic business, larger competitors who had been developing their academic divisions over the years were making an impact. Some of the smaller academic dealers who adhered to their original business models silently closed their doors. Others who still had a viable brand name were being acquired for pennies on the dollar. In a short period of time five academic dealers would be acquired almost all by fire sale.

These five businesses essentially dissolved with little wealth maximization or owner transition. The founders did not have their eye on the horizon and most likely failed to have an exit plan. As sales trended downward, they failed to react, and did not have a plan to get out before irreparable damage was done. Businesses are investments and tremendous psychology is at play when worth is at stake. Individual investors can lose their entire principle watching their investment slide, finding it difficult to sell at a level below what they paid. Same is true for business owners who have a true or estimated value of their company at stake. As business deteriorates and its subsequent value slides, the owner is resistant to sell for a price lower than his historical valuation. However, history is just that. To maximize shareholder value, the owner needs to prepare a viable strategy to get back on course or consider a short sale to stem future losses.

Once I had made the decision to sell TRC, the course was swift as I had done my Entrepreneurial Exercises in advance and knew the route I wanted to take to put TRC on the market. I had already researched and chosen a respected Chicago law firm and a professional broker. We would spend the next month creating TRC's portfolio which would be submitted to interested and specially targeted firms. A few housekeeping items were recommended to clean up the physical appearance of the office as well as assembling historical financial information that would be requested. Once preparations were complete, TRC's information would be included on the multiple listing feeds that announced to the M & A community that TRC was available for purchase. I had no apprehensions and I was anxious to see what the next steps would entail.

CHAPTER THIRTY-EIGHT
Going to Market

The three constant determinants for success in every phase, including exit, includes preparation, the I.D.E.A. components, and selling. Once you've conducted as many preparation items as possible, or as instructed by your advisor, you are ready to go to market with your business. The process of selling will require every element of the I.D.E.A. as well as your selling skills. A mindset can develop, especially when using a broker or other representation, that the business will sell itself. Unless your business is a high-profile brand, you will need to muster all of your marketing and sales skills to attract the appropriate buyer.

All of your abilities will be called upon to continue managing your business while simultaneously working to sell it. A new desire will emerge to make this goal materialize and the effort primarily expelled during startup will need to emerge to carry you through. A wide variety of buyers and situations will present themselves and innovative measures will be called upon to engage their interest and move them to make an offer.

By the time you go to market, you will have an established sales plan and process to sell your company. Many people, including myself, enlist the services of a business broker or M&A specialist, advisor, negotiator (or similar title) to help create and execute that plan. It's important to do your homework to find the right person or company to do the job as skill set and services rendered vary greatly. Again, the planning process should bring to the surface what services and talent you will require to augment your own knowledge and ability. An important gap to fill for most business owners is reaching the multiple listing services that will promote your business to private equity, third party buyers, and foreign investors. Certainly Web-based services have emerged but for credibility and quality buyers it is best to tap professionals who know how to reach M&A specialists.

When an entrepreneur's business is for sale, more often than not, the entrepreneur is up for sale as well. Entrepreneurs hold tremendous influence, knowledge, and relationships in their business and ensuring a successful transition often requires the entrepreneur to stay on for a period of time post sale. As such, you will be scrutinized as closely as your company's books. Be prepared to be in the spotlight and interrogated. If your plan is to walk away with the check, think again as that may be a deal killer. Unless you've managed to build a business that is very independent of you, you should plan to stick around as long as your acquirer desires, which customarily would be one to two years.

Business Brokers

I've mentioned brokers several times and it's worthy to discuss their services. Most are similar to real estate agents in that they list your company in the multiple channels of active buyers. They have access and relationships with private equity, venture capital, private investors, foreign investors, and listing services. Attracting the largest potential pool of buyers is critical to foster a competitive bidding environment. Many will represent you as the seller and assist with the process including the formal exchange of documentation and negotiations. They should assist in "packaging" your company into a traditional sell sheet and prospectus. Like a real estate agent, a broker will take a percentage of the gross sale and often requests an upfront retainer for his services.

If you talk to enough seasoned entrepreneurs, you'll find plenty of stories, both good and bad, about the brokers they have encountered. You'd like to think that these guys are on your side to maximize the value of your business, when, in reality, most are focused on closing the deal in the shortest amount of time to collect their commission. I can't fault them too much, and there certainly are pros out there doing a great job, but ultimately they are salespeople who have quotas to hit.

The caution I raise is with their pitch and positioning. These guys know all the emotional points to hit with entrepreneurial owners. Understand that they will be continually selling you through the process, which may come across as advice. You will have to decipher the difference and hold true to your goals and objectives. You will also have to remind yourself not to put too much faith and reliance into their efforts as they will never match your own. It is easy during the long courting process to get tired and have the urge to push things off on your broker. Never take yourself out of the loop; stay in control of the process.

I encourage enlisting the services of a professional negotiator when a viable offer has been extended. There is a process to skilled negotiations and buyers often have the upper hand in experience and positioning. Should you be courted by a large corporation, it is likely they have made acquisitions in the past and have mastered the negotiation process or enlisted professionals themselves. The price to be paid for the company is merely one of many points of negotiation that will arise during closing and this is when you want top talent on your side.

Courting

The courting process is about creating a buzz and sense of urgency with multiple buyers. During preparation you should have assembled a list of potential or desired acquirers and established selling points as to why they would want to buy your company. Don't limit yourself to your industry. Create scenarios like roll-up strategies to go public; integrating technologies; synergistic cost savings; geographic expansion; or adding new segments, products, and customers. Buyers will have their own intentions to consider, but your creative thinking will help target a wider audience and potentially heighten their interest.

Look at your company through the lens of a potential acquirer and think of ways that your company could add value to that organization. It is critical to keep in mind that the focus is on the buyer not you! Although this is much more than just a business to you, at the end of the day, you are selling a product that will answer a buyer's need. Your job is to find out what that need is and position your company as the solution.

Courting can start to get chummy, especially if there seems to be a good fit, which is what everyone is striving for. However, objectivity must be kept when negotiations start to occur and here again a hired representative can help provide a buffer between you and what may become your future employer. Your legal advisor may be another source of representation during negotiations that allows you to play good cop/bad cop.

Perfect Timing

When TRC hit the market in late 2005, I was curious to see the reaction and who we would attract. I had assembled a list of about 20 companies that I felt would make a complimentary fit with TRC. This included Best Buy who was starting a new education-focused reseller division; Systemax, a conglomerate of resellers and an international personal computer manufacturer; Office Depot who had a fledgling focus on education and software licensing; and ASAP Software which would eventually be sold to Dell. I also considered an unlikely sale to a software publisher like Adobe Systems and telecommunication companies like Sprint or Verizon who may be looking to penetrate the college student market. I did not restrict myself to Fortune 500 prospects as it is necessary to cast the widest net of potential buyers. The goal was to attract several buyers at once to propagate a bidding environment.

Initially, we received several responses from small companies that I had not previously heard of. Some were in the IT industry while others represented unrelated products or services. A few caught our interest and some made low-ball offers that quickly evaporated our interest. It is an exciting, albeit stressful, experience to engage with new companies to learn their business and motives for acquisition. Each opportunity was a chance to hone my selling skills and to adapt the presentation to the unique needs of each potential buyer. It was challenging to decipher the buyer's intentions in order to play up or down either our financials or our value-added features. Truth be told, it was exhilarating and I enjoyed it. I really wanted to get to the table with Best Buy and Office Depot but discussions would only surface over the phone with Office Depot. TRC was a natural fit to either organization as they were developing a focus in education and knew little about software licensing. TRC was far more advanced than any competitor on the market. We had an impressive customer portfolio and years of growth to support our boasting, not to mention the Microsoft LAR authorization, which they would likely never get on their own. Much to my disappointment, discussions fizzled in the corporate bureaucracy of Office Depot as it was clear we were not talking to influencers but decision makers who were far removed from the customer nerve center. The innovations developed at TRC did not resonate with this team because they had not experienced the customer or internal pain points of software licensing.

By late fall, we had been on the market a couple months

and the level of response started to dry up. There was serious consideration being given to a collegiate book distributor, but their financials were not exciting nor were the future prospects with them. Around this time, my broker was pushing me to submit our material to CDW who I had intentionally left off the target list. In fact, they were on the "to block" list, meaning no information was to reach them. My plan was to partner with the number two or three player in the market to challenge CDW who was in a commanding lead position at $7 billion in annual sales and improving their position on the Fortune 500 list yearly.

My strategy was that a buyer would recognize the value TRC could bring to them in closing the gap on CDW. They would have a secret weapon in the intellectual property that we had developed that could be quickly scaled to any segment. Further, the niche we carved out in education would return tremendous growth in incremental sales. My primary resistance to CDW was that I didn't think they needed TRC, and I feared them replicating our innovations once we exposed them. It was clear CDW knew of TRC, but only in their education division where we had festered into a nuisance. I perceived great risk engaging with CDW at this point.

A danger in selling that the entrepreneur needs to recognize is their personal attachment to the business. It is an emotionally exhausting experience and objectivity can get lost in the process. With the trail starting to get cold, my broker pressed again about CDW, and I reluctantly agreed to submit our packet to them. In November 2005, our material went out to CDW along with my concerns of what we might reveal and how they may capitalize on our secrets.

CDW was in the mood to buy in 2005 and they were being very vocal in the press about it. They had just built a 400,000 square foot warehouse in Las Vegas that needed additional volume to maximize its full potential. Acquisitions were one way to fill that need. They were flush with cash being one of the most efficient and profitable resellers in the world and having gone public years prior. It was now a public strategy for CDW to grow by acquisition to achieve grander sales goals; their trick was to find the right companies.

CDW had not been able to find an attractive acquisition for some time. They had the right mindset for what they wanted to and did not want to acquire. Buying their biggest competitor that did exactly what they did was not part of their strategy. This mirrored my philosophy. What CDW wanted was a complimentary business that could scale and add value to their core competency.

When our prospectus reached CDW, we received an immediate response. Our material was clearly organized to show our niche in education and software licensing and those two points allowed our document to be routed directly to a key influencer, the Director of Higher Education. It certainly helped that we had already established a reputation within the CDW education sales staff as an aggressive competitor that was taking large software licensing contracts left and right from them. We were a real thorn in their side, and I loved being in that position. After a preliminary phone call, they wanted to meet and a week later we were scheduled to visit their home office 45 minutes from TRC.

To my utter surprise, conversations went remarkably well, and I could sense a chemistry developing. Our material had reached their hands at exactly the right time. A green light to acquire was given from within and here was a growing company that had developed a revolutionary method to present, sell, and transact volume software licensing that could be transferred and scaled to every customer segment within CDW. We were speaking the same language and sharing the same customer pain points. Our intellectual property would overcome major obstacles that CDW could not address on their own. Both parties were anxious to move forward.

My fears of CDW copying our innovations subsided as we continued to meet and understand their reasons for considering a TRC acquisition. This gave me confidence to reveal more and deeper details about our Web functionality and sales strategies. I quickly became smitten with the prospect of joining forces with the firm I considered one of my greatest competitive threats. I was discussing merger plans with likeminded individuals who were pleasant and had a certain reasonableness about them. Our conversations were going extremely well and everything seemed to gel perfectly. CDW had weaknesses that TRC could bridge, and I was anticipating that both parties were ready to take the relationship to the next level.

Late one afternoon in spring of 2006, I received a call from my broker. He had received a letter of intent to acquire TRC from CDW. I sensed it would be coming and now that it was actually delivered I was excited—darn right giddy, I would say. The deal with CDW had been the best scenario TRC could have envisioned. As a local Fortune 500 company, CDW was financially secure, consistently growing, repeatedly recognized as a top corporation for employees to work for, known for its litany of employee benefits and perks, and in sync my perspective on customer care and sales execution. Best of all they wanted to pay cash—no financing hurdles! The whole selling process had brought such highs and lows and right now it was all highs.

CHAPTER THIRTY-NINE
Negotiations

I like to play Texas Hold'em poker with my neighbors. One thing I've learned from experience is that I may be holding decent cards from the initial deal, but they don't mean much until I see the flop. A common trap less-experienced players fall into is getting blinded by aces. For instance, if I get dealt an ace and then say a nine, I tend to focus strictly on that ace. I pay so much attention to it that I forget to decipher what type of hand my opponents may have. Inevitably, I miss an obvious flush or straight, especially if an ace is revealed on the board.

The same psychology holds true for your business when the time comes to put out the For Sale sign. Your business has some great attributes that make it unique. Those are your aces. An entrepreneur can dig his heels in and demand a certain value for his company based on those aces without considering what the buyer is holding in his hands. The buyer may have no interest or need for your aces, but he may be interested in several other aspects that you are neglecting to disclose due to your polarized focus. Getting locked into your perceived strengths may derail a deal or allow you to sell short other meaningful aspects of your business.

During the courting phase for TRC, I pushed the Microsoft Select Large Account Reseller (LAR) status that we possessed as a significant and unique value add because only 19 dealers in the country had this designation and no new dealers were being added. Much to my disappointment, several interested buyers had no use for our LAR status. They did not understand its significance, and even if they did, it served no purpose for them. To retain their interest, I had to get off my compulsion with LAR status and focus on finding what would interest them.

Once an actual offer is received by either buyer or seller, the negotiation process begins. Many different factors including employment agreements, perks and benefits, salary, assets exclusion, and so on are involved in determining the worth of the company. Since negotiating truly is an art, I recommend the services of a professional. This may be your only chance to sell a business and you want to make it count. However, your role is not removed or diminished during the process. The entrepreneur has to be on his toes to ensure the process goes well.

Let's dive deeper into negotiations, specifically the process of deriving the company's value. This includes two separate analyses: the financial and the intrinsic. The buyer is first going to review the financial performance and condition of the company to establish a benchmark accounting evaluation of worth. The far less quantitative intrinsic analysis comes next by establishing a value to things like brand name, patents, rights, agreements, contracts, talent, and so forth.

The Financial Analysis

Understanding the value of a business, particularly a privately held business, is not as simple as one would assume, and it is often a mystery to the business owner himself. Sure, balance sheets, income and cash flow statements are generated monthly or quarterly but few privately held businesses actually calculate company worth using formulas like EBITDA (Earnings Before Interest, Taxes, Depreciation and Amortization). The EBITDA statement is often ignored by owners as it exists foremost as a valuation tool, rather than an operational tool, which is the focus of the entrepreneur in the trenches. I'll argue that EBITDA should be used as a monthly operational tool or as a dashboard metric for the entrepreneur to continually monitor profitability.

The financial evaluation is black and white on its surface in terms of applying the following accounting methods to establish a company's value.

The Comparable Worth Method

This is a rather simplistic (often pre-acquisition) method of finding businesses with comparable worth to your own company. It may be finding a competitor with similar revenues to your own who recently sold. The trick is that this often applies only to public companies whose books are open, or based on sales information exposed in the news media. The weaknesses of this method are apparent as so much supporting information is not considered or available in the analysis. Your company is going to be valued on profit, not raw sales revenue. Therefore, a stronger method is needed to obtain the ratio of a competitor's sales to their costs and compare that to your own to establish a level of profitability.

The Asset Valuation Method

This is the least desirable method to use. It simply assigns a worth to the hard assets of your company. This method is used when a large portion of a firm's value is pegged to their fixed assets, but a seller should not let it be the exclusive method to evaluate the value of the business. Think of a business that wanted to start producing steel. They have a choice of building a new steel mill or buying one ready to go. Buyers are considering the overall "cost of reproduction" which would involve constructing the same assets as what they are considering buying only at current prices.

Buyers are also faced with the "cost of replacement," to purchase the same desired assets at current prices. Primary buyer consideration is given to the time needed to replicate the assets to start the business on their own or to buy what may be existing. A great example is Significant Education, LLC's acquisition of the assets of struggling Grand Canyon University in 2004. With an acquisition, overnight, Significant Education would have a physical college campus that they would be able to take public in 2008 and establish themselves as the sixth-largest online university in the country.

Financial Performance Methods

More common and accepted valuation methods are financial performance measures which review historical results and predict future performance in determining a value. This helps a buyer understand what the business will be worth after the closing. The most common methods include Net Present Value (NPV), Internal Rate of Return (IRR), Discounted Cash Flow, and Return on Investment (ROI). A buyer and seller may and should use all of these models when establishing an evaluation.

Multipliers

Multipliers are less of a method to establish the value of a company as they are to project it. The purpose for multipliers is to establish a future worth of the company based on historical performance. The multiplier can be subjective but refined if tied to a net present value of money to determine an appropriate buyer's return on investment. Multipliers are assigned to accounting evaluations like EBITDA, revenue, or even earnings if applicable. Raw multipliers do not take into account buyer benefits from the economies of scale, market conditions, timing of the negotiations, taxes, internal motivation and goals of both buyer and seller, or other factors that may not be explicitly defined.

Strictly evaluating a worth on a financial model may not be prudent as a publicly held company's management strives to show high earnings on its financial reports in order to attract people to buy its stock thereby improving its price-to-earnings ratio. A closely held company's management may be working to minimize the earnings shown on its financial reports in order to minimize its tax burden. Financial reports really serve as a basis to ask questions about the business, its history, and its strategies to arrive at an appropriate financial valuation.

The Intrinsic Analysis

Business worth is not fully realized by financial measure alone. The intrinsic elements of the company—the most difficult to replicate— are yet to be considered. The true essence of a company is its differentiation which can take various forms such as distribution methods, copyrights, business processes and methodology, in addition to examples already cited. I'll refer to intrinsic value generically as intellectual property or IP. The IP of a company is what separates it from its competition and it will be the greatest factor to influence the final valuation of the firm.

The importance of the entrepreneur focusing on innovation and developing the company's IP is evident at this juncture. Certainly IP's foremost role during startup and running was to attract customers and differentiate from the competition, but now its value will pay dividends in boosting the ultimate valuation. There are models to determine intrinsic value; however, most are applied to public equity. The most applicable method for small-to-medium private firms will be to apply an additional multiplier value to the already derived financial valuation. This becomes very subjective, which is to the benefit of the savvy seller.

Accountants and CFOs do not like subjectivity. They prefer mathematical reasoning to support all underlying numbers. The seller can help the buyer in this process, and at the same time increase their chances for having their multiples supported or increased if they have a methodology to present. Although it does not remove all subjectivity, I have derived a Negotiations Worksheet to aid in merging the financial and intrinsic valuations.

CHAPTER FORTY
Negotiations Worksheet

T he negotiations worksheet is a tool to be used throughout the negotiation process that separates the financial evaluation from the intrinsic evaluation. Its purpose is to garner the highest valuation by increasing the number of company items or features that can individually be assigned a value or separate multiple. The premise being that the more individual items are being measured, the greater the chances are of negotiating a higher overall value.

The Negotiations Worksheet

FINANCIAL ANALYSIS	Buyer	Buyer Multiplier	Buyer Total	Seller	Industry Multiplier	Seller Total
EBITDA	$3,000,000	3	$9,000,000	$3,000,000	3.5	$10,500,000
Asset Valuation	$1,500,000	3	$4,500,000	$1,500,000	3.8	$5,700,000
Net Present Value	$2,500,000	3	$7,500,000	$2,500,000	3.6	$9,000,000
Discounted Cash Flow	$2,400,000	3	$7,200,000	$2,400,000	3.5	$8,400,000
Comparable Worth	$8,500,000	1	$8,500,000	$13,500,000	1.0	$13,500,000

INTRINSIC ANALYSIS	Buyer	Multiplier Value		Seller	Multiplier Value	
Brand & Trade Marks				X	0.3	
Technology				X	0.1	
Proprietary Technology	X	0.4				
Intellectual Property	X	0.5				
Processes	X	0.2				
Geography				X	0.2	
Customers	X	0.3				
Certifications	X	0.3				
Human Capital				X	0.3	
Copyrights				X	0.1	
Additional Multiple Total	1.7			Additional Multiple Total	1.0	$18,450,000

Let's break down how to use the worksheet and determine where individual points of valuation can be inserted. The following scenario is condensed and simplified to demonstrate the functionality of the worksheet.

How to Use the Negotiations Worksheet

1.) Prior to an offer, the Seller will:
   a. Complete and document as many financial evaluation models as possible on the Seller's portion of the Financial Analysis to determine which is the most and least favorable to the Seller.
   b. Line list all Intellectual Property items in the Intrinsic Analysis portion of the worksheet.
   c. Determine historic industry multiples applied to each financial evaluation model for similar industry M&A activity.

2.) The Buyer will make an offer, which will be documented on the Buyer's portion of the worksheet. The Seller will verify if the offer was made strictly using a financial evaluation, if intrinsic values were included and what, if any, multiple was applied. The Seller will document those findings in the appropriate sections of the worksheet.

3.) Seller's Review
   a. Does the Buyer's financial valuation match the Seller's same financial valuation, i.e., did both arrive at the same EBITDA? Ideally, you want to identify and strip away any stated intrinsic analysis included in the offer that raised the valuation.

b. Does the Buyer's multiple match the historic industry multiple?

c. Do other financial formulas provide a more favorable result for the Seller?

4.) Seller's Response

Prior to the Seller responding to accept or counter the offer, the following questions should be asked of the Buyer.

a. Why did the Buyer select this financial model and did they consider other models?

b. Why does the Buyer want to purchase the Seller's business?

c. What aspects specifically appeal to the Buyer about the business? List them in detail under the Intrinsic Analysis and ask the Buyer to rank them from least to highest importance. If the Buyer stated they were buying you strictly for revenues or profit generation you would leave those as factors under the financial analysis.

d. Did the Buyer recite intrinsic items that the Seller already denoted? If so, put an X in the Seller column of the Intrinsic Analysis showing that the Buyer values this item.

e. Did the Buyer mention IP items not designated by the Seller? If so, add them to the Intrinsic Analysis and put an X in column B showing that the Buyer designated this as a valued IP.

f. Does the Buyer value any of the remaining intrinsic items identified in the worksheet?

g. What pain points does the Buyer want eliminate through this acquisition?

h. What goal(s) does the Buyer want to achieve through this acquisition?

i. How will the Buyer finance the acquisition?

j. What would the Buyer like to see about your company
that was not presented?

5.) Buyer's Response
The Buyer should be able to answer all of the Seller's questions,
and using this information, the Seller can formulate the first counter
offer. All of the questions that the Seller asks are designed to learn
how much the Buyer values each line item of IP, and if any IP was
missed during the Seller's own internal evaluation. The last question
(j) is asked to determine the complete list of Buyer's needs. It may
be that the Seller cannot fulfill all of the Buyer's needs, or it may
provide an opportunity for the Seller to revisit their presentation to
show that indeed they do fulfill the missing need.

6.) Seller's Counter Offer

Financial Analysis Response
Armed with the Buyer's responses, the Seller will make
a counter offer using the worksheet as justification. The Seller's
response will begin with the Financial Analysis portion from
which any one or a combination of the following can be used.
a. Counter with a higher financial valuation model if
one exists.
b. Average several valuation models to obtain a higher
valuation than the single one selected by the Buyer.
c. Counter with a higher multiple using the industry as a
benchmark but not as a ceiling.
d. The counter multiplier should be done as a whole and
fractional amount. For instance, counter with a 7.8 times
multiplier versus 7.0.

Intrinsic Analysis Response

The Seller will assign a multiplier to each of the intrinsic items that the Buyer stated was of value based on the ranking conducted in 4c. The multiplier used will be fractional starting at .01 and increasing up to any whole number. For instance, the Seller may assign a value of .02 to trademarks and 2.5 for certifications. The value of the multiple should have relevance to the importance ranking the Buyer provided earlier. For instance, the highest ranking IP item should have the highest multiple out of all of the listed IP items.

Questions 4c – 4f are intended to extract every intrinsic item of value from the Buyer. Even if the Buyer states they simply desire revenue and profits, those revenues and profits are derived because of the intrinsic items. Therefore, value needs to be assigned to them.

This will produce a listing of intrinsic items with separate multipliers. The sum total of those multiples would be added to the multiple used in the financial analysis. Together that multiple is then multiplied by the valuation dollar amount determined in the designated financial formula. This will produce a new valuation total.

Take careful consideration over the next couple paragraphs as they reveal an important strategic aspect to negotiations.

It is critical to understand the roles and titles of all those involved on the Buyer side. Typically, the financial consideration and review is going to be delegated to someone on the Buyer's side that is removed or not as intimate with the acquisition process. It may be the accountant or CFO who is familiar with financial models that is requested to state an opinion. The Buyer will use their expert to assess the Seller's financials and formulate an offer. The financial reviewer will often have less influence overall in determining whether to move forward or not with the deal.

The person on the Buyer side reviewing the intrinsic components will often hold the greatest influence and ownership of the acquisition. It is likely that the intrinsic factors are what are most attractive and compelling to the Buyer. Typically the person who will be responsible for the acquisition and "own it" will be the same person reviewing the intrinsic factors. The financial valuation will be fairly rigid and straightforward. The greatest leverage and basis for negotiation will come from the intrinsic side and the decision maker assigned to its review.

This goes back to understanding why the Buyer wants to acquire the firm. If simply adding revenue or profit to the books is their interest and all intrinsic factors hold little regard, the Seller is most likely not maximizing shareholder value with this buyer. It is usually only through asserting the value of intrinsic items that a seller will be able to bolster an otherwise low or average financial valuation. The Seller needs to understand that the decision maker will typically be directed internally toward the financial evaluation, but they will be most attracted to the intrinsic variables. This person holds the greatest influence in swaying the overall financial opinion and your job as the Seller is to move the weighting of their decision making toward the intrinsic factors.

Advantages of the Negotiations Worksheet
Negotiations that follow the worksheet provide a logical explanation for both the Buyer and Seller to arrive at a designated price. Following common sales strategies, the Seller gets the Buyer to talk about why they want to make the acquisition, and what is valued most about the company. Prior to an offer being made, the Seller listens and asks questions of the Buyer related to the worksheet. The goal is for the Buyer to reveal all of the intrinsic items that they feel are important. The Seller will question the Buyer on

intrinsic items that the Buyer failed to mention in conversation to determine if they hold any value. Documenting the Buyer's responses in the worksheet creates a dashboard to drive negotiations.

The key in negotiations is to establish several points of discussion, opposed to one lump package or number. The worksheet provides multiple levers to tweak with the Buyer to achieve this purpose. Dissecting the initial offer with the Buyer to ideally separate the intrinsic items from the financial analysis will extend the number of areas to negotiate. Further, the Seller must demonstrate a reliance on the intrinsic items as determinants for the overall financial results of the firm.

On the financial analysis the Seller can counter the valuation derived, the multiple used, or introduce other models for comparison. For instance, the Seller may shift to an asset valuation to heighten the value of the company's hard assets and request a greater multiple. The financial analysis may provide the least amount of wiggle room, whereas, the intrinsic factors are completely subjective and open to wide variances. That is why it is so important to extensively interview the Buyer to determine their value and understanding of all your intrinsic items.

By line listing your firm's intrinsic items, you have assigned separate fractional multiples to each one. Now you can negotiate each intrinsic item and the corresponding multiple assigned. These add up fast and you can see by the sample worksheet how you can leverage the intrinsic analysis to boost the overall multiple. The more items in the intrinsic analysis, the stronger your position. A buyer may reject a higher multiple on three line items but concede on the fourth. When multiples are used, incorporating fractions instead of whole numbers will aid the process. If the Buyer is firm on a five times multiple and won't go to six, ask for 5.7 or 5.5. It may seem insignificant, but its effect can be dramatic.

At the Table

How would you feel if you think you threw away a million dollars?—the key word being *think*. As the seller in negotiations, you really don't know what you leave on the table. I am confident that I am guilty of leaving just that sum of money or possibly more in the sale of TRC. This is a bit of a self-cleansing confession of sorts, but more so to provide you the reader with a valuable lesson.

Discussions with CDW were going great and moving quickly. They were anxious to seal the deal and so was I. When the offer from CDW's acquisition team was on my broker's desk, things broke down for TRC. Although I had explored the selling process on and off through the years, I was by no means an expert. I thought the broker I researched and hired had a process to represent TRC during negotiations. I should say he at least said he did prior to hiring him. I entered the situation naively and entrusted too much to this person. I failed to research the negotiation process myself, having focused too intently on marketing and selling the company.

Part of this blame could fall on timing and exhaustion. When you go to sell, it is like starting another business while running your existing one. I had just resolved the lawsuit with my previous equity partner and that had an emotional drain on me. Further, we had been on the market for a while before receiving the CDW offer and I wanted a deal to happen.

My broker had been saying that when the right offer comes around you'll know it and you'll want it bad. That's exactly what happened. CDW's offer was all cash, meaning there would be no financing delays, earn-out requirements, stock options, or other clauses. Further, CDW was located in our area and had offices in the suburbs and downtown Chicago offering options to our employee base for easy transition.

At the time the offer was made our broker became ill and

turned the transaction over to his son, who was clearly green. I never understood the diagnosis, but he was doctor ordered to stay away from business and not to even take phone calls. Our broker turned out to be like the rest of his peers who ran seminars claiming Fortune 500 companies were ripe for buying businesses, fully knowing that far less than one percent of any business such as ours gets sold to a Fortune 500 company. The first day I met him I told him that TRC was the right company to sell to a Fortune 500, and he failed to believe in his own industry's rhetoric that it could happen.

Two fundamental mistakes were made that I'm sure cost me. The first was his statement that when I saw the right deal I would want it bad. He was right, and he needed to be there to tell me to take it easy, play it cool, and follow the plan. When you want something badly, you let your emotions take over, and there's no room for emotions in negotiations. The problem was that he was overcome by emotion and disbelief that a Fortune 500 was making an offer. This wanting to do the deal weakened our position drastically.

CDW made the offer first, which was to our advantage as you never want to be the first to extend an offer in the negotiation process. It establishes a benchmark for the seller who can use that to launch an appropriate counter offer. Here's where the second mistake was made: we did not counter. The CDW offer made was a generous multiple off of our projected EBITDA at closing, which would be scheduled for June 2006. My broker returning from his illness stated that it was a good offer, and we should take it. Emotionally I was in no position to say no and the broker should have known that. Unfortunately he was in the same position right next me. Happily, we accepted the offer, scheduled a closing date, and started due diligence. There is no doubt in my mind that if we countered with a higher price we would have fetched more for the company. I blew Negotiations 101, and I was using a broker! How could that happen?

Hindsight is 20/20, and I've had the opportunity to study my experience and learn from professionals who train and conduct negotiations to see what went wrong. That experience helped me create the Negotiations Worksheet and subsequent process described, as a methodology to structure the selling process, hold emotions at bay, and strengthen the negotiating position.

CHAPTER FORTY-ONE
Closing the Deal

Due diligence is what stands between you and your check, and it is by far the least favorable aspect of selling a business. The purpose of due diligence is to investigate all nooks and crannies of the company being acquired to uncover missing facts or information that may cause expense or legal exposure down the road for the acquiring firm. Once again, preparation would have been helpful for what was about to be thrown at me by the law firm representing CDW.

When I talk about tasks an entrepreneur likes and dislikes, organizing paperwork is one that does not rank high for me. As owner, I was always signing off on various documents ranging from bids, reseller agreements, distribution agreements, and personal guarantees to creditors—all of which are legal documents. Over the years I could probably recite the legalese in these documents with my eyes closed. They all seemed to be the same boiler-plate document. They were formality tasks standing in the way of a sale, a much-needed product, or a credit release to expand our purchasing. I took little care in overseeing whether these documents were filed properly—if at all. As fate would have it, the CDW law firm zeroed in on all of these items as standard practice.

Since we found little use for these records over the past ten years, they were scattered throughout the building depending on what individual at the time was responsible for them. What a mess and embarrassment to have such shoddy records. The serious aspect of due diligence is that information revealed can be cause to change the terms of the deal, delay closing, or kill the deal. We managed to provide all of the necessary documents for this area of focus. The next would not be so easy.

A primary intrinsic selling point of TRC was our proprietary Web development featuring the display, fulfillment, and administration of software licensing. I had hired a development firm to custom build an e-commerce tool reflective of my vision and intended architecture. Over the years, our functionality was refined and perfected based on customer feedback making TRC the only dealer in the country with such a powerful deliverable. This was the intellectual property that CDW wanted to acquire. They could scale it across all segments of the company, and an acquisition was seen as being both faster and cheaper than trying to replicate such a system on their own.

The purpose of due diligence was to validate that TRC owned the development and more specifically the code. Up popped an unanticipated potential deal killer: TRC didn't own the code! I had confirmed with the developer, prior to this stage, that TRC did own the Web site and its functionality. However, the real question being asked was who owned the underlying code. I was about to discover that our developer, and many others, have a technical stipulation of defining ownership just above the code level that they develop. The argument extended by the developer is that if they turn over code ownership to each client, their ability to scale their own development efforts for new clients would be limited and restricted. For instance, if they create a shopping cart for one client it may look entirely different for another, but the underlying code may be very similar if not identical.

What CDW wanted was to have our developer sign an agreement that stated TRC owned the code, and the developer would not replicate that code for any other client. Obviously, this would severely impact the developer's ability to efficiently scale their own business. CDW didn't want our functionality to be replicated by a competitor that may call on our developer for work. The developer would not sign. My lawyers were now involved working with the developer's lawyers and things were going nowhere fast. In fact, the relationship was deteriorating as lawyer egos played up one another. My developer was no longer returning my calls, and I was very concerned that without this piece, CDW would walk.

Fed up with everyone who had their hands in this mess, I removed my lawyer from the case and personally went to my developer's office to understand the root concern from them, face to face. Up to this point, we really did not understand why TRC did not own the code, and why it was such a big deal to the developer. As soon as our lawyers got involved, they would not talk. Bridging our relationship formed over several years, I was able to get a meeting with our point of contact and the owner of the development firm. With their explanation, I understood and agreed with their concerns. I explained how this impasse was detrimental to the success of the acquisition and asked how we could reach a mutual agreement between all parties. Logic prevailed, and the CDW lawyers drafted an intellectual property agreement that was amicable for the developer and CDW.

This goes to prove a point mentioned earlier. The entrepreneur needs to be vigilant and stay involved in the entire selling process. Our lawyer fees were starting to go through the roof on a developer agreement that should have been concluded after a series of emails. The more each side was pushed, the more they entrenched their position. Even though professionals are hired, you cannot turn over the wheel of the ship to them. Professionals are on board to show you things to look out for as you guide yourself into port. Letting them take control is attune to a mutiny, and it's hard to win control back if allowed to continue too long. Temporarily removing my lawyers and getting CDW to take some management over their own legal team allowed us to get this portion of the deal done without damaging the acquisition. We were back on track!

Word Gets Out

An appropriate time to tell your employees what is going on is when due diligence begins. You will need the help of your staff during this process, and the size of your firm will dictate the scope of your disclosure. New faces from the buyer's office will likely be coming on site, and there will be a lot of unusual activity that may raise suspicion. Communicating to a small group of trusted employees is ideal, but not a guarantee of stopping information leakage. The danger of premature disclosure is that customers and vendors may catch wind and have real concerns regarding the future owner. Certainly, employees will want to know if they will still have a job after a sale and who exactly is buying their company.

Competitors are the other group likely to hear about your plans. When you decide to sell your company you are telling your competitors that you are either a magnificent swan or a lame duck. This is a daunting time for your position in the market as competitors will certainly plan to react in some fashion either fearing your ability to strengthen your market position or sensing your vulnerabilities.

If information cannot be contained, a well thought-out announcement that clearly addresses most conceivable concerns should be issued along with a prompt request to keep focused on work. The concern for all parties will be to retain customers and employees during this unusual time.

Everyone at TRC was aware that the day would come when we would sell and, by my personal hype, it would be for all the right reasons. Even with this preparation, I was not ready for the variety of responses from my workforce when word surfaced. The group who I thought would least support a buyout, the administrative operations group, became the most supportive. The sales team, the group I thought would be most energized became the most disruptive and disgruntled. The acquisition was a tremendous career and earnings growth opportunity for everyone, but not all perceived it as such.

The sales team felt threatened by the change and feared losing accounts they had managed for years. Our counterparts at CDW failed to fully disclose to our staff what their future would look like at CDW. Base pay, commission, and territory were cryptically shared with our team, and the lack of immediate answers was not enough to entice some of them to stay on board. I would lose my top three sales representatives before our physical move to the CDW offices. Productivity ground to a halt as rumors, fears, and misinformation filled the grape vine.

After the Sale

We would emerge from due diligence successfully and promptly close the deal within the month. It was June 2006, and TRC would no longer exist in six months. We would close the office and physically move to CDW offices at yearend, at which time the Web site would be transferred to CDW. My agreement was to stay on a minimum of two years after the close to assist with the transition and knowledge transfer. It had been a long and emotional journey to get to this point and now it was time for me and my family to celebrate.

It was my goal at the start of the process to take my family, parents, and in-laws on a trip once we closed. They had all sacrificed to make TRC successful by working directly or indirectly on the business and Lisa and I could not have done it without them. We planned our trip for Spring Break 2007 to Coronado Island in San Diego. I knew my parents and in-laws were very happy for our success, and I was really looking forward to the trip to show them my appreciation.

True to form, change was constant and not letting up even after the sale of our company. My mother was diagnosed with a Stage IV melanoma along her left eye brow in late July just weeks after our closing. As it is to anyone in a similar situation, we were all shocked as my mom was the picture of health. A Stage IV melanoma is no walk in the park and every Google search result provided grim statistics as to the likely outcome. Why was this happening and happening now? After years of sacrificing for TRC's growth, I was ready to spend some real quality time with all of my family. That may sound selfish, but it was more disappointment and utter concern for my mother's wellbeing.

Life seemed to settle into a weird sense of limbo. We were taking things day by day uncertain as to what fate awaited. My mother was in her 70s, but looked as if in the prime of her 50s. Regardless of age, it was too early and I couldn't accept that this was happening. Entrepreneurs control things, they adapt, and they find solutions. I could not control this and that was both frustrating and frightening. The only positive outcome of such life experiences is that they provide the opportunity to self reflect and re-evaluate true priorities. Death has a way of punching a hole right through a Risk Box, blatantly revealing that most risk is insignificant in comparison to mortality.

The entire process of visiting doctors, conducting tests, and undergoing surgeries blended together forming an unintelligible chronology of what happened that summer of 2006. When my mom had a procedure I would sit with my dad in the waiting room trying to console and think of what to say, failing at both. My thoughts were with my dad. How he was feeling and how he would survive without her. My mom ran the house, ran the schedule and the social calendar, while my dad had now been retired a number of years. I was concerned about him and yet was unable to really communicate my feelings and fully understand his thoughts. He did share with me in the most sincere and touching manner his concern and at the same time optimism, which was likely provided more for my comfort and benefit. He wanted to protect me from the pending reality that he had seen repeated with friends and acquaintances.

What was most comforting was the depth of love he revealed that had not always been expressed in our family. Let me explain. I am of 100 percent German heritage. Beer stein images aside, Germans are often stoic, matter-of-fact people who are concerned with practicality more than personal expression. That's by no means to say that I had American gothic parents; they were a very lively and fun couple. However, we were not a family of shared and visibly expressed feelings. We were not a hugging family or one to tell each other how we felt. In this most emotional of situations, when the household leader was battling a life-or-death illness, we were ill prepared to talk about it.

By late August 2006, we would receive more bad news, and this would be far worse than the late July melanoma diagnosis. For a number of months, my dad had complained of difficulty swallowing his food, stating he felt it was just not going all the way down. A visit and scope from an otolaryngology specialist brought back news of esophageal cancer. Unaware of the significance of this diagnosis and without time to truly research, my dad was rushed to surgery within days. A significant portion of his esophagus was removed and his stomach was raised and reattached to the remaining portion of his esophagus.

The remainder of 2006 would be full of surgeries, therapy, and doctor visits. My parents' surgeries were both successful in eliminating the cancer in their respective regions. My mom looked to be a remarkable case of having beaten the odds thanks to a very skilled team of doctors. Remarkably for my dad's age, he came through his surgery well. He spent several months gradually increasing the type and size of food he was able to eat, but surgery had aged him overnight, and he was incredibly weakened. What we didn't know was that the cancer had spread to his lungs and within months of his surgery, he would have difficulty breathing and would be retaining fluid. The prognosis for this round would be hospice which was a cruel fate for us all. We had just gotten our mother back and now we had to contemplate life without our family patriarch.

My father died March 1, 2007 only seven months after his initial diagnosis. We still took our trip at the end of that month simply to get away from the months of pain and sorrow we had all experienced. My goal of having the whole family together would obviously not be realized. My mother understandably decided not to go along with us, and we would schedule a separate one-on-one trip with her later that year.

By 2008, my two-year agreement to stay with CDW was over but I was going to continue in my current position. I was ready to ride out into the sunset with a nice corporate job, regular hours, and all the special benefits that came with it. I had thought that the sale of TRC and subsequent events would end my entrepreneurial dreams; in fact, I really wanted them to. What I found was that I couldn't stop my mind from thinking like an entrepreneur.

Going through all of the health issues with my parents caused a vision I had years earlier to resurface: develop a national personal electronic healthcare records system. The explosion of the digital age and Web 2.0 capabilities were revealing incredible new businesses and ways to do business. All sorts of opportunities were starting to flood my mind. The spark to create was firing rapidly, and I was finding my corporate job was not fulfilling this internal desire.

"Dreams come true by doing not wishing"—Jeff Weber

PHASE V: MOVING ON

"Our passions are the winds that propel our vessel. Our reason is the pilot that steers her. Without winds the vessel would not move and without a pilot she would be lost."—A proverb

I seem to have a subconscious attraction to the sea through my analogies of turtles and ship captains even though I am easily susceptible to seasickness. I've retired as captain of TRC and am in the process of moving on to a new chapter of my life. I've learned that entrepreneurism is a journey and that the business itself is the ship.

The ship's sail is designed to catch the momentum and response to the market. The market demand for your product or service is the wind which catches your sail and pushes the company forward. The relative strength of the wind determines how fast the company moves or grows.

The wind is independent—it can't be controlled. Yet it can be manipulated by how you adjust and work your sail. The sail represents the aspects of your business that are fixed to capture sales. The infrastructure, Web site, employee training, staffing, your location all go to support your business sail. Included is your business plan, which encompasses all of these elements starting with lead generation all the way through product fulfillment. Your readiness to conduct business and capture sales is contingent upon these items.

The rudder of the ship is critical for pointing the company in the right direction. Without a rudder a ship is in jeopardy. The rudder represents company strategy. The keel is a long thin wing of sorts mounted down the center underside of the vessel. The purpose of the keel is to keep the boat upright and prevent it from capsizing. The financial health and management of your business is represented by the keel.

The captain makes decisions, sets a course, and establishes both short and long destinations. Preliminary planning and preparation is needed to conduct a safe and successful voyage. The captain needs to constantly steer the ship. With his hands on the wheel, he is looking toward the horizon as he commands his vessel. If the captain is down below throwing coal into the furnace, he won't be able to see the iceberg right in front of him. It may be admirable that he "gets his hands dirty" and his crew bonds with him, but his misplaced effort jeopardizes the voyage. Ultimately, the captain is responsible for his crew and his vessel. He will have to make decisions that ensure the sustainability of those aboard as well as the ship itself and recognize those things that distract him from this purpose.

The crew takes care of various aspects of the ship and conducts many tasks while following established processes that serve a specific purpose. Failure in one of these areas could put the ship at risk. A cook preparing food for the crew is vital to keeping his team fed, happy, healthy, and strong. He may not directly influence the outcome of the voyage, but without him the journey would be unpleasant at best.

Pulling the ship into harbor at the conclusion of its voyage is the most tenuous time. Attention must be paid to every detail and each decision is highly scrutinized. The captain must use all of his abilities and experience to position the ship properly for a safe mooring. Most likely, the ship will prepare shortly for a new destination and at some point see new captains at its helm. By caring foremost for the ship, its crew, and its mission, the captain has ensured the ship's ability to continue and welcome new leadership.

CHAPTER FORTY-TWO
Back at Work

It is a late January afternoon in 2009, and I am at my Fortune 500 job. As you would have guessed, I am at CDW. A great deal has changed in my life since the acquisition and at CDW too. Shortly after the TRC acquisition in 2006, it was announced that CDW would purchase a professional services firm named Berbee Information Networks based in Wisconsin with a reported $390 million revenue. Resellers like CDW and TRC needed to find ways to grow revenue and profits. Professional services had always been the logical progression. The dilemma for TRC was how to nationally scale services and enter this unfamiliar business. The answer for CDW was to purchase a major player and expand their successful Midwest model nationally.

As if this acquisition activity was not enough excitement, less than a year later in May 2007, CDW announced it would be sold to private equity investment house Madison Dearborn Partners (MDP) for $7.3 billion on 2006 revenues of $6.8 billion. The once cash-rich CDW was now leveraged with debt, and growing EBITDA would become the paramount focus.

Two and a half years had passed since I first walked through CDW's doors and today will be my last. As I swipe my ID card for the final time, I reflect on the journey that led me here. I entered this industry in my late twenties, and now I am forty-two. Looking back on the accomplishments from those years gives a tremendous sense of pride for me and those who helped make it all happen. Sadly, the number of achievements dwindled in the most recent two years as bureaucracy seemed to stifle the I.D.E.A. at CDW. The energy, enthusiasm, and passion I had when I first entered this building had slowly and systematically been replaced with conformity, procedure, and politics. This transformation frustrated me. I knew that my skills and talent were being sidelined, and that I could have done more to impact the company I now termed my employer.

My exit from CDW would not be with the same fanfare as my entrance. I have been laid off, along with 189 other coworkers due to the economic fallout and current debt position of the company. The reality is, I was a square peg in a round hole coming into CDW, and my new position and reporting structure would not lend itself to utilizing my talents. My new role was that of a quickly created Business Development Manager. Its initial appeal waned as I found there was little vision for the appointed position, and I would have to lobby advocates within my own department for my initiatives. I made some decent accomplishments during my term, but it was always a struggle. The position was not part of the existing structure and as such, it was hardly fluid. Instead of being supported by the full resources and capabilities of the company, I found I had to swim upstream where my co-managers and operational "support departments" acted more like competitors than facilitators.

I was enjoying the creature comforts CDW offered. My Risk Box walls grew protective of the salary I was earning and all the wonderful benefits afforded. Although I was increasingly less satisfied with my work, I stayed anchored to the material security of the job allowing my work soul to spoil. When my two year commitment was up in July 2008, I wanted to leave but I was too comfortable.

Six months later, I was probably the only happy one out of the 190 coworkers given their dismissal that morning. I had been wasting my time, and the situation I now found myself in along with the state of the economy would establish a unique opportunity for me to pursue new ideas. As I pulled out of the parking lot for the last time, the feeling of the entrepreneur that had been dormant began to show life. I was invigorated. I felt purpose flowing back into me. The mirage that the Risk Box was projecting started to dissolve, and I was excited.

I used this time to search for my next opportunity. I had started writing this book about two years earlier, squeezing content in on weekends and afterhours, but never really making progress. This had satisfied my longing to create as I tried to make the most of my routine days. Now time was available, and I could pursue this project fully. My idea for the book would blossom into a business and an entirely new and exciting personal and professional direction for me. Systematically, the E-Formula would be complete. Two years prior I vowed never to start another bootstrap business, but here I was doing it again.

My situation allowed me to actively pursue the opportunity arising from the current economy. People yearning to express their entrepreneurial dreams due to the uncertainty of the economy was creating a thirst for knowledge, guidance, and mentoring. Something that I believed in and that solved a problem was calling me to take action. I had been giving thought to what I truly wanted to do that would resurrect that same passion I had for TRC. Now all I had to do was jump in the pool.

Upon reflection, I see that if I had waited to take TRC to market by just nine months or less, I would have missed the opportunity with CDW, probably forever. The decisive blow would have come in 2008 when merger and acquisition activity came to a grinding halt. TRC would have been forced to face this economic storm by cash flow alone. If I had chosen debt to finance my vision for TRC's continued growth, I'm not sure TRC would have made it through that storm. I guess my gut had been right all along.

CHAPTER FORTY-THREE
The Self-Made Man

How often have you heard so and so is a "self-made man"? It typically describes a successful athlete, entrepreneur, or celebrity who either started with nothing or overcame extreme adversity and then rose to greatness. I believe that behind most of these stories are individuals who helped and supported the self-made man along his way. It is important not to discount or forget those who brought you to where you are today.

Some have called me a successful self-made man. The self-made part is far from the truth. My support began with parents who provided the basic building blocks for my success. They cared, believed, loved, and cheered me on. They provided an environment that nurtured a young entrepreneur's dreams. They paid for my college education which is a luxury 80 percent of American students don't have. My in-laws encouraged me to do something on my own and never discounted any idea I happened to bring up. Foremost, my wife truly believes in me and doesn't doubt anything I want to do. She has made sacrifices and adapted her life to allow me to pursue my dreams. Who has more courage, the person who strikes out on his own or the person who goes along with him?

The self-made man is supported by his employees, vendors, and customers. All of these stakeholders provide assistance, commitment, guidance and trust that make the entrepreneur a success. These stakeholders take a chance on the entrepreneur by way of their careers, credit, and spending. There is no such thing as a self-made man.

I am extremely grateful and blessed to have had the opportunity and experience that I had. My life has been made rich far beyond monetary terms by being able to live a dream that so many millions only imagine. It is my hope that my experience will help others find their path and understand their E-Formula for entrepreneurial activation.

CHAPTER FORTY-FOUR
Extraordinary

"Entrepreneurs are ordinary people that do extraordinary things."
—Jeff Weber

E xtraordinary is one of my favorite adjectives. It is two words *extra* and *ordinary* joined to characterize what is beyond normal or usual. People and events described as extraordinary are exceptional, remarkable, and beyond everyday achievement. An entrepreneur's efforts and achievements are often defined as extraordinary and they most certainly are. Successful entrepreneurs represent a very small percentage of the population. They take on the enormous task of launching a venture and survive daunting odds to remain in business. They are able to achieve the extraordinary because they researched, planned, and prepared to be successful. Most importantly, they put in a lot of hard work and long hours to make it happen.

"If I believe I cannot do something, it makes me incapable of doing it. But when I believe I can, then I acquire the ability to do it, even if I did not have the ability in the beginning."—Mahatma Gandhi

Entrepreneurs are ordinary people who do extraordinary things. When I launched TRC, I knew there were individuals who were smarter, more talented, and better financed than me, but I had the heart, desire, and effort to outperform most of them. I was fueled by passion and activated by the entrepreneurial formula.

As a result of achieving the extraordinary, people are celebrated and revered by others. However, the greatest recognition and reward tends to be internal to the entrepreneur. An idea was sparked, acted upon and tremendous unseen sacrifice was made to make it a success.

If few achieve the entrepreneurial equivalent of extraordinary and even less have the opportunity to pull off an extraordinary rescue or feat of heroism, where is their opportunity for extraordinary in our day to day lives? Does one have to wait for the right situation and circumstances?

We all can achieve the extraordinary by acting on ordinary things that occur in daily situations. Opportunities are all around. All it takes is the conscious decision to act. Long-term planning and preparation is not required for these types of extraordinary. The extraordinary can be the choice to stop your car to remove dangerous debris from the street or to help a turtle cross the road. Choose not to gossip. Become a volunteer reader. Cut the elderly neighbor's lawn. Intentionally meet new people. Purposely ask to be of assistance. Brush snow off the car next to yours. Work at a charity as well as donating your money. Give up your seat on the bus. Act on one of your ideas to make your workplace better or more productive. Seek to create extraordinary events to benefit others and you will come to know extraordinary.

Extraordinary happens when you break your daily routine. Take time to do something new with your children or your spouse. Go somewhere different on a vacation. Do something you've never done before. Help someone, who you've never met. I guarantee that if you routinely vacation to Florida and instead take a trip to New York City and reserve one or two days out of that trip to help in a city shelter, you'll talk about that trip and the experiences you had for the rest of your life.

Your extraordinary may not make headlines but it will invigorate your soul and your purpose for being. It will revitalize your relationships and create new ones. It will deliver purpose, meaning, and substance to your work and for your employer. Best of all, it may profoundly touch someone in a way that you will never know or be able to fully appreciate.

Ben Hollis, a talented and gifted writer, television personality, thespian, and now philosopher of sorts, (and a bit of a Chicago legend) personifies the extraordinary. He created a show called *Wild Chicago* that aired on the public broadcasting network and ran for 15 years. The show was a fast-paced, thirty-minute reality show before the advent of reality shows. Ben would find the most obscure, bizarre, and creative people and businesses in and around Chicago. Donning his signature pith helmet, safari shirt, and jungle shorts, Ben set out to find the wild side of Chicago and report on those people who were living wild in the city. For his efforts and innovation Ben won eight Emmys, the Studs Terkel award from the Pulitzer Prize winner himself, and numerous other recognitions. That alone is rather extraordinary!

About five years after the last *Wild Chicago* episode aired, Ben reinvented himself and the WILD theme. Reflecting on his own life and accomplishments, he summed up what was responsible for his extraordinary career in the prefix of the show. Ben's discovery of his success was really by reflection of his failures. Many of his early personal and professional decisions were not focused on what Ben wanted, but subconsciously on what he thought others wanted from him. All of this led to an unfulfilled life that at times brought depression, anxiety, and a sense of incompleteness.

Only by establishing a sense of purpose and direction of what he desired was Ben able to move toward relationships and career aspirations that matched his passions. When he started taking care of what he wanted and needed, things started to fall into place. By stepping out of his Risk Box Ben was able to meet new people and force introductions which eventually would lead him to a producer at PBS with an idea to feature local Chicago businesses and hot spots around town.

By discovering *Wild Chicago*, Ben discovered the wild in him that drives his passion and stirs his soul. Ben's recent rediscovery was that wild defined him and he in turn defined W.I.L.D. as an acronym for What I Love Doing. On April 25, 2009, Ben introduced his keynote address and soon-to-be-released book titled *W.I.L.D. about Living and Loving.* He delivered an insightful, motivating, funny, and theatrical performance that stirred the audience. With relative ease, Ben explained how everyone can live an extraordinary W.I.L.D. life that is enriching and focused on spending all of your 86,400 seconds every day doing what you love doing. It's a way to live your life and the way you should live your life.

I love living W.I.L.D.—doing what I love doing in business and in all facets of my life. The Risk Box and fear prevents us from living W.I.L.D., but I've proven that the Risk Box can be shattered. It is a false prison.

A recent ad I came across from Cisco seemed to sum up this sentiment best:

There's never been a better time to change.
To find new ways to innovate
New ways to collaborate
New ways to thrive
New ways to share human knowledge
To work together
Solve problems together and bring the world a little closer.

A Closing Message from Ben:

Awaken The Wild Within You!

In my television show *Wild Chicago* (on WTTW-Chicago, the PBS outlet) I entertained viewers by introducing them to unusual, offbeat, surprising people, places and things around town. There was the Polka Music Hall of Fame; the store that sold nothing but condoms; the tall, bearded man who held the Guinness World Record for writing the world's longest poem; cross-dressing square dancers; and the list goes on.

The show was a hit and critics loved it too. And while I was thrilled with all the phone calls and letters I received lauding me and my show, every once in a while I'd hear something from a fan that disturbed me. It wasn't anything critical, either. It was something else. It usually went like this: "Hey, Ben, I love *Wild Chicago*! You totally crack me up. But it must be really hard keeping a straight face when you're interviewing all those weirdoes. How do you do it?"

This troubled me. Whenever I heard this sentiment expressed I felt a sudden surge of protectiveness for my "weirdoes." I didn't see them that way at all. Certainly many of my guests were eccentric, some even disturbed. But "keeping a straight face" was never a challenge. Why? Because I was too busy enjoying them, meeting them at their level, getting swept in their enthusiasm, their love for what they were doing. This was true whether they were involved in mud wrestling, rocket building or UFO investigating. It wasn't so much about what they were doing as it was about the spirit with which they did it. I felt affection for my non-mainstream *Wild Chicago* friends. And upon reflection, I discovered a common thread in the best of my interview subjects.

It was passion. These people absolutely loved what they did.

As a result, they were compelling to watch. They made for great TV watching. These offbeat collectors, inventors, museum curators and tattoo artists had magnetism. I admired them and loved being around them – even when their surroundings might have been deemed by less adventurous viewers (and camera crews!) as frightening, dangerous, creepy, smelly or just vaguely disturbing.

Obviously, I, and some of my viewers, had different ideas about the definition of "wild" as in *Wild Chicago*. I didn't subscribe to the "wild equals weird" position. I defined wild as that which lives in its natural habitat, in the neighborhoods, unpretentious, not concerned with what anyone thinks, guileless.

About a year ago, my definition of "wild" deepened. As I prepared to launch a new business giving inspirational talks and workshops based on lessons learned in my two decades on television, I knew my brand would revolve around the concept of "wild." And as professional speakers are wont to do, I needed to find the perfect acronym for W.I.L.D.

My first attempt was not all that elegant and need not be repeated here. I needed help. So I called a writer friend of mine, J.B., to have lunch to talk it over. We brainstormed then went our separate ways without anything of note coming from it. But a few hours later I received an email with fresh information that breathed life into the "wild" concept and its new role as an acronym. It was from J.B. He wrote: "W.I.L.D. = What I Love Doin'!"

Yes! The hidden DNA of Wildness was revealed: My favorite people I'd interviewed and hung with on *Wild Chicago* were the ones doing the W.I.L.D. Thing – doing what they loved doing. That's where their passion came from, and why they came across so compellingly on television. And that's why I found them so magnetic. Doing what you love doing draws good things to you and creates positive energy.

In my work as an inspirational speaker and in my upcoming book, I encourage you to embrace your wildness and start doing what you love doing as much as you can every day. It's the only way you'll find the necessary persistence and power to sustain your dream of being an entrepreneur. Doing what you love doing will put you in the flow of good fortune in the form of: meeting the right people who will help you; seeing amazing opportunities unfold before your eyes; receiving brilliant new ideas, and more.

So embrace your W.I.L.D.-ness. It's only natural.

NOTES

Chapter 1

Gerber, Michael E., *E-Myth Revisited: Why Most Small Businesses Don't Work and What to Do about It* (HarperCollins, 2004)

Arts Entrepreneurship: How to be a hero, A profile of Elliot McGucken, PhD, Kauffman Thought Book (2007)

The Grove National Historic Landmark

Kennicott, Robert (1835-1865); Bannister, Henry M. (1844-1920) Papers, 1857-1905, Series 11/2/2, Boxes 1-2. Northwestern University Archives, Evanston, Illinois

Chapter 2

The Parable of the Talents (Matthew 25:14-30)

Chapter 3

Ewing, Marion, Kauffman Foundation

Schumpeter, Joseph, *Capitalism, Socialism and Democracy* (New York: Harper, 1975) [orig. pub. 1942]

Knight, Frank H., *Risk, Uncertainty, and Profit* (Boston: Hart, Schaffner & Marx; Houghton Mifflin Co.

Chapter 4

Hofstrand, Don, "What is an Entrepreneur?" Iowa State University (January 2006)

Gartner, William B., "Some Suggestions for Research on Entrepreneurial Traits and Characteristics," Entrepreneurship Theory and Practice (1989)

Gray, Patricia B., "Do you need school to succeed? Classes for would-be entrepreneurs are a hot trend at America's universities. But can risk taking and originality be learned?" *FORTUNE Small Business*, additional reporting by Anne Field (March 1, 2006)

R. T. Hughes, Johnathan, "Arthur Cole and Entrepreneurial History," Northwestern University (1983)

"Thomas Kinkade: A Success: Morley Safer Interviews Artist Who's Also Master Marketer," CBS News (July 4, 2004)

Cullum, Paul, "Thomas Kinkade's 16 Guidelines for Making Stuff Suck," *Vanity Fair* (November 14, 2008)

Chapter 6

Cole, Arthur, "An Approach to the Study of Entrepreneurship, Journal of Economic
History" Vol. 6 (1946, Supplement) reprinted in Lane, Frederic C. and Riesmersman, Jelle C. eds., *Enterprises and Secular Change: Readings in Economic History*
(Homewood, IL: Irwin, 1953)

Chapter 7

Gardner, John W., http://www.pbs.org/johngardner/

Chapter 12

Collins, Jim, *Good to Great: Why Some Companies Make the Leap...and Others Don't* (Harper Collins 2001)

Fairlie, Robert W., the Kauffman Index of Entrepreneurial Activity, National Report (1996- 2005)

Al-Zubeidi, Mohammad*, BS, MBA, MS, "Higher Education and Entrepreneurship: The Relation between College Educational Background and All Business Success in Texas," (May 2005)
*Dissertation prepared for the Degree of Doctor of Philosophy, University of North Texas

"Bankruptcy Filings," *Wall Street Journal*, (September 30, 2008) Source: American Bankruptcy Institute

The Business Dynamic Statistics (BDS), U.S. Census Bureau
Small Business Statistics and Failure Rates, GlobalBX

Grabmeier, Jeff, "Restaurant Failure Rate Much Lower than Commonly Assumed, Study Finds," Ohio State University (September 8, 2003)

Bates, Timothy; Nucci, Alfred, "An Analysis of Small Business Size and Rate of Discontinuance," CES 90-2 (January 1990)

Chapter 13

Mitchell, Jerry R., President, the Midwest Entrepreneurs' Forum
Bootstrapping Newsletter, (April 2009)

Chapter 17

Wadhwa, Vivek; Aggarwal, Raj; Krisztina "Z" Holly; Salkever, Alex; Ewing, Marion, "The Anatomy of an Entrepreneur: Family Background and Motivation," Kauffman Foundation (July 2009)

"The Forbes 400," *Forbes*, (September 18, 2008)

Kelly, Kate, "Lost Opportunities Haunt Final Days of Bear Stearns," *Wall Street Journal* (May 27, 2008)

Kelly, Kate, "His Job at Bear Gone, Mr. Fox Chose Suicide," *Wall Street Journal* (November 6, 2008)

Pink, Daniel H., *A Whole New Mind: Why Right-Brainers Will Rule the Future,* (The Berkley Publishing Group, 2005, 2006)

Chapter 20

Boswell, Grant, Hatch, Gary (editors), *Dialogues and Conversations Second Edition* (Needham Heights, MA: Simon &Schuster, 1996)

Mander, Jerry, *Four Arguments for the Elimination of Television* (New York: Quill, 1978)

Mifflin, Lawrie, "Fattening up the Menu for Children's TV," *The New York Times* (Late Edition Sunday, November 3, 1996 Sec. 12) p. 5

"Military Censorship Lives," *The New York Times* (Late Edition, Wednesday, September 21, 1994, Sec. A, Editorial Desk) p. 22

Rogers, Adam, Television, *Newsweek Extra* (Winter 1997-98) p. 49

Chapter 21
Dow Jones Venture Source, copyright 2009. Statistic cited in the *Wall Street Journal* (June 7, 2009)

Chapter 30
Mann, Catherine L., PhD, "The Globalization of Innovation and Entrepreneurship," Kauffman Thought Book (2007), p. 195

Chapter 32
Gray, Loren, "Understanding the Process of Innovation," *Harvard Business School, Working Knowledge Newsletter* (August, 5, 2002), reprinted with permission from "Where Does the Competitive Advantage Lie?" *Harvard Management Update*, Vol. 7, No. 7, (July, 2002)

Kelley, Tom, *The 10 Faces of Innovation,* (Doubleday, a division of Random House, Inc. 2005)

Cone, Judith, "Entrepreneurship on Campus: Why the Real Mission is Culture Change," *Kauffman Thought Book* (2007), p.78

Chapter 33
Blanchard, Kenneth H., Hutson, Don, Willis, Ethan, *The One Minute Entrepreneur,* (Random House, Inc., 2008)

Chapter 34
Vroom, Victor H., & Jago, Arthur G, "The Role of the Situation in Leadership," The *American Psychologist*, (January 2007), pp. 61, 17-24

Chapter 36
Contaldo, Bob (Corporate Finance Associates) "How Do I Know When It's Time to Sell My Company?" *Peoria Magazines.com*, (July 2008)

Chapter 37
PriceWaterhouseCoopers study cited by Changing the Focus, LLC

Additional sources referenced or utilized
Pickens, T. Boone, *The First Billion Is The Hardest - How Believing It's Still Early in the Game Can Lead to Life's Greatest Comebacks,* (Crown Publishing Group 2008)

2007 Human Development Report (HDR), United Nations Development Program, (November 27, 2007) p. 25

World Bank Development Indicators (2008)

"The Women Presidents Organization," *E magazine,* November 2008, p. 64

Chemer, Martin M., *Cognitive, Social, and Emotional Intelligence of Transformational Leadership: Efficacy and Effectiveness.* In R. E. Riggio, S. E. Murphy, F. J. Pirozzolo (Eds.), Multiple Intelligences and Leadership, (2002)

Grant, A., *Entrepreneurship: The Major Academic Discipline for the Business Education Curriculum for the 21st Century.* In M. Scott, P. Rosa, & H. Klandt (Ed), *Educating Entrepreneurs for Wealth Creation,* (Brookfield, VT: Ashgate Publishing Company) pp. 28-37

Gartner, W., "Who is an entrepreneur? Is the wrong question," *American Journal of Small Business,* 12(1), (1988) 11-32

THE AUTHOR

Jeffrey Weber earned his MBA from Chicago's Loyola University School of Business and entered the technology industry during the start of the dot com era. The company he founded grew rapidly earning a rank on INC magazine's "Top 500 Fastest Growing Private US Companies" list in 2001 and 2002. He successfully positioned and sold that company to a Fortune 500 in 2006.

Weber incorporates his entrepreneurial knowledge and proprietary methodologies into this, his first book on the topic. He is an adjunct faculty teaching entrepreneurism at the college level, speaker, and coach for start-ups, existing small/medium size businesses, and corporations wishing to innovate and establish an entrepreneurial spirit.

Staying active in entrepreneurial circles and networks, Weber is always looking to start or get involved with something new and exciting.